D1523831

CLAUDIO MONTEVERDI

COMPOSER RESOURCE MANUALS
(General Editor: Guy Marco)
(Vol. 23)

GARLAND REFERENCE LIBRARY
OF THE HUMANITIES
(Vol. 792)

MONTE VERDE ✶ CLAVDIO

FIORI POETICI
Raccolti nel Funerale
DEL MOLTO ILLVSTRE;
E Molto Reuerendo
SIGNOR CLAVDIO
Monte verde
Maestro di Cappella della Du-
cale di S. Marco.
Consecrati
DA D. GIO: BATTISTA
Marinoni, detto Gioue:
Maestro di Cappella del Do-
mo di Padoua
ALL' ILLVSTRSSIMI
& Eccellentissimi
SIG. PROCVRATORI
Di Chiesa di S. Marco.

In VENETIA, Presso Francesco Miloco.
Con Lic. de Sup.   MDCXLIV.

CLAUDIO MONTEVERDI
A Guide to Research

K. Gary Adams and Dyke Kiel

GARLAND PUBLISHING, INC. • NEW YORK & LONDON
1989

Library of Congress Cataloging-in-Publication Data

Adams, K. Gary.
    Claudio Monteverdi : a guide to research / K. Gary Adams and Dyke
Kiel.
       p. cm. — (Composer resource manuals ; vol. 23) (Garland
reference library of the humanities ; vol. 792)
    Includes indexes.
    ISBN 0–8240–7743–1 (alk. paper)
    1. Monteverdi, Claudio, 1567–1643—Bibliography. I. Kiel, Dyke.
II. Title. III. Series. IV. Series: Garland composer resource
manuals ; v. 23.
ML134.M66A5   1989
016.782'0092—dc20   89–33040
                                                     CIP
                                                     MN

Printed on acid-free, 250-year-life paper
Manufactured in the United States of America

GARLAND COMPOSER
RESOURCE MANUALS

In response to the growing need for bibliographic guidance to the vast literature on significant composers, Garland is publishing an extensive series of research guides. This ongoing series encompasses more than 50 composers; they represent Western musical tradition from the Renaissance to the present century.

Each research guide offers a selective, annotated list of writings, in all European languages, about one or more composers. There are also lists of works by the composers, unless these are available elsewhere. Biographical sketches and guides to library resources, organization, and specialists are presented. As appropriate to the individual composer, there are maps, photographs, or other illustrative matters, and glossaries and indexes.

GARLAND COMPOSER RESOURCE MANUALS

General Editor: Guy A. Marco

CONTENTS

PREFACE

The music of Claudio Monteverdi has been the object
of extensive study, performance, and research since
Emil Vogel's 1887 landmark monograph (item 349) was
published a century ago in the Vierteljahrsschrift für
Musikwissenschaft. Several earlier references to
Monteverdi which appeared between his death in 1643
and the late nineteenth century add to the quantity of
writing about the composer and his music. Our purpose
in compiling this volume is to provide a guide to the
breadth and quality of Monteverdi literature published
through 1986. We have included one entry published in
1987, Gary Tomlinson's important Monteverdi and the
End of the Renaissance (item 429). English, Italian,
German, and French are the principal languages
covered, although selected, representative items in
other languages are also cited.

The bibliography that comprises the greater part of
this volume is selective rather than comprehensive.
We have attempted to choose the most significant
literature about Monteverdi issued in the form of
scholarly books, articles, and dissertations. Representative concert reviews, particularly those considered to present useful information or deemed to have
historical importance, have also been included in
order to supply the reader with a sampling of Monteverdi performances in the twentieth century. With
some notable exceptions, encyclopedia and dictionary
articles, newspaper articles, reviews of books, record
jacket notes, articles from general sources, and writings of a popular or introductory character have been
excluded.

   After Section I, Monteverdi's Works, which presents
a list of all the composer's works and a selective
list of modern editions, the main bibliography is
divided into four subject areas, each of which is
subdivided into chapters: Section II, General Background for Monteverdi Research, includes historical
background, studies of musical thought in Monteverdi's
time, and studies of Monteverdi's contemporaries;
Section III, Monteverdi's Life, covers letters, documents, pictures, and biographical studies; Section IV,
Studies of Monteverdi's Music, divides his work by
genre and includes chapters on the prima and seconda
pratica and performance practice; and Section V,
Monteverdi Today, addresses the revival of his works,
research, and discographies. The entries in each
chapter are arranged alphabetically by author and include the standard bibliographical information. The
book concludes with an author index, an index of
compositions, and a general index of proper names.
   Several bibliographies were utilized in the selection of items for this volume. Especially helpful
were those found in The Monteverdi Companion (item
779), The New Monteverdi Companion (item 780), and
those accompanying the Monteverdi entries in Die Musik
in Geschichte und Gegenwart (item 333) and The New
Grove Dictionary of Music and Musicians (item 294).
Also useful in gathering materials for inclusion were
RILM Abstracts, The Music Index, and the bibliographies of various dissertations, monographs, and
Monteverdi biographies.
   The authors have personally perused nearly all of
the entries contained in the bibliography. In the
case of unpublished dissertations which were not
available through interlibrary loan, annotations were
based on abstracts located in Dissertation Abstracts
International. Entries for a few foreign language
works and other selected unavailable materials rely
upon the annotations printed in RILM Abstracts. In
both cases, the annotation begins with the indication
"Not examined." Other items that were not personally
inspected by the authors, yet seemed appropriate for
inclusion in the book, are listed without annotation.
   Research for this project was carried out in the
music libraries of the following institutions: The
Library of Congress, University of Virginia, Rutgers
University, University of North Texas, Rice University, University of Missouri at Kansas City, and the

University of Kansas. We are grateful to the staffs
of those institutions for their invaluable assistance.
Special thanks is reserved for the librarians at
Bridgewater College and Cottey College; we would
particularly like to thank the interlibrary loan
personnel, Deborah Bittle and Alison Freeland at
Bridgewater and Saundra Byers and Jeannie Deatherage
at Cottey, for their cheerful and efficient
assistance.

We must acknowledge several individuals who
provided valuable help in translating a few of the
foreign language entries: Anna Lootsma Barr for her
expert translations of the Dutch articles, Kajsa
Svarfvar for providing us with excellent translations
of the Swedish articles, and Ellsworth Kyger for
helpful suggestions concerning the translations of
three abstruse German articles. Our gratitude also
goes to Guy Marco, general editor of the Garland
Composer Resource Manuals Series, and Marie Ellen
Larcada of Garland   for   their   advice and, above
all, for their great patience with us as we prepared
this project for publication. We would like to
express sincere thanks to our respective institutions:
to Bridgewater College for a research grant in the
summer of 1985 and to Cottey College for providing the
computer and software necessary for the completion of
this book.

This volume is respectfully dedicated to our mentor
and friend Cecil Adkins, Professor of Music at the
University of North Texas, who, some years ago,
encouraged us to pursue this bibliography. Finally,
to our wives, Rebecca Kiel and Mary Kay Adams, we
offer our greatest thanks for their help with indexing
and proofreading and, most of all, for their support
and encouragement throughout the preparation of this
volume.

                              K. Gary Adams
                              Dyke Kiel
                              June 1988

INTRODUCTION

    After the death of Claudio Giovanni Antonio
Monteverdi on 29 November 1643, interest in the composer, one of the greatest musicians of his age, continued to be demonstrated for approximately a decade,
primarily through performances of his operas and, most
significantly, by two substantial posthumous publications: the Messa a 4 voci e Salmi of 1650 and the
Madrigali e canzonette of 1651. Following the middle
part of the seventeenth century, however, Monteverdi
suffered the negligence common to so many other early
composers. Prior to the nineteenth century, the only
references to Monteverdi are those found in the works
of a few theorists and music historians. In 1732, for
example, Johann Gottfried Walther provided only scant
information concerning Monteverdi's life and works in
the Musikalisches Lexikon oder musikalische Bibliothek
(item 350). Giovanni Battista Martini, in his
authoritative treatise on counterpoint (item 387)
published at Bologna in 1774, examined three works by
Monteverdi and included a complimentary statement on
the composer's accomplishments. Only a few years
later, the English music historians John Hawkins (item
511) and Charles Burney (item 357) offered assessments
of the composer and printed examples of his music.
Hawkins, for instance, credited Monteverdi as being
the father of the theatrical style and described the
composer's use of instruments and recitative in Orfeo.
Burney discussed Monteverdi's harmonic innovations and
recognized his importance as a composer of opera,
particularly with regard to Arianna. The last
noteworthy reference to Monteverdi in the eighteenth
century was published in Ernst Ludwig Gerber's

xiv   INTRODUCTION

significant dictionary of musical biography in which
the author offered a brief discussion of the composer's life and works and hailed Monteverdi as "the
Mozart of his time" (item 306).

Carl von Winterfeld, in his pivotal work on
Giovanni Gabrieli (item 255) published in 1834, paved
the way for the rediscovery of Monteverdi in the nineteenth century. In addition to printing four compositions by Monteverdi, an ample portion of the second
volume is devoted to an essay on the music of the
composer. In 1854, Francesco Caffi's monumental
history of church music at St. Mark's Cathedral in
Venice (item 298) contained a discussion of Monteverdi
and reproduced three of the composer's letters.
August Wilhelm Ambros, in the fourth volume of his
Geschichte der Musik of 1878 (item 291), presented a
lengthy essay dedicated to the composer's life and
works entitled "Claudio Monteverdi und seine Schule."

The penultimate decade of the nineteenth century
marks the proper beginning of modern Monteverdi
research. In 1881, Robert Eitner published his
landmark edition of Orfeo in Berlin and in 1887, Emil
Vogel's impressive biography of the composer appeared
(item 349), first presented to the University of
Berlin as a doctoral dissertation and subsequently
published in the Vierteljahrsschrift für Musik-
wissenschaft in the same year. These historically
important publications established the foundation
for further research into the life and music of
Monteverdi. Other notable scholarly studies issued
before 1900 which either dealt specifically with
Monteverdi or contained major sections devoted to the
composer included monographs on music in Mantua by
Pietro Canal (item 47) and Antonio Bertolotti (item
36), published in 1881 and 1891 respectively; Hermann
Kretzschmar's valuable essay on Venetian opera (item
102) and his major article dealing with L'incoronazione di Poppea (item 519); Romain Rolland's history
of Baroque opera (item 149) which, like Vogel's
biography, was originally his doctoral dissertation;
and two influential studies published in 1892 and 1895
by Hugo Goldschmidt, one of the pioneers in
seventeenth-century music research (items 85, 86).

Immediately after the turn of the century,
Goldschmidt's position as one of the leading Monteverdi scholars was solidified with four additional
publications: the monumental two-volume history of
seventeenth-century Italian opera (item 88), the

important articles on Il ritorno d'Ulisse (items 507,
508), and the substantial essay on the Italian opera
orchestra (item 87). Other scholars--among whom the
most important were Alfred Heuss, Hugo Riemann, C.
Hubert H. Parry, Hugo Leichtentritt, Eugen Schmitz,
Gaetano Cesari, and Angelo Solerti--produced a wide
variety of specialized studies between 1900 and the
end of World War I which added to the corpus of
Monteverdi literature.

Revivals of Monteverdi's music also began to occur
in the first part of the twentieth century. The
impetus for this renascence of the composer's compositions in the opera house and the concert hall can be
traced to early editions prepared by several scholars
and composers prior to World War I. Eitner's 1881
edition of Orfeo signals the commencement of modern
editions of Monteverdi's music. Immediately following
1900, several editions of Orfeo, L'incoronazione di
Poppea, and other works were prepared by Vincent
d'Indy, Giacomo Orefice, Luigi Torchi, Hugo
Leichtentritt, and others. Performances utilizing
these editions soon followed, notably those of Orfeo
in Paris and Breslau.

Between the two World Wars, the German Hans F.
Redlich, the Englishman J.A. Westrup, the Frenchman
Henry Prunières, and the Italians G. Francesco
Malipiero and Domenico de' Paoli emerged as the most
prolific and important Monteverdi scholars. Perhaps
the most valuable contributions from this group during
these years would be Redlich's impressive study of the
composer's madrigals (item 408), a revision of his
Ph.D. dissertation, and, most certainly, Malipiero's
complete edition of Monteverdi's works, published in
sixteen volumes from 1926 to 1942. Major biographies
of the composer were written between 1921 and 1945 by
three authors: Louis Schneider (item 338), Prunières
(item 329), and de' Paoli (item 301). In addition to
the above-mentioned scholars, it should be noted that
from 1920 to 1945, numerous noteworthy studies dealing
with Monteverdi, representing a wide range of topics,
were published by other musicologists.

Shortly after World War II, three authoritative
biographies of the composer appeared which continue to
be consulted by students and scholars of Monteverdi:
Hans F. Redlich's informative Claudio Monteverdi:
Leben und Werk (item 331) in 1949, published in an
expanded English translation by Kathleen Dale three
years later; Leo Schrade's masterful Monteverdi:

Creator of Modern Music (item 341) in 1950, still,
perhaps, the finest biographical account of the
composer in the English language; and Claudio
Sartori's admirable Monteverdi (item 337) in 1953.
Following these outstanding works, the second half of
the twentieth century has seen a constant outpouring
of articles and books adding to our knowledge and
understanding of Monteverdi and his music. Although
the names of many prominent Monteverdi scholars are
too numerous to mention here, among the most influential contributions are the studies of Anna Amalie
Abert on Monteverdi's operas, especially Claudio
Monteverdi und das musikalische Drama (item 438); the
wide-ranging monographs of Wolfgang Osthoff; the
voluminous writings of Denis Arnold; Jeffrey
Kurtzman's erudite examinations of Monteverdi's sacred
music; and the important body of work produced by
Denis Stevens.
     With the publication of Malipiero's complete
edition from 1926 to 1942 and the editions of individual works by scholars such as Redlich, Arnold,
Stevens, and Raymond Leppard, performances of
Monteverdi's music increased accordingly. In the
1970s, two new sets of Monteverdi's complete works
were announced. The first, published by the
Fondazione Claudio Monteverdi in Cremona, has issued
five volumes to date under the guidance of various
editors. The second, a proposed complete works by Les
Editions Renaissantes in Paris, includes only one
volume thus far, a 1972 edition of the first madrigal
book edited by Bernard Bailly de Surcy.
     As one would expect with a composer of Monteverdi's
stature, several twentieth-century Festschriften and
other similar publications have been devoted to an
examination of the composer and his music. One of the
earliest such efforts was a special 1929 issue of La
rassegna musicale (item 819) given entirely to
articles on Monteverdi. This was followed in 1943 by
the Florentine publication of Musica II (item 813), a
collection of articles dedicated principally to
Monteverdi in commemoration of the 300th anniversary
of the composer's death. Also in this category are
Guido Pannain's important series of fifteen articles
which appeared in La rassegna musicale from 1958 to
1962 under the title Studi monteverdiani. The 1967
quatercentenary of Monteverdi's birth inspired several
noteworthy publications: Claudio Monteverdi, nel
quarto centenario della nascita (item 297), for

example, was produced in collaboration with three
Monteverdi scholars; a volume of Rivista italiana di
musicologia (item 838) included twenty papers originally presented at the 1967 Siena Convegno internazionale di studi monteverdiani, a congress sponsored
by the Società Italiana di Musicologia; and, most
importantly, the Congresso internazionale sul tema
Claudio Monteverdi e il suo tempo (item 811), a 1969
publication which printed papers read at the 1968
International Congress held in Venice, Mantua, and
Cremona. Immediately following the quatercentenary
year, Denis Arnold and Nigel Fortune co-edited The
Monteverdi Companion (item 779), a substantial
collection of ten articles intended to shed light on
Monteverdi's music and his environment; a revised
version of this volume appeared in 1985 as The New
Monteverdi Companion (item 780). The latest
Festschrift dedicated to Monteverdi research is
Claudio Monteverdi: Festschrift Reinhold Hammerstein
zum 70. Geburtstag (item 794), a 1986 volume of
twenty-three articles published in honor of the
seventieth birthday of Hammerstein and edited by
Ludwig Finscher. All of these publications, although
differing widely in purpose, format, and content, have
proven to be useful additions to Monteverdi literature
and research.
    The Artusi-Monteverdi controversy has attracted the
attention of several writers. In addition to the
scholarly examination this topic has received in the
general Monteverdi literature, several specialized
studies have focused directly on the famous debate.
Of the more recent investigations, the cogent analysis
provided in Claude Palisca's article (item 671) in The
New Monteverdi Companion, a slight revision of an
earlier article in The Monteverdi Companion, offers
the best introduction to the controversy.
    Monteverdi's own writings, consisting chiefly of a
substantial body of letters and prefaces to a few
collections, are important documents which contribute
to an understanding of the composer's character and
work. Modern interest in this literature dates from
Pereyra's 1911 French translation (item 277) of the
composer's foreword to the fifth book of madrigals and
Giulio Cesare Monteverdi's Dichiaratione. In 1950,
Oliver Strunk provided English translations (item 288)
for the forewords to the fifth and eighth books of
madrigals as well as the Dichiaratione. Major
publications of the composer's letters include those

by Malipiero (item 271), de' Paoli (item 272), and
Stevens (item 273). Additionally, a number of the
letters have been published in The Monteverdi
Companion and The New Monteverdi Companion.
    Beginning with Stevens's authoritative edition of
Monteverdi's letters in 1980, the present decade has
proven, thus far, to be especially fertile for
Monteverdi scholarship. Other outstanding contributions include two recent biographies, one by Silke
Leopold (item 316) and the other by Paolo Fabbri (item
303); Manfred H. Stattkus's valuable and long-needed
catalog (item 874) of Monteverdi's works; and, published a century after Emil Vogel's landmark monograph, Gary Tomlinson's learned Monteverdi and the End
of the Renaissance (item 429).
    The size of this selective bibliography indicates
the enormous quantity of Monteverdi research to date
and attests to a continuing enthusiasm for his music.
It is the hope of the authors that this volume, which
organizes the vast amount of Monteverdi literature,
will stimulate and enhance further investigation about
the composer and his compositions. As the twentieth
century comes to a close, it seems apparent that the
study of Monteverdi, which is extensive but not yet
complete, will continue to engage the attention of
scholars for some time to come.

CLAUDIO MONTEVERDI

I

MONTEVERDI'S WORKS

1. A List of Works by Claudio Monteverdi

Extensive listings of Monteverdi's music can be
found in the biographies of the composer by Arnold
(item 295), de' Paoli (item 302), Leopold (item 316),
and Fabbri (item 303), as well as the lists accompanying the Monteverdi entries in The New Grove
Dictionary of Music and Musicians and Die Musik in
Geschichte und Gegenwart. A recent, valuable contribution to Monteverdi literature is Manfred H.
Stattkus's Claudio Monteverdi Verzeichnis der
erhaltenen Werke (item 874), an informative catalog
which assigns numbers to all of the composer's works.
As yet, no thematic catalog of Monteverdi's music is
in print, although Stattkus states that such a volume
is forthcoming.
The purpose of the following concise list of
Monteverdi's works is to facilitate the use of this
volume and to cite, when identification is possible,
the poets of the texts set by the composer. The
locations of the original printed and manuscript
sources are available in the volumes of RISM (items
867 and 868), Bibliografia della musica italiana
vocale profana pubblicata dal 1500 al 1700 (item 876),
and in the Stattkus catalog cited above. Stattkus
numbers, abbreviated SV, are included before each
extant composition. For the convenience of the
reader, citations of works in the second edition of
Tutte le opere di Claudio Monteverdi, edited by Gian

Francesco Malipiero, follow the entries in this list
of works, as in XI/1 for Malipiero, volume XI, page 1.

a. Operas and Dramatic Works[1]

SV

318   L'Orfeo. Text by Alessandro Striggio.
        Presented first for the Accademia degli
        Invaghiti of Mantua in 1607, then at the
        court of Mantua. Venice: Ricciardo Amadino,
        1609; reprint ed., Venice: Ricciardo
        Amadino, 1615. M. XI/1
291   L'Arianna. Text by Ottavio Rinuccini.
        Presented at the court of Mantua in 1608.
        Music lost except for the Lamento d'Arianna,
        published with Due lettere amorose. Venice:
        Bartolomeo Magni, 1623. M. XI/159
        Prologue to Giovanni Battista Guarini's comedy
        L'Idropica. Text by Gabriello Chiabrera.
        Presented at the court of Mantua in 1608.
        Music lost.
333   La Maddalena. Text by Giovanni Battista
        Andreini. Presented at the court of Mantua
        in 1617. Monteverdi composed only an aria
        with a ritornello. See Musiche de alcuni
        eccellentissimi musici composte per la
        Maddalena (p. 23).
        Andromeda. Text by Ercole Marigliani.
        Presented at the court of Mantua in 1620.
        Music lost.
153   Il combattimento di Tancredi e Clorinda. Text
        by Torquato Tasso. Presented at the
        Mocenigo palace in Venice, 1624. See
        Madrigali guerrieri, et amorosi (p. 14).
        M. VIII/132
        La finta pazza Licori. Text by Giulio
        Strozzi. 1627. Not performed, music lost.
        Gli amori di Diana e di Endimione. Text by
        Ascanio Pio. Presented at the court of
        Parma in 1628. Music lost.

[1]Monteverdi works which are mentioned only in his
correspondence are not listed.

323   Proserpina rapita. Text by Giulio Strozzi.
        Presented at the Mocenigo palace, Venice, in
        1630. Music lost.

325   Il ritorno d'Ulisse in patria. Text by
        Giacomo Badoaro. Presented at the Teatro
        San Cassiano, Venice, in 1641. Manuscript
        at the Hofbibliothek in Vienna. M. XII
        Le nozze d'Enea con Lavinia. Text by Giacomo
        Badoaro. Presented at the SS. Giovanni e
        Paolo at Venice in 1641. Music lost.

308   L'incoronazione di Poppea. Text by Giovanni
        Francesco Busenello. Presented at the SS.
        Giovanni e Paolo, Venice, in 1642.
        Manuscripts in the Biblioteca Nazionale
        Marciana, Venice, and the Biblioteca del
        Conservatorio S. Pietro a Maiella, Naples.
        M. XIII

                        b. Ballets

SV

167   Il ballo delle ingrate. Text by Ottavio
        Rinuccini. Presented at the court theater
        in Mantua, 1608. See Madrigali guerrieri,
        et amorosi (p. 14). M. VIII/314

145   Tirsi e Clori. Text by Alessandro Striggio.
        Presented at the court theater in Mantua,
        1616. See Settimo libro de madrigali (p.
        13). M. VII/191
        Mercurio e Marte, Torneo. Text by Claudio
        Achillini. Presented at the court of Parma
        in 1628. Music lost.

145.2   Volgendo il ciel per l'immortal sentiero.
        Text by Ottavio Rinuccini. According to
        Paolo Fabbri (item 303), this work may have
        been presented at the Imperial Palace at
        Vienna in 1636. See Madrigali guerrieri, et
        amorosi (p. 14). M. VIII/157
        La vittoria d'amore. According to Paolo
        Fabbri (item 303), the text is by B.
        Morando. Presented at Piacenza in 1641.
        Music lost.

c. Secular Collections

Canzonette a tre voci...libro primo. Venice:
    Giacomo Vincenti and Ricciardo Amadino,
    1584. M. X

SV	Text
1	Qual si può dir maggiore X/2
2	Canzonette d'amore X/3
3	La fiera vista X/4
4	Raggi, dov'è il mio bene? X/6
5	Vita de l'alma mia X/8
6	Il mio martir tengo X/9
7	Son questi i crespi crini? X/10
8	Io mi vivea com'aquila X/11
9	Su su, che'l giorno è fore X/12
10	Quando sperai del mio servir mercede X/13
11	Come farò, cuor mio? X/14
12	Corse a la morte il povero Narciso X/15
13	Tu ridi sempre mai X/16
14	Chi vuol veder d'inverno un dolce aprile X/17
15	Già mi credev'un sol esser in cielo X/18
16	Godi pur del bel sen felice X/19
17	Giù lì a quel petto giace X/20
18	Sì come crescon alla terra i fiori X/21
19	Io son fenice e voi sete la fiamma X/22
20	Chi vuol veder un bosco X/23
21	Hor, care canzonette X/24

Madrigali a cinque voci...libro primo.
    Venice: Angelo Gardano, 1587; reprint ed.,
    Venice: Alessandro Raverii, 1607; reprint
    ed., Venice: Bartolomeo Magni, 1621. M. I

SV	Text	Poet
23	Ch'io ami la vita mia nel tuo bel nome I/1	
24	Se per havervi oimè donato il core I/5	
25	A che tormi il ben mio I/8	G.B. Strozzi
26	Amor per tua mercè vatene a quella I/11	G.M. Bonardo
27	Baci soavi e cari I/14	G.B. Guarini
28	Se pur non mi consenti I/18	L. Groto
29	Filli cara e amata I/21	A. Parma
30	Poi che del mio dolore I/24	

31.1	Fumia la pastorella (1^a parte) I/27	A. Allegretti
31.2	Almo divino raggio (2ª parte)	A. Allegretti
31.3	All'hora i pastor tutti (3ª parte)	A. Allegretti
32	Se nel partir da voi, vita mia sento I/36	G.M. Bonardo
33	Tra mille fiamme e tra mille cathene I/39	
34	Usciam, ninfe, homai fuor di questi boschi I/42	
35	Questa ordì il laccio I/46	G.B. Strozzi
36	La vaga pastorella sen va tra fiori I/50	
37	Amor, s'il tuo ferire I/54	
38	Donna, s'io miro voi, giaccio divengo I/58	
39.1	Ardo, sì, ma non t'amo I/61	G.B. Guarini
39.2	Ardi o gela a tua voglia (risposta)	T. Tasso
39.3	Arsi e alsi a mia voglia (contrarisposta)	T. Tasso

Il secondo libro de madrigali a cinque voci.
Venice: Angelo Gardano, 1590; corrected
reprint ed., Venice: Alessandro Raverii,
1607; corrected reprint ed., Venice:
Bartolomeo Magni, 1621. M. II

SV	Text	Poet
40.1	Non si levav'ancor l'alba novella (1ª parte) II/1	T. Tasso
40.2	E dicea l'una sospirando (2ª parte)	T. Tasso
41	Bevea Fillide mia II/15	G. Casoni
42	Dolcissimi legami di parole amorose II/19	T. Tasso
43	Non giacinti o narcisi II/24	G. Casoni
44	Intorno a due vermiglie e vaghe labra II/29	
45	Non sono in queste rive fiori così vermigli II/35	T. Tasso
46	Tutte le bocche belle in questo nero volto II/39	F. Alberti
47	Donna, nel mio ritorno II/44	T. Tasso
48	Quell'ombra esser vorrei II/49	G. Casoni
49	S'andasse amor a caccia II/53	T. Tasso

50	Mentre io miravo fiso de la mia donna gl'occh'ardenti e belli II/58	T. Tasso
51	Ecco mormorar l'onde II/68	T. Tasso
52	Dolcemente dormiva la mia Clori II/78	T. Tasso
53	Se tu mi lassi, perfida II/65	T. Tasso
54	La bocc'onde l'asprissime parole solean uscir II/75	E. Bentivoglio
55	Crudel, perchè mi fuggi? II/83	G.B. Guarini
56	Questo specchio ti dono, Rosa II/87	G. Casoni
57	Non m'è grave'l morire II/92	B. Gottifredi
58	Ti spontò l'ali amor, la donna mia II/97	F. Alberti
59	Cantai un tempo, e se fu dolc'il canto II/102	P. Bembo

Il terzo libro de madrigali a cinque voci.
Venice: Ricciardo Amadino, 1592; reprint
editions were also printed by Amadino in
1594, 1600, 1604, 1607, and 1611; reprint
edition "con il basso continuo per il
clavicembalo, cittharone od altro simile
istromento," Antwerp: Pierre Phalèse, 1615;
reprint ed., Venice: Bartolomeo Magni, 1621.
M. III

SV	Text	Poet
60	La giovinetta pianta si fa più bell'al sole III/1	
61	O come è gran martire III/8	G.B. Guarini
62	Sovra tenere herbette e bianchi fiori III/13	
63	O dolce anima mia III/19	G.B. Guarini
64	Stracciami pur il core III/26	G.B. Guarini
65	O rossignuol ch'in queste verdi fronde III/33	P. Bembo
66	Se per estremo ardore morir potesse un core III/41	G.B. Guarini
67.1	Vattene pur, crudel, con quella pace (1ª parte) III/48	T. Tasso
67.2	Là tra'l sangu'e le morti (2ª parte)	
67.3	Poi ch'ella in sè tornò (3ª parte)	

68	O primavera, gioventù de l'anno III/62	G.B. Guarini
69	Perfidissimo volto III/68	G.B. Guarini
70	Ch'io non t'ami, cor mio III/76	G.B. Guarini
71	Occhi un tempo, mia vita, occhi di questo cor III/82	G.B. Guarini
72.1	Vivrò fra i miei tormenti e le mie cure (1ª parte) III/87	T. Tasso
72.2	Ma dove, o lasso me, dove restarò? (2ª parte)	T. Tasso
72.3	Io pur verrò là dove sete (3ª parte)	T. Tasso
73	Lumi miei, cari lumi III/99	G.B. Guarini
74.1	Rimanti in pace a la dolente e bella Fillida (1ª parte) III/104	L. Celiano
74.2	Ond'ei di morte la sua faccia impressa (2ª parte)	L. Celiano

Il quarto libro de madrigali a cinque voci.
Venice: Ricciardo Amadino, 1603; reprint
editions were also printed by Amadino in
1605, 1607, 1611, and 1615; reprint ed.,
"con il basso continuo per il clavicembalo,
cittharone od altro simile istromento,"
Antwerp: Pierre Phalèse, 1615; corrected
reprint ed., Venice: Bartolomeo Magni, 1622;
reprint edition "con il basso continuo per
il clavicembalo, cittharone od altro simile
istromento," Antwerp: Pierre Phalèse, 1644.
M. IV

SV	Text	Poet
75	Ah dolente partita IV/1	G.B. Guarini
76	Cor mio, mentre vi miro IV/7	G.B. Guarini
77	Cor mio, non mori? IV/11	
78	Sfogava con le stelle un inferno d'amore IV/15	O. Rinuccini
79	Volgea l'anima mia soavemente IV/20	G.B. Guarini
80.1	Anima mia, perdona (1ª parte) IV/26	G.B. Guarini
80.2	Che se tu se'il cor mio (2ª parte)	G.B. Guarini
81	Luci serene e chiare, voi m'incendete IV/35	R. Arlotti

82	La piaga c'ho nel core IV/41	A. Gatti
83	Voi pur da me partite, anima dura IV/44	G.B. Guarini
84	A un giro sol de' bell'occhi lucenti IV/49	G.B. Guarini
85	Ohimè, se tanto amate di sentir dir ohimè IV/54	G.B. Guarini
86	Io mi son giovinetta IV/59	
87	Quel augellin che canta si dolcemente IV/66	G.B Guarini
88	Non più guerra, pietate IV/72	G.B. Guarini
89	Sì ch'io vorrei morire IV/78	M. Moro
90	Anima dolorosa IV/84	G.B. Guarini
91	Anima del cor mio IV/88	
92	Longe da te, cor mio, struggomi di dolore IV/92	
93	Piagne e sospira IV/96	T. Tasso

Il quinto libro de madrigali a cinque
voci...col basso continuo per il
clavicembalo, chittarone od altro simile
istromento, fatto particolarmente per li sei
ultimi, e per li altri a beneplacito.
Venice: Ricciardo Amadino, 1605; corrected
reprint ed., Venice: Ricciardo Amadino,
1606; reprint ed., Venice: Ricciardo
Amadino, 1608; reprint ed., Venice:
Ricciardo Amadino, 1610; corrected reprint
ed., Venice: Ricciardo Amadino, 1611;
reprint ed., Venice: Ricciardo Amadino,
1613; corrected reprint ed., Venice:
Ricciardo Amadino, 1615; reprint ed.,
Antwerp: Pierre Phalèse, 1615; corrected
reprint ed., Venice: Bartolomeo Magni, 1620;
reprint ed., Antwerp: Pierre Phalèse, 1643.
M. V

SV	Text	Poet
94	Cruda Amarilli V/1	G.B. Guarini
95	O Mirtillo, Mirtill'anima mia V/5	G.B. Guarini
96	Era l'anima mia già presso a l'ultim'hore V/9	G.B. Guarini
97.1	Ecco, Silvio, colei ch'in odio hai tanto (1ª parte) V/14	G.B. Guarini

97.2	Ma se con la pietà non è in te spenta (2ª parte)	G.B. Guarini
97.3	Dorinda, ah dirò mia, se mia non sei (3ª parte)	G.B. Guarini
97.4	Ecco piegando le ginocchie a terra (4ª parte)	G.B. Guarini
97.5	Ferir quel petto, Silvio (5ª parte)	G.B. Guarini
98.1	Ch'io t'ami e t'ami più de la mia vita (1ª parte) V/39	G.B. Guarini
98.2	Deh, bella e cara (2ª parte)	G.B. Guarini
98.3	Ma tu più che mai dura (3ª parte)	G.B. Guarini
99	Che dar più vi poss'io? V/51	
100	M'è più dolce il penar per Amarilli V/56	G.B. Guarini
101	Ahi, com'a un vago sol cortese giro V/62	G.B. Guarini
102	Troppo ben può questo tiranno amore V/71	G.B. Guarini
103	Amor, se giusto sei V/81	
104	T'amo, mia vita V/90	G.B. Guarini
105	E così a poc'a poco torno farfalla (6 voices) V/96	G.B. Guarini
106	Questi vaghi concenti (9 voices) V/104	

Scherzi musicali a tre voci, raccolti da
Giulio Cesare Monteverde suo fratello...con
la dichiaratione di una lettera che si
ritrova stampata nel quinto libro de suoi
madrigali. Venice: Ricciardo Amadino, 1607;
reprint editions were also printed by
Amadino in 1609, 1615, and 1619; reprint
ed., Venice: Bartolomeo Magni, 1628. M. X

SV	Text	Poet
230	I bei legami X/29	G. Chiabrera
231	Amarilli onde m'assale X/31	G. Chiabrera
232	Fugge il verno dei dolori X/34	G. Chiabrera
233	Quando l'alba in oriente X/36	G. Chiabrera
234	Non così tosto io miro X/38	G. Chiabrera
235	Damigella tutta bella X/40	G. Chiabrera
236	La pastorella mia spietata X/41	J. Sannazaro
237	O rosetta, che rosetta X/43	G. Chiabrera

238	Amorosa pupilletta X/44	
239	Vaghi rai di cigli ardenti X/46	G. Chiabrera
240	La violetta X/48	G. Chiabrera
241	Giovinetta ritrosetta X/50	
242	Dolci miei sospiri X/52	G. Chiabrera
243	Clori amorosa X/54	G. Chiabrera
244	Lidia, spina del mio core X/56	

Il sesto libro de madrigali a cinque voci, con
uno dialogo a sette, con il suo basso
continuo per poterli concertare nel clava-
cembano, et altri stromenti. Venice:
Ricciardo Amadino, 1614; corrected reprint
ed., Venice: Ricciardo Amadino, 1615;
reprint ed., Venice: Bartolomeo Magni, 1620;
reprint ed., Antwerp: Pierre Phalèse, 1639.
M. VI

SV	Text	Poet
107	Lamento di Arianna:	
107.1	Lasciatemi morire (1^a parte) VI/1	O. Rinuccini
107.2	O Teseo, Teseo mio (2^a parte)	O. Rinuccini
107.3	Dove, dove è la fede (3^a parte)	O. Rinuccini
107.4	Ahi, ch'ei non pur risponde (4^a parte)	O. Rinuccini
108	Zefiro torna e'l bel tempo rimena VI/22	F. Petrarch
109	Una donna fra l'altre honesta e bella vidi VI/29	
110	A Dio, Florida bella VI/38	G.B. Marino
111	Sestina, Lagrime d'amante al sepolcro dell'amata:	
111.1	Incenerite spoglie, avara tomba (1^a parte) VI/46	S. Agnelli
111.2	Ditelo, o fiumi e voi ch' udiste (2^a parte)	S. Agnelli
111.3	Darà la notte il sol (3^a parte)	S. Agnelli
111.4	Ma te raccoglie, o ninfa (4^a parte)	S. Agnelli
111.5	O chiome d'or, neve gentil del seno (5^a parte)	S. Agnelli
111.6	Dunque amate reliquie (6^a parte)	S. Agnelli

112	Ohimè, il bel viso VI/70	F. Petrarch
113	Qui rise o Tirsi VI/77	G.B. Marino
114	Misero Alceo VI/91	
115	Batto qui pianse Ergasto VI/101	G.B. Marino
116	Presso un fiume tranquillo (7 voices) VI/113	G.B. Marino

Concerto. Settimo libro de madrigali a 1. 2. 3. 4. & sei voci, con altri generi de canti. Venice: Bartolomeo Magni, 1619; reprint editions were also printed by Magni in 1622 and 1623. M. VII

SV	Text	Poet
117	Tempro la cetra VII/2	G.B. Marino
118	Non è di gentil core chi non arde VII/8	Degl'Atti
119	A quest'olmo, a quest'ombre VII/14	G.B. Marino
120	O come sei gentile, caro augellino VII/35	G.B. Guarini
121	Io son pur vezzosetta pastorella VII/41	
122	O viva fiamma, o miei sospiri ardenti VII/47	
123	Vorrei baciarti, o Filli VII/52	G.B. Marino
124	Dice la mia bellissima Licori VII/58	G.B. Guarini
125	Ah, che non si conviene romper la fede? VII/62	
126	Non vedrò mai le stelle VII/66	
127	Ecco vicine, o bella tigre, l'hore VII/71	C. Achillini
128	Perchè fuggi tra salci, ritrosetta? VII/76	G.B. Marino
129	Tornate, o cari baci VII/81	G.B. Marino
130	Soave libertate VII/85	G. Chiabrera
131	S'el vostro cor, madonna VII/90	G.B. Guarini
132	Interrotte speranze VII/94	G.B. Guarini
133	Augellin, che la voce al canto spieghi VII/98	
134	Vaga su spina ascosa VII/104	G. Chiabrera
135	Eccomi pronta ai baci, Ergasto mio VII/111	G.B. Marino

136   Parlo, miser'o taccio? VII/116 G.B. Guarini
137   Tu dormi? Ah crudo core
         VII/123
138   Al lume delle stelle
         VII/129
139   Con che soavità, labbra   G.B. Guarini
         odorate VII/137
140.1   Ohimè, dov'è il mio ben?   B. Tasso
         (1^a parte) VII/152
140.2   Dunque ha potuto sol desio   B. Tasso
         d'honore (2^a parte)
140.3   Dunque ha potuto in me più   B. Tasso
         che'l mio amore (3^a parte)
140.4   Ahi sciocco mondo e cieco   B. Tasso
         (4^a parte)
141   Se i languidi miei sguardi   C. Achillini
         (Lettera amorosa a voce sola)
         VII/160
142   Se pur destina e vole il cielo
         (Partenza amorosa a voce
         sola) VII/167
143   Chiome d'oro, bel thesoro
         VII/176
144   Amor che deggio far? VII/182
145   Tirsi e Clori VII/191

Scherzi musicali cioè arie, & madrigali in
  stil recitativo, con una ciaccona a 1. & 2.
voci...Raccolti da Bartolomeo Magni.
Venice: Bartolomeo Magni, 1632. M. IX & X

SV   Text   Poet

150   Armato il cor d'adamantina   O. Rinuccini
         fede IX/27
246   Maledetto sia l'aspetto X/76
247.1   Quel sguardo sdegnosetto X/77
247.2   Armatevi, pupille X/78
247.3   Begli occhi, all'armi X/79
248   Eri già tutta mia X/80
249.1   Ecco di dolci raggi X/81
249.2   Io che armato sin hor X/91
250   Et è pur dunque vero X/82
251   Zefiro torna (Ciacona a 2)   O. Rinuccini
         IX/9

Madrigali guerrieri, et amorosi con alcuni
opuscoli in genere rappresentativo, che
saranno per brevi episodi fra i canti senza
gesto, libro ottavo. Venice: Alessandro
Vincenti, 1638. M. VIII & IX

Canti guerrieri

SV	Text	Poet
146	Altri canti d'amor VIII/2	
147.1	Hor ch'el ciel e la terra e'l vento tace (1ª parte) VIII/39	F. Petrarch
147.2	Così sol d'una chiara fonte viva (2ª parte)	F. Petrarch
148.1	Gira il nemico insidioso (1ª parte) VIII/75	G. Strozzi
148.2	Nol lasciamo accostar (2ª parte)	G. Strozzi
148.3	Armi false non son (3ª parte)	G. Strozzi
148.4	Vuol degl'occhi attaccar il baloardo (4ª parte)	G. Strozzi
148.5	Non è più tempo, ohimè (5ª parte)	G. Strozzi
148.6	Cor mio, non val fuggir (6ª parte)	G. Strozzi
149	Se vittorie sì belle IX/21	F. Testi
150	Armato il cor d'adamantina fede IX/27	O. Rinuccini
151.1	Ogni amante è guerrier (1ª parte) VIII/88	O. Rinuccini
151.2	Io che nell'otio naqui e d'otio vissi (2ª parte)	O. Rinuccini
151.3	Ma per quel ampio Egeo spieghi le vele (3ª parte)	O. Rinuccini
151.4	Riedi ch'al nostr'ardir (4^a parte)	O. Rinuccini
152	Ardo, avvampo, mi struggo VIII/107	
153	Combattimento di Tancredi et Clorinda VIII/132	T. Tasso
154	Ballo (Movete al mio bel suon le piante snelle) VIII/162	O. Rinuccini

Canti amorosi

SV	Text	Poet
155.1	Altri canti di Marte (1^a parte) VIII/181	G.B. Marino

155.2	Due belli occhi fur l'armi (2^a parte)	G.B. Marino
156	Vago augelletto, che cantando vai VIII/222	F. Petrarch
157	Mentre vaga Angioletta ogn'anima gentil cantando alletta VIII/246	G.B. Guarini
158	Ardo, e scoprir, ahi lasso, io non ardisco IX/32	
159	O sia tranquillo il mare IX/36	
160.1	Ninfa che scalza il piede (1^a parte) VIII/259	
160.2	Qui, deh, meco t'arresta (2^a parte)	
160.3	Dell'usate mie corde al suon (3^a parte)	
161	Dolcissimo uscignolo VIII/271	G.B. Guarini
162	Chi vol haver felice e lieto il core VIII/280	G.B. Guarini
163	Lamento della Ninfa:	
163.1	Non havea Febo ancora (1^a parte) VIII/286	O. Rinuccini
163.2	Lamento della ninfa (Amor, dicea) (2^a parte)	O. Rinuccini
163.3	Si tra sdegnosi pianti (3^a parte)	O. Rinuccini
164	Perchè t'en fuggi, o Fillide? VIII/295	
165	Non partir, ritrosetta VIII/305	
166	Su su, su pastorelli vezzosi VIII/310	
167	Ballo delle ingrate VIII/314	O. Rinuccini

Madrigali e canzonette a due, e tre,
voci...libro nono. Venice: Alessandro
Vincenti, 1651. M. IX

SV	Text	Poet
149	Se vittorie si belle IX/21	
150	Armato il cor d'adamantina fede IX/27	O. Rinuccini
158	Ardo, e scoprir, ahi lasso, io non ardisco IX/32	
159	O sia tranquillo il mare IX/36	

168   Bel pastor dal cui bel guardo   O. Rinuccini
        IX/1
169   Alcun non mi consigli IX/42
170   Di far sempre gioire amor
        speranza dà IX/50
171   Quando dentro al tuo seno
        IX/56
172   Non voglio amare per non
        penare IX/58
173   Come dolce hoggi l'auretta   G. Strozzi
        spira IX/60
174   Alle danze, alle gioie IX/68
175   Perchè se m'odiavi IX/79
176   Si si ch'io v'amo, occhi
        vaghi, occhi belli IX/82
178   O mio bene, o mia vita IX/95
251   Zefiro torna IX/9   O. Rinuccini

        d. Secular Works in Anthologies

        Il primo libro delle canzonette a tre voci di
        Antonio Morsolino con alcune altre de
        diversi eccellenti musici. Venice: Giacomo
        Vincenti & Ricciardo Amadino, 1594.

SV   Text   Poet

309   Io ardo, sì, ma'l fuoco di
        tal sorte XVII/1
314   Occhi miei, se mirar, più
        non debb'io XVII/2
324   Quante son stelle in ciel   G.B. da Cerreto
        XVII/3
331   Se non mi date aita XVII/4

        I Nuovi Fioretti Musicali a tre voci d'Amante
        Franzoni Mantovano...Raccolti dall'illu-
        strissimo Signor Fulvio Gonzaga marchese.
        Venice: Ricciardo Amadino, 1605.

SV   Text

322   Prima vedrò ch'in questi prati XVII/5

        Lamento d'Arianna...et con due lettere amorose
        in genere rapresentativo. Venice:
        Bartolomeo Magni, 1623.

SV	Text	Poet
22.1	Lasciatemi morire XI/159	O. Rinuccini
141	Se i languidi miei sguardi VII/160	C. Achillini
142	Se pur destina e vole il cielo VII/167	

Madrigali del signor cavaliere Anselmi...a 2.
3. 4. 5. voci. Con il basso continuo.
Venice: Bartolomeo Magni, 1624.

SV	Text	Poet
315	O come vaghi, o come	G.B. Anselmi
334	Taci, Armelin, deh taci	G.B. Anselmi

Quarto Scherzo delle ariso vaghezze, commode
da cantarsi à voce sola...di Carlo
Milanuzzi...con una cantata, & altre arie
del Signor Monteverde, e del Sig. Francesco
suo figliolo. Venice: Bartolomeo Magni,
1624.

SV	Text	
310	La mia turca che d'amor	IX/117
316	Ohimè ch'io cado, ohimè ch'inciampo	IX/111
332	Si dolce è'l tormento	IX/119

Arie de diversi raccolte da Alessandro
Vincenti...con le lettere dell' alfabetto
per la chitarra spagnola. Venice:
Alessandro Vincenti, 1634.

SV	Text	
320	Perchè, se m'odiavi	XVII/24
321	Più lieto il guardo	XVII/22

e. Sacred Collections

Sacrae cantiunculae tribus vocibus...liber
primus. Venice: Angelum Gardanum, 1582.
M. XIV

SV	Text
207	Lapidabant Stephanum XIV/1
208	Veni in hortum meum XIV/3
209	Ego sum pastor bonus XIV/6
210	Surge propera, amica mea XIV/8
211	Ubi duo vel tres congregati fuerint XIV/11
212	Quam pulchra es XIV/13
213	Ave Maria, gratia plena XIV/15
214	Domine Pater et Deus vitae meae XIV/17
215.1	Tu es pastor ovium (1^a pars) XIV/19
215.2	Tu es Petrus (2^a pars)
216.1	O magnum pietatis opus (1^a pars) XIV/22
216.2	Eli clamans (2^a pars)
217	O crux benedicta XIV/25
218	Hodie Christus natus est XIV/26
219.1	O Domine Jesu Christe (1^a pars) XIV/29
219.2	O Domine Jesu Christe (2^a pars)
220	Pater, venit hora XIV/33
221	In tua patientia XIV/34
222	Angelus ad pastores ait XIV/36
223	Salve, crux pretiosa XIV/38
224	Quia vidisti me, Thoma, credidisti XIV/40
225	Lauda, Sion, salvatorem XIV/42
226	O bone Jesu, illumina oculos meos XIV/44
227	Surgens Jesus, Dominus noster XIV/46
228	Qui vult venire post me XIV/48
229	Iusti tulerunt spolia impiorum XIV/50

Madrigali spirituali a quattro voci. Cremona:
  Pietro Bozzola, 1583; Brescia: Vincenzo
  Sabbio, 1583. Only the bass part is extant.

SV	Text
179	Sacrosanta di Dio verace imago
180.1	Laura del ciel sempre feconda (1^a parte)
180.2	Poi che benigno il novo cant' attende (2^a parte)
181.1	Aventurosa notte (1^a parte)
181.2	Serpe crudel (2^a parte)
182.1	D'empi martiri (1^a parte)
182.2	Ond'in ogni pensier (2^a parte)
183.1	Mentre la stell'appar (1^a parte)
183.2	Tal contra Dio de la superbia il corno (2^a parte)
184.1	Le rose, gli amaranti e gigli (1^a parte)

184.2   Ai piedi havendo (2^a parte)
185.1   L'empio vestia di porpora
              (1^a parte)
185.2   Ma quel medico (2^a parte)
186.1   L'human discorso (1^a parte)
186.2   L'eterno Dio quel cor pudico
              scelse (2^a parte)
187.1   Dal sacro petto esce veloce
              dardo (1^a parte)
187.2   Scioglier m'addita (2^a parte)
188.1   Afflitto e scalz'ove la sacra
              sponda (1^a parte)
188.2   Ecco, dicea (2^a parte)
189.1   Dei miei giovenil anni (1^a parte)
189.2   Tutt'esser vidi (2^a parte)

            Sanctissimae Virgini missa senis vocibus ad
            ecclesiarum choros ac vesperae pluribus
            decantandae cum nonnullis sacris concentibus
            ad sacella sive principum cubicula
            accommodata. Venice: Ricciardo Amadino,
            1610. M. XIV

SV   Text

205   Missa de cappella a sei voci, fatta sopra il
              motetto 'In illo tempore' del Gomberti:
              Kyrie eleison XIV/57
              Et in terra pax
              Patrem omnipotentem
              Sanctus
              Agnus Dei
206   Vespro della Beata Vergine:
206.1   Domine ad adiuvandum XIV/123
206.2   Dixit Dominus
206.3   Nigra sum sed formosa
206.4   Laudate, pueri, Dominum
206.5   Pulchra es, amica mea
206.6   Laetatus sum
206.7   Duo Seraphim clamabant
206.8   Nisi Dominus aedificaverit domum
206.9   Audi, coelum, verba mea
206.10   Lauda, Jerusalem, Dominum
206.11   Sonata sopra Sancta Maria, ora pro nobis
206.12   Ave maris stella
206.13   Magnificat I (7 voices)
206a.12   Magnificat II (6 voices)

Selva morale e spirituale.   Venice: Bartolomeo
    Magni, 1640. M. XV

SV   Text

252   O ciechi il tanto affaticar che giova   XV/1
253   Voi ch'ascoltate in rime sparse   XV/15
254   È questa vita un lampo   XV/35
255   Spuntava il dì   XV/42
256   Chi vol che m'innamori   XV/54
257   Messa a 4 voci da cappella:
            Kyrie eleison   XV/59
            Et in terra pax
            Patrem omnipotentem
            Sanctus
            Agnus Dei
258   Gloria in excelsis Deo   XV/117
259   Crucifixus (1ª pars)   XV/178
260   Et resurrexit (2^a pars)
261   Et iterum venturus est (3^a pars)
262   Ab aeterno ordinata sum   XV/189
263   Dixit Dominus Domino meo (I)   XV/195
264   Dixit Dominus Domino meo (II)   XV/246
265   Confitebor tibi, Domine (I)   XV/297
266   Confitebor tibi, Domine (II)   XV/338
267   Confitebor tibi, Domine (III)   XV/352
268   Beatus vir (I)   XV/368
269   Beatus vir (II)   XV/418
270   Laudate, pueri, Dominum (I)   XV/438
271   Laudate, pueri, Dominum (II)   XV/460
272   Laudate Dominum, omnes gentes (I)   XV/481
273   Laudate Dominum, omnes gentes (II)   XV/503
274   Laudate Dominum, omnes gentes (III)   XV/521
275   Credidi propter quod locutus sum   XV/544
276   Memento, et omnis mansuetudinis eius   XV/567
277   Sanctorum meritis inclita gaudia (I)   XV/606
278   Sanctorum meritis inclita gaudia (II)   XV/610
278a   Deus tuorum militum sors et corona   XV/614
278b   Iste confessor Domini sacratus (I)   XV/618
279   Iste confessor Domini sacratus (II)   XV/622
279a   Ut queant laxis resonare fibris   XV/629
280   Deus tuorum militum sors et corona   XV/636
281   Magnificat (I)   XV/639
282   Magnificat (II)   XV/703
283   Salve regina (I)   XV/724
284   Salve regina (II)   XV/736
285   Salve regina (III)   XV/741
286   Jubilet tota civitas   XV/748

287   Laudate Dominum in sanctis eius XV/753
288   Iam moriar, mi Fili (Pianto della Madonna
            sopra il Lamento d'Arianna) XV/757

         Messa a 4 voci, et Salmi a 1, 2, 3, 4, 5, 6,
            7, et 8 voci, concertati, e parte da
            cappella, et con le letanie della B.V.
            Venice: Alessandro Vincenti, 1650. M. XVI

SV   Text

190   Messa a 4 voci da cappella:
            Kyrie eleison XVI/1
            Et in terra pax
            Patrem omnipotentem
            Sanctus
            Agnus Dei
191   Dixit Dominus (I) XVI/54
192   Dixit Dominus (II) XVI/94
193   Confitebor tibi, Domine (I) XVI/129
194   Confitebor tibi, Domine (II) XVI/144
195   Beatus vir XVI/167
196   Laudate, pueri, Dominum XVI/211
197   Laudate Dominum, o omnes gentes XVI/227
198   Laetatus sum (I) XVI/231
199   Laetatus sum (II) XVI/276
200   Nisi Dominus aedificaverit domum (I) XVI/299
201   Nisi Dominus aedificaverit domum (II) XVI/318
202   Lauda, Jerusalem, Dominum (I) XVI/344
203   Lauda, Jerusalem, Dominum (II) XVI/358
204   Laetaniae della Beata Vergine XVI/382

         f. Sacred Works in Anthologies

         Parnassus musicus Ferdinandeus...a Joanne
            Baptista Bonometti...congestus. Venice:
            Giacomo Vincenti, 1615.

SV

292   Cantate domino canticum novum XVI/409

Musiche de alcuni eccellentissimi musici
composte per la Maddalena sacra rappresentazione di Gio. Battista Andreini
fiorentino. Venice: Angelo Gardano, 1617.

SV

333   Su le penne de' venti   XI/170

Primo libro delli concerti ecclesiastici...di
Gio. Battista Ala. Milan: Filippo Lomazzo,
1618.

SV

328   Sancta Maria, succurre miseris   XVI/511

Symbolae diversorum musicorum...Ab admodum
reverendo D. Laurentio Calvo...in lucem
editae. Venice: Alessandro Vincenti, 1620.

SV

305   Fuge, anima mea, mundum   XVI/444
312   O beatae viae, o felices gressus   XVI/454

Libro primo de motetti...di Giulio Cesare
Bianchi. Con un altro à cinque, e tre à sei
del Sig. Claudio Monteverde. Venice:
Bartolomeo Magni, 1620.

SV

289   Adoramus te, Christe   XVI/439
292   Cantate Domino canticum novum (6 voices)
           XVI/422
293   Christe, adoramus te   XVI/428
298   Domine, ne in furore tuo arguas me
           XVI/432

Libro secondo di mottetti...di Giulio Cesare
Bianchi. Con le Letanie à sei voci del Sig.
Claudio Monteverde. Venice: Alessandro
Vincenti, 1620.

SV

204   Letanie della Beata Vergine   XVI/382

Promptuarii musici concentus ecclesiasticos
II. III. et IV. vocum...e diversis, iisque
illustrissimis et musica laude praestan-
tissimis hujus aetatis authoribus, collectos
exhibentis. Pars prima...Collectore Joanne
Donfrido. Strasbourg: Paul Ledertz, 1622.

SV

313   O bone Jesu, o piissime Jesu   XVI/506

Seconda raccolta de' sacri canti...de diversi
eccellentissimi autori fatta da Don Lorenzo
Calvi. Venice: Alessandro Vincenti, 1624.

SV

301   Ego flos campi et lilium convallium   XVI/464
326   Salve, o regina, o mater   XVI/475
335   Venite siccientes ad aquas Domini   XVI/467

Sacri affetti con testi da diversi eccellentissimi autori raccolti da Francesco
Sammaruco. Rome: Luca Antonio Soldi, 1625.

SV

300   Ego dormio et cor meum vigilat   XVI/481

Ghirlanda sacra scielta da diversi eccellentissimi compositori de varii motetti à voce
sola. Libro primo opera seconda per
Leonardo Simonetti. Venice: Bartolomeo
Magni, 1625.

SV

297   Currite, populi, psallite timpanis   XVI/491
299   Ecce sacrum paratum convivium   XVI/497
317   O quam pulchra es, amica mea   XVI/486
327   Salve regina   XVI/502

Psalmi de vespere a quattro voci del Cavalier
D. Gio. Maria Sabino da Turi. Naples:
Ambrosio Magnetta, 1627.

SV

295   Confitebor tibi, Domine

Quarta raccolta de sacri canti...de diversi
eccellentissimi autori, fatta da Don Lorenzo
Calvi. Venice: Alessandro Vincenti, 1629.

SV

285   Salve regina (3 voices)   XV/741
303   Exulta, filia Sion   XVII/8
304   Exultent caeli et gaudeant angeli   XVII/15

Motetti a voce sola de diversi eccellentissimi
autori...Libro primo. Venice: Gardano,
1645.

SV

336   Venite, videte martyrem quam sit carus
          XVII/25

Raccolta di motetti a 1. 2. 3. voci di Gaspro
Casati et de diversi altri eccellentissimi
autori. Venice: Bartolomeo Magni, 1651.

SV

302   En gratulemur hodie   XVI/517

                    g. Contrafacta

Musica tolta da i madrigali di Claudio Monteverde, e d'altri autori, à cinque, ed à sei
voci, e fatta spirituale da Aquilino
Coppini. Milan: Agostino Tradate, 1607;
reprint ed., Agostino Tradate, 1611.

SV

94.k   Felle amaro   (Cruda Amarilli)
96.k   Stabat Virgo   (Era l'anima mia)

97.1k	Qui pependit	(Ecco, Silvio)
97.3k	Maria, quid ploras?	(Dorinda, ah dirò mia)
97.4k	Te, Jesu Christe	(Ecco piegando)
97.5k	Pulchrae sunt	(Ferir quel petto)
98.2k	Sancta Maria	(Deh, bella e cara)
98.3k	Spernit Deus	(Ma tu più che mai dura)
101.k	Vives in corde meo	(Ahi, com'a un vago)
102.k	Ure me Domine	(Troppo ben può)
104.k	Gloria tua	(T'amo, mia vita)

Il secondo libro della musica di Claudio
Monteverde e d'altri autori à 5 voci fatta
spirituale da Aquilino Coppini. Milan:
Agostino Tradate, 1608.

SV

60.k	Florea serta	(La giovinetta pianta)
61.k	O dies infelices	(O come è gran martire)
68.k	Praecipitantur, Jesu Christe	(O primavera)
75.k	O infelix recessus	(Ah dolente partita)
95.k	O mi fili	(O Mirtillo)
98.1k	Te sequar, Jesu	(Ch'io t'ami)
99.k	Qui regnas	(Che dar più vi poss'io?)
100.k	Animas eruit	(M'è più dolce il penar)

Il terzo libro della musica di Claudio
Monteverde à cinque voci fatta spirituale da
Aquilino Coppini. Milan: Agostino Tradate,
1609.

SV

76.k	Jesu, dum te	(Cor mio, mentre vi miro)
77.k	Jesu, tu obis	(Cor mio, non mori?)
78.k	O stellae	(Sfogava con le stelle)
79.k	Ardebat igne	(Volgea l'anima mia)
80.k	Domine Deus	(Anima mia, perdona)

80.k2	O gloriose martyr	(Che se tu se'il cor mio)
81.k	Luce serena	(Luci serene e chiare)
82.k	Plagas tuas	(La piaga c'ho nel core)
83.k	Tu vis a me	(Voi pur da me partite)
84.k	Cantemus	(A un giro sol)
86.k	Rutilante in nocte	(Io mi son giovinetta)
87.k	Qui laudes	(Quell'augellin che canta)
89.k	O Jesu, mea vita	(Sì ch'io vorrei morire)
90.k	Anima miseranda	(Anima dolorosa)
91.k	Anima quam dilexi	(Anima del cor mio)
92.k	Longe a te	(Longe da te, cor mio)
93.k	Plorat amare	(Piagne e sospira)
97.2k	Qui pietate	(Ma se con la pietà)
103.k	Amemus te	(Amor, se giusto sei)
109.k1	Una es	(Una donna fra l'altre)

Concerti sacri...libro secondo...del P. Pietro
Lappi. Venice: Bartolomeo Magni, 1623.

SV

134.k1	Ave regina mundi	(Vaga su spina ascosa)

Erster Theil geistlicher Concerten und
Harmonien à 1. 2. 3. 4. 5. 6. 7. &c.
vocibus...colligiret und zum öffentlichen
Druck befördert durch Ambrosium Profium.
Leipzig: H. Köler, 1641.

SV

134.k2	Jesum viri senesque	(Vaga su spina ascosa)

Ander Theil geistlicher Concerten und
Harmonien...colligiret und zum öffentlichen
Druck befördert durch Ambrosium Profium.
Leipzig: H. Köler, 1641.

SV

155.k12	Ergo gaude, laetare	(Due belli occhi)
155.k21	Pascha concelebranda	(Altri canti di Marte)
155.k22	Lauda, anima mea	(Due belli occhi)

Dritter Theil geistlicher Concerten und
Harmonien...colligiret und publiciret durch
Ambrosium Profium. Leipzig: H. Köler, 1642.

SV

150.k	Heus, bone vir	(Armato il cor)
249.2k	Spera in Domino	(Io che armato sin hor)
253.k	Haec dicit Deus	(Voi ch'ascoltate in rime sparse)

Corollarium geistlicher collectaneorum...
gewähret von Ambrosio Profio. Leipzig:
Ritzsch, 1649.

SV

136.k1	Longe, mi Jesu	(Parlo, miser, o taccio?)
137.k	O Jesu, lindere meinen Schmerzen	(Tu dormi?)
138.k	O rex supreme	(Al lume della stelle)
147.k	O du mächtiger Herr	(Hor che'l ciel e la terra)
147.k2	Dein allein ist ja	(Cosí sol d'una chiara fonte)
152.k1	Alleluja, kommet jauchzet	(Ardo, avvampo)
152.k2	Freude kommet, lasset uns	(Ardo, avvampo)
156.k1	Resurrexit de sepulcro	(Vago augelletto)
156.k2	Veni, veni, soror mea	(Vago augelletto)

h. Secular Works in Manuscript[2]

<u>SV</u>

290   Ahi, che si partì il mio bel sol adorno
          (Manuscript in the Biblioteca Estense,
          Modena)
A 2   Lamento d'Olimpia:
A 2.1   Voglio morir: van'è'l conforto tuo (1^a
          parte)
A 2.2   Anzi che non amarmi (2ª parte)
A 2.3   Ma perchè, o ciel, invendicate lassi
          (3ª parte)
          (Manuscript in the British Library, London)
337   Voglio di vita uscir
          (Manuscript in the Archivio dei Filippini,
          Naples)

          i. Sacred Works in Manuscript

<u>SV</u>

306   Fuggi fuggi, cor, fuggi a tutte l'or
          (Manuscript in the Biblioteca Queriniana,
          Brescia. See Kurtzman, item 380)
307   Gloria in excelsis Deo
          (Manuscript in the Archivio dei Filippini,
          Naples)
330   Se d'un angel il bel viso
          (Manuscript in the Biblioteca Queriniana,
          Brescia. See Kurtzman, item 380)

[2]For an extensive list of Monteverdi manuscripts,
see Stattkus, item 874.

2. Modern Editions of Monteverdi's Works

The first modern editions of Monteverdi's music
were inspired by the revival of the composer's works
in the late nineteenth century. Many of these, such
as the edition of Orfeo by Robert Eitner in Publikationen älterer praktischer und theoretischer
Musikwerke and the edition of Il ritorno d'Ulisse in
patria by Robert Haas in Denkmäler der Tonkunst in
Österreich, appeared in landmark historical collections. Numerous twentieth-century performances of
Monteverdi's works have also resulted in the publication of performing editions. Clearly the most
significant step taken in the resurrection of Monteverdi's music was the publication of Tutte le opere di
Claudio Monteverdi, edited by Gian Francesco Malipiero
between 1926 and 1942. Although the editorial procedures followed by Malipiero in his complete edition
of Monteverdi's compositions have received considerable criticism, the collection is nevertheless a
monumental achievement and has provided the first
practical editions of many of the composer's works.
Another immense project is underway with the ongoing
publication of a second Monteverdi complete edition by
the Fondazione Claudio Monteverdi in Cremona. This
edition, of which five volumes have been issued to
date under the guidance of various editors, promises
to be the long-awaited scholarly edition of the
composer's complete works.
     The following lists summarize the contents of the
Malipiero complete edition and the volumes published
and projected by the Fondazione Claudio Monteverdi.
This section concludes with a selective list of modern
editions.

Tutte le opere di Claudio Monteverdi, edited by Gian
Francesco Malipiero. Vol. I-XVI. Asolo: G. Francesco
Malipiero, 1926-42. A second edition, published by
Universal Edition, 1954-68, contains revisions only in
vols. VIII, XV, and XVI. A supplementary volume
(XVII) was published in 1966.

    I   Il primo libro de madrigali à cinque voci
          (1587)
   II   Il secondo libro de madrigali à cinque voci
          (1590)

III   Il terzo libro de madrigali à cinque voci
       (1592)
IV   Il quattro libro de madrigali à cinque voci
       (1603)
V   Il quinto libro de madrigali à cinque voci
       (1605)
VI   Il sesto libro de madrigali à cinque voci,
       Lamento d'Arianna, and Lagrime d'amante
       (1614)
VII   Il settimo libro de madriali à 1.2.3.4. & 6
       voci, Concerto, and Tirsi et Clori (1619)
VIII   Il ottavo libro: Madrigali guerrieri, et
       amorosi, Combattimento di Tancredi e
       Clorinda (1638)
IX   Il nono libro: madrigali e canzonette à due
       e tre voci (1651)
X   Canzonette a tre voci (1584), Scherzi
       musicali a tre voci (1607), and Scherzi
       musicali cioè arie & madrigali à 1 & 2
       voci (1632)
XI   Orfeo: Favola in musica (1609), Lamento
       d'Arianna (1608), and Musiche de alcuni...
       La Maddalena (1617)
XII   Il ritorno d'Ulisse in patria: Drama in
       musica (1641)
XIII   L'incoronazione di Poppea: Drama in musica
       (1642)
XIV   Sacrae cantiunculae tribus vocibus...liber
       primus (1582); Sanctissimae virgini missa
       senis vocibus, Vespro della Beata Vergine,
       Sonata sopra Sancta Maria, Ave Maris
       stella, Magnificat a 7, and Magnificat a 6
       (1610)
XV   Selva morale e spirituale (1640)
XVI   Messa et Salmi a 1.2.3.4.5.6.7. & 8 voci
       concertati, e parte da cappella, & con le
       letanie della B.V. (1650); Frammenti
       pubblicati in varie raccolte (1615, 1620,
       1622, 1624, 1625, 1627, 1651); and
       appendix: Madrigali Spirituali a Quattro
       voci (Bass parts only) (1583)

Opera omnia. Edited by the Fondazione Claudio
   Monteverdi. Instituta et Monumenta I/5.

   I   Sacrae cantiunculae (1582); Madrigali
        spirituali a quattro (1583); Canzonette a
        tre voci (1584). Forthcoming.

II	Madrigali a 5 voci, Libro I (1587), ed. by Raffaello Monterosso. Cremona: Athenaeum Cremonense, 1970. Contains facsimiles, an extensive preface, and a selective bibliography and discography.
III	Madrigali a 5 voci, Libro II (1590), ed. by Anna Maria Monterosso Vacchelli. Cremona: Fondazione Claudio Monteverdi, 1979. Contains facsimiles, an extensive preface, and a selective bibliography and discography.
IV	Madrigali a cinque, Libro III (1592). Forthcoming.
V	Madrigali a cinque, Libro IV (1603), ed. by Elena Ferrari Barassi. Cremona: Fondazione Claudio Monteverdi, 1974. Contains facsimiles, an extensive preface, and a selective bibliography and discography.
VI	Madrigali a cinque, Libro V (1605), ed. by Maria Caraci. Cremona: Fondazione Claudio Monteverdi, 1984. Contains facsimiles and an extensive preface.
VII	Scherzi musicali a tre (1607). Forthcoming.
VIII	Orfeo, Lamento d'Arianna, Maddalena (1609, 1608, 1617). Forthcoming.
IX	Missa de Capella a sei voci, Vespro della Beata Vergine (1610). Forthcoming.
X	Madrigali Libro VI (1614). Forthcoming.
XI	Concerto. Settimo libro de madrigali (1619). Forthcoming.
XII	Scherzi musicali a una & due voci (1632). Forthcoming.
XIII	Antologia di composizioni profane (1594-1634). Forthcoming.
XIV	Madrigali guerrieri, et amorosi libro VIII, (1638). Forthcoming.
XV	Selva morale e spirituale (1640). Forthcoming.
XVI	Il ritorno di Ulisse in patria (1641). Forthcoming.
XVII	L'incoronazione di Poppea (1642). Forthcoming.
XVIII	Messa a quattro voci et Salmi (1650). Forthcoming.

XIX   Madrigali e canzonette libro IX (1651), ed.
       by Anna Maria Monterosso Vacchelli.
       Cremona: Fondazione Claudio Monteverdi,
       1983. Contains facsimiles, an extensive
       preface, and a selective bibliography and
       discography.
XX   Antologia di composizioni sacre (1615-
       1651). Forthcoming.

             a. Operas and Other Dramatic Works

L'Orfeo
------.   Edited by Robert Eitner. Publikationen
älterer praktischer und theoretischer Musikwerke,
X. Berlin: Gesellschaft für Musikforschung,
1881.
------.   Edited by Vincent d'Indy. Paris: Edition de
la Schola cantorum, 1905; other editions published in 1915 and 1926. Abridged vocal score
with text in French.
------.   Edited by Giacomo Orefice. Milan:
Associazione Italiana di Amici della Musica,
1909. Vocal score based on the original 1609
edition.
------.   Edited by Gian Francesco Malipiero. London:
J. & W. Chester, 1923. Vocal score with an
English translation by Robert Stuart.
------.   Edited by Carl Orff. Munich: n.p., 1923;
revised editions, Mainz: B. Schott's Söhne, 1929,
1931, and 1940. Vocal score with text in German.
------.   Facsimile of the 1609 edition. Augsburg: B.
Filser, 1927. Introduction by Adolf Sandberger.
------.   Edited by Giacomo Benvenuti. Milan: Ricordi,
1934. Vocal score.
------.   Edited by Ottorino Respighi. Milan: Carisch,
1935. Both a full score and a vocal score.
Vocal score reduction by Giovanni Salviucci.
------.   Edited by Giacomo Benvenuti. Milan: I
Classici musicali italiani, 1942. Vocal score.
------.   Edited by August Wenzinger. Kassel:
Bärenreiter, 1955; reprint editions 1958, 1967.
Vocal score.
------.   Edited by Michel Podolski. Brussels: Centre
International des Etudes de la Musique Ancienne,
1966.

------. Edited by Denis Stevens. London: Novello,
1967; rev. ed., 1968.
------. Edited by Bruno Maderna. Milan: Suvini
Zerboni, 1967. Vocal score.
------. Edited by Valentino Bucchi. Milan: Carisch,
1968. Vocal score reduction by Franco
Pacioselli.
------. Facsimile of the 1615 edition. Farnborough:
Gregg, 1972. Introduction by Denis Stevens.
------. Edited by Edward H. Tarr. Paris: Costallat,
1974.

L'Arianna (solo version of Lament)
------. Edited by François-Auguste Gevaert in Les
Gloires de l'Italie. Paris: Heugel, 1868.
------. Edited by Angelo Solerti in Gli albori del
melodramma. Vol. 1. Milan: Remo Sandron, 1904;
reprint ed., Hildesheim: Olms, 1969.
------. Edited by Ottorino Respighi. Leipzig: C.
Schmidel & Co., 1910.
------. Edited by Ottorino Respighi. Trieste: Casa
musicale Giuliana, 1920.
------. Die Klage der Ariadne. Edited by Carl Orff.
Mainz: B. Schott's Söhne, 1931. Edition has
German and Italian text.
------. Edited by Carl Orff. Mainz: B. Schott's
Söhne, 1952; New York: Associated Music
Publishers, 1952.
------. Edited by Hans Joachim Moser and Traugott
Fedtke. Kassel: Bärenreiter, 1961; London:
Novello, 1961. This edition combines the solo
version of the Lament with the corresponding
sections of the madrigal version.
------. Edited by Claudio Gallico. London: Universal
Edition, 1969.
------. Edited by Günter Hauswald in Die Musik des
Generalbass-Zeitälter. Vol. 45. Cologne: Arno
Volk, 1973.

Il ballo delle ingrate
------. Edited by Luigi Torchi in L'arte musicale in
Italia. Vol. 6. Milan: Ricordi, 1907.
------. Der Tanz der Spröden. Edited by Carl Orff.
Mainz: B. Schott's Söhne, 1931; another edition,
Mainz: B. Schott's Söhne, 1940.
------. Edited by Alceo Toni. Milan: Ricordi, 1932.
Vocal score.

------. Edited by Denis Stevens. London: B. Schott's
    Söhne, 1960; New York: Associated Music
    Publishers, 1960.
------. Edited by N. Anfuso and A. Gianuario.
    Florence: OTOS, 1971.

Tirsi e Clori
------. Edited by Alceo Toni. Milan: Carisch, 1963.
    Vocal score.
------. Edited by Kenneth Cooper. University Park:
    Pennsylvania State University Press, 1968.

Il combattimento di Tancredi e Clorinda
------. Edited by Luigi Torchi in L'arte musicale in
    Italia. Vol. 6. Milan: Ricordi, 1907.
------. Edited by Alceo Toni. Milan: Societa anonima
    notari, 1921.
------. Edited by Gian Francesco Malipiero. London:
    J. & W. Chester, 1931.
------. Edited by Virgilio Mortari. Milan: Carisch,
    1946.
------. Edited by Giorgio Federico Ghedini. Milan:
    Suvini Zerboni, 1949; vocal score edition Milan:
    Suvini Zerboni, 1950.
------. Edited by Gian Francesco Malipiero. London:
    J. & W. Chester, 1954. English text by Peter
    Pears.
------. Edited by Denis Stevens. London: Oxford
    University Press, 1962. English translation by
    Denis Stevens.
------. Edited by Luciano Berio. London: Universal
    Edition, 1968.
------. Edited by Nella Anfuso. Florence: OTOS,
    1971.

Ballo: Movete al mio bel suon
------. Edited by Denis Stevens. London: Faber
    Music, 1967.

Il ritorno d'Ulisse in patria
------. Die Heimkehr des Odysseus. Edited by Robert
    Haas in Denkmäler der Tonkunst in Österreich,
    LVII. Vienna: Universal Edition, 1922; Leipzig:
    Breitkopf & Härtel, 1922. Text in German and
    Italian.
------. Edited by Vincent d'Indy. Paris: Heugel,
    1926. Vocal score with French and Italian text.

------. Edited by Luigi Dallapiccola. Milan: Suvini
Zerboni, 1942. Vocal score.
------. Edited by Hans Werner Henze. Mainz: B.
Schott's Söhne, 1982.

L'incoronazione di Poppea

------. Edited by Hugo Goldschmidt in Studien zur
Geschichte der italienischen Oper im 17.
Jahrhundert. Vol. 2. Leipzig: Breitkopf &
Härtel, 1904; reprint ed., Hildesheim: Olms,
1967.
------. Le couronnement de Poppée. Edited by Vincent
d'Indy. Paris: Schola cantorum, 1908; Paris:
Lerolle, 1922. Vocal score with text in French.
------. Edited by Charles van den Borren. Brussels:
n.p., 1914.
------. Edited by Giacomo Benvenuti. Milan: Suvini
Zerboni, 1937; reprint ed., 1965. Vocal score.
------. Edited by Ernst Krenek. Vienna: Universal
Edition, 1937. Vocal score with German and
Italian text.
------. Facsimile of the Venetian manuscript. Milan:
Fratelli Bocca, 1938. Introduction by Giacomo
Benvenuti.
------. Edited by Giorgio Federico Ghedini. Milan:
Ricordi, 1953. Vocal score.
------. Edited by Hans F. Redlich. Kassel:
Bärenreiter, 1958.
------. Edited by Walter Goehr. London: Universal
Edition, 1960. Vocal score with German and
Italian text.
------. Edited by Riccardo Nielsen. Bologna:
Edizioni Bongiovanni, 1965. Vocal score.
------. Edited by Raymond Leppard. London: Faber
Music, 1966; New York: G. Schirmer, 1966; revised
ed., London: Faber Music, 1968. Vocal score with
English and Italian text.
------. Facsimile of the Venetian manuscript.
Bologna: Forni, 1969. Foreword by Sergio
Martinotti.
------. Edited by Raymond Leppard. London: Faber
Music, 1977; New York: G. Schirmer, 1977. Vocal
score with text in English, German, and Italian.

b. Madrigals, Canzonette, and Scherzi Musicali

12 fünfstimmige Madrigale. Edited by Hugo
    Leichtentritt. Leipzig: C.F. Peters, 1909.
    German and Italian text.
12 fünfstimmige Madrigale. Edited by Arnold
    Mendelssohn. Leipzig: C.F. Peters, 1911. German
    and Italian text.
Sechs Kammerduette. Edited by Ludwig Landshoff.
    Frankfurt: C.F. Peters, 1927.
Canzonette a tre voci. Edited by Gaetano Cesari in
    Istituzioni e monumenti dell'arte musicale
    italiana. Vol. 6. Milan: Ricordi, 1936.
Canzonette a tre voci. Edited by Hilmar Trede.
    Kassel: Bärenreiter, 1951; reprint ed., 1973.
15 madrigals. Edited by Hans F. Redlich. London: B.
    Schott's Söhne, 1954.
Scherzi musicali (a una voce). Edited by Marius
    Flothuis. Amsterdam: Broekmans en Van Poppel,
    1958.
12 composizioni vocali profane e sacre. Edited by
    Wolfgang Osthoff. Milan: Ricordi, 1958.
Scherzi musicali. Italian and German text, ed. by
    Hilmar Trede. Kassel: Bärenreiter, 1967; reprint
    ed. 1974.
Ten Madrigals. Edited by Denis Stevens. London:
    Oxford University Press, 1978.
Il primo libro de madrigali a 5 voci. Edited by
    Bernard Bailly de Surcy. Paris: Les Editions
    Renaissantes, 1972. This is the first volume of
    a proposed complete works edition.
Il primo libro de madrigali a 5 voci. Facsimile
    edition, edited by Bernard Bailly de Surcy.
    Paris: Les Editions Renaissantes, 1972. This is
    a facsimile of the part-books to the third
    edition of Monteverdi's first book of madrigals.
Due lettere amorose in genere rappresentativo. Edited
    by N. Anfuso and A. Gianuario. Venice: Centro
    studi Rinascimento musicale, 1973. Contains a
    facsimile of the 1623 edition of Se i languidi
    miei sguardi and Se pur destina e vole il cielo
    and an extensive preface.
Il quinto libro de madrigali. Edited by Karin
    Jacobsen and Jens Peter Jacobsen. Denmark:
    Edition Egtved, 1985.

c. Sacred Works

Sacrae cantiunculae
------. Edited by G. Terrabugio. Milan: A.
   Bertarelli, 1910.
------. Edited by Gaetano Cesari in Istituzioni e
   monumenti dell'arte musicale italiana. Vol. 6.
   Milan: Ricordi, 1936.
------. Edited by János Gábor. Budapest: Magyar
   Kórus, 1943.

Vespro della Beata Vergine and Missa 'In illo tempore'
------. Magnificat a sei voci. Edited by Karl
   Matthaei. Kassel: Bärenreiter, 1941.
------. Magnificat (seven voices). Edited by Giorgio
   Federico Ghedini. Milan: Suvini Zerboni, 1949.
   Vocal score.
------. Vespers. Edited by Hans F. Redlich. Vienna:
   Universal Edition, 1949; revised ed., Vienna:
   Universal Edition, 1952. Vocal score.
------. Vespers. Edited by Giorgio Federico Ghedini.
   Milan: Suvini Zerboni, 1951. Vocal score. Full
   score published by Zerboni, 1952.
------. Dixit Dominus. Edited by Gottfried Wolters.
   Wolfenbüttel: Möseler Verlag, 1954.
------. Vespers. Edited by Walter Goehr. Vienna:
   Universal Edition, 1957.
------. Vespers. Edited by Denis Stevens. London:
   Novello, 1961.
------. Missa 'In illo tempore' a 6. Edited by Hans
   F. Redlich. London: Eulenburg, 1962. Contains a
   foreword by Redlich.
------. Vespers. Edited by Gottfried Wolters.
   Wolfenbüttel: Möseler Verlag, 1966. Thorough-
   bass realized by Mathias Siedel.
------. Magnificat a sei voci. Edited by Denis
   Arnold. London: Eulenburg, 1968. Miniature
   score.
------. Magnificat a sei voci. Edited by Don
   Smithers. New York: Lawson-Gould, 1969.
------. Vespers. Edited by Jürgen Jürgens. Vienna:
   Universal Edition, 1977; miniature score, Vienna:
   Universal Edition, 1977.
------. Missa 'In illo tempore' a 6. Edited by
   Francesco Luisi. Arezzo: Associazione amici
   della musica di Arezzo, 1984; Rome: Pro Musica
   Studium, 1984.

------. Vespers. Edited by Clifford Bartlett.
Huntingdon, Cambs: King's Music, 1986.

Selva morale et spirituale (1640)
------. Messa a 4 voci da capella. Edited by A.
Tirabassi. Brussels: Breitkopf & Härtel, 1914.
Preface by Charles van den Borren.
------. Messa a 4 voci da capella. Edited by
Bonaventura Somma. Rome: Edizioni De Santis,
1948.
------. Messa a 4 voci da cappella. Edited by J.A.
Bank. Amsterdam: A. Banks, 1950.
------. Magnificat I. Edited by Walter Goehr.
London: Universal Edition, 1960.
------. Messa a 4 voci da cappella. Edited by Denis
Arnold. London: Eulenburg, 1962. Miniature
score.
------. Beatus vir I. Edited by John Steele.
London: Novello, 1965.
------. Laudate Dominum I. Edited by Denis Arnold.
London: Eulenburg, 1966.
------. Gloria concertata. Edited by John Steele.
University Park: Pennsylvania State University
Press, 1968.
------. Magnificat I. Edited by Denis Stevens and
John Steele. London: Novello, 1969.
------. Messa a 4 voci da cappella. Edited by Rudolf
Walter. Stuttgart-Hohenheid: n.p., 1972.
------. Christmas Vespers. Edited by Denis Stevens.
Borough Green, Sevenoaks, Kent: Novello, 1979. A
selection of works from the Selva morale of 1640
and the Messa...et Salmi of 1650.
------. Dixit Dominus II. Edited by John Steele.
Borough Green, Sevenoaks, Kent: Novello, 1983.

Messa a quattro voci et salmi (1650)
------. Messa a quattro voci da cappella. Edited by
Hans F. Redlich. London: Eulenburg, 1952.
------. Laetatus sum, a 5 strumenti et 6 voci.
Edited by Alfredo Casella. Rome: Edizioni De
Santis, 1951.
------. Messa a quattro voci da cappella. Edited by
Rudolf Walter. Stuttgart: Hänssler-Verlag, 1972.

GENERAL BACKGROUND FOR MONTEVERDI RESEARCH

1. Historical, Social, and Literary Background

1. Ademollo, Alessandro. "I Basile alla corte di
    Mantova secondo documenti inediti o rare
    (1603-1628)." <u>Giornale ligustico</u> 11 (1895): 416-
    42.

    Documents the relationship between Adriana
    Basile, a famous singer and instrumentalist, and
    the Gonzaga court at Mantua. Basile, known as
    "bell'Adriana," was asked to become a part of the
    Gonzaga court by the Duchess Leonora in 1610 and
    remained associated with that court until she left
    ca. 1624. Provides correspondence of both Vincenzo
    and Ferdinando Gonzaga. Mentions a letter of
    Antonio Pavese to Cardinal Gonzaga at Rome, June
    25, 1610, which notes Monteverdi's astonishment
    over Basile.

2. Arnaldi, Girolamo, and Stocchi, Manlio Pastore, ed.
    <u>Il seicento</u>. Storia della cultura Veneta. Part
    4. 2 vols. Vicenza: Neri Pozza, 1984-85. 660,
    598 pp.

    A comprehensive study of Venice in the seven-
    teenth century. Includes, in addition to political
    history, informative articles pertaining to art,
    literature, and music. Contains an index of illus-
    trations and names as well as a list of manuscripts
    and documents in the Venetian archives.

*   Arnold, Denis. "Music at a Venetian Confraternity
     in the Renaissance."

     Cited below as item 25.

3.   Burckhardt, Jakob. The Civilization of the Renais-
     sance in Italy. Translated from the German by
     S.G.C. Middlemore, with an introduction by
     Benjamin Nelson and Charles Trinkaus. 2 vols.
     New York: Harper & Row, 1958. 519 pp. DG533 B85
     1958b

     First published in Basel as Die Kultur der
     Renaissance in Italien: Ein Versuch in 1860, this
     landmark study of the Italian Renaissance attempts
     to reveal the totality of Renaissance civilization.
     The six parts of this work are entitled "The State
     as a Work of Art," "The Development of the Indi-
     vidual," "The Revival of Antiquity," "The Discovery
     of the World of Man," "Society and Festivals," and
     "Morality and Religion."

4.   Damerini, Gino. "Venezia al tempo di Monteverdi."
     Musica II (item 813), pp. 105-20.

     Concludes that the period from 1613 to the death
     of Monteverdi was a dark era in the history of
     Venice. Notes that changes in trade routes were
     damaging the economy and that Venice's political
     position was weakening. Argues that only the art
     of music, with Monteverdi as the central figure,
     had a sense of direction in Venice during this
     epoch.

5.   Einstein, Alfred. "Italian Madrigal Verse."
     Proceedings of the Musical Association 63
     (1936/37): 79-95.

     Translated from the German by A.H. Fox
     Strangways, the essay concentrates on Italian
     madrigal verse in the sixteenth century after some
     discussion of the madrigal's predecessors. Poets
     such as Bembo, Petrarch, Cassola, Ariosto,
     Sannazaro, Guarini, Tasso, and Chiabrera are
     examined.

6.   Fabbri, Mario. "La cappella musicale dei Gonzaga a
     Mantova: considerazioni e prospettive in margine
     al catalogo del 'Fondo di S. Barbara.'" Nuova
     rivista musicale italiana 3 (1974): 371-77.

Identifies three periods at Mantua which coincide with the lives of Isabella d'Este, Guglielmo Gonzaga, and Vincenzo Gonzaga. New light has been shed on the last period, which covers the time Monteverdi was active at Mantua, by the publication Catalogo della Biblioteca del Conservatorio di Musica, edited by G. Barblan (item 860).

7. Fletcher, Iain. "From Tasso to Marino." Nine 7 (1951): 129-38.

An informative article concerning late sixteenth-century Italian madrigal poetry. Concentrates on the poetry of Torquato Tasso (1544-1595) and Giambattista Marino (1569-1625).

* Hanning, Barbara Russano. Of Poetry and Music's Power: Humanism and the Creation of Opera.

Cited below as item 94.

8. Lavin, Irving. "Lettres de Parmes (1618, 1627-28) et débuts du théatre baroque." Le lieu théâtral à la Renaissance, edited by Jean Jacquot. Paris: Centre national de la recherche scientifique, 1964, pp. 105-58.

An account of the series of festivals arranged to celebrate the marriage of Duke Odoardo II Farnese of Parma. The article, based upon correspondence addressed to Enzo Bentivoglio, reproduces thirty-eight of the letters.

9. Maylender, Michele. Storia delle accademie d'Italia. 5 vols. Bologna: Licinio Cappelli, 1926. 541, 458, 506, 472, 498 pp. AS215 M3

Organized in alphabetical order by name of academy, the work gives concise histories of Italian academies. Each volume contains its own index.

10. Mazzali, Ettore. "Literature: Torquato Tasso; An Introduction." The Late Italian Renaissance, 1525-1630, edited by Eric Cochrane. London: Macmillan, 1970, pp. 134-48. DG540 C63

Discusses the poet Torquato Tasso within the general framework of Renaissance culture. This article was extracted from the preface of the author's edition of Tasso's Prose.

11. Molmenti, Pompeo Gherardo. La Storia di Venezia
     nella vita privata dalle origini alla caduta
     della republica. 3rd ed. Turin: Roux e Favale,
     1885; 7th ed., 3 vols. Trieste: Edizioni LINT,
     1973. 599 pp. (Roux e Favale) DG675.6 M59 1973

     This landmark study of culture in Venice from
     the ninth through the eighteenth centuries is
     divided into three parts. The third part, devoted
     to the seventeenth and eighteenth centuries, has
     chapters concerning public festivals, arts and
     letters, academies, theaters, and other aspects of
     public and private life.

12. Momigliano, Attilio. Storia della letteratura
     Italiana. Dalle origini ai nostri giorni.
     Florence: Giuseppe Principato, 1948; reprint ed.,
     Milan: Giuseppe Principato, 1977. 665 pp.
     PQ4042 M73 1948

     A comprehensive history of Italian literature.
     Chapters XI and XII, pertaining to the literature
     of Monteverdi's era, discuss Torquato Tasso,
     Guarini, Marino, Rinuccini, and their
     contemporaries.

13. Ortolani, Giuseppe. "Venezia al tempo di
     Monteverdi." Rassegna musicale (item 819), pp.
     469-82.

     Recounts the political, economic, and social
     conditions in Venice at the time of Monteverdi.
     Although Venice was in political and economic
     decline, the carnivals flourished, public opera was
     established, and public festivals were presented
     with splendor.

*   Reiner, Stuart. "La vag'Angioletta (and others)."
     Cited below as item 410.

14. Schulz-Buschhaus, Ulrich. Das Madrigal: Zur
     Stilgeschichte der italienischen Lyrik zwischen
     Renaissance und Barock. Bad Homburg: Gehlen,
     1969. 268 pp. PQ4128 M3 S3

     A comprehensive survey of madrigal poetry.
     Includes explanatory footnotes and a large bibli-
     ography.

15. Symonds, John Addington. Renaissance in Italy. 7
     vols. London: Smith, Elder, 1875-86; reprint ed.
     in 2 vols., New York: The Modern Library, 1935;
     reprint ed. in 7 vols., Hildesheim: Olms, 1971.
     970, 1060 pp. (Modern Library) DG533 S945 1971

     An important history of Italy by a contemporary
     of Jakob Burckhardt. The original sections were
     entitled "The Age of the Despots," "The Revival of
     Learning," "The Fine Arts," "Italian Literature,"
     and "The Catholic Reaction." Contains both a
     political and cultural history of Renaissance
     Italy. Section V, "The Catholic Reaction,"
     discusses the poets Tasso, Guarini, Marino, and
     Chiabrera.

16. Tessier, André. "La décoration théâtrale à Venise
     à la fin du XVII siècle." La revue de l'art
     ancien et moderne (1928): 181-90.

     A general survey of stage design in Venetian
     opera from 1637 to ca. 1690, focusing particularly
     upon the work of Giacomo Torelli (1608-1678).

          2. Musical Thought in the Late Sixteenth and
              Early Seventeenth Centuries

17. Abert, Anna Amalie. The Opera from Its Beginnings
     until the Early 19th Century. Cologne: Arno,
     1962. 87 pp. M2 M94512 No.5

     A volume in the Arno Volk Verlag Anthology of
     Music series. Primarily a collection of excerpts
     from operas composed from 1600 to 1823. Contains a
     scene from Monteverdi's L'incoronazione di Poppea.
     An excellent historical overview opens the anthol-
     ogy, translated into English by Robert Kolben.

18. ————. "Schauspiel und Opernlibretto im
     italienischen Barock." Die Musikforschung 2
     (1949): 133-41.

     Traces the development of the seventeenth-century
     Italian opera libretto. Notes the influence of
     Spanish drama.

19. Adrio, Adam. Die Anfänge des geistlichen Konzerts.
     Neue deutsche Forschungen, vol. 31. Berlin:
     Junker & Dünnhaupt, 1935. 180 pp. ML2902 A3

     A most significant study of the vocal concerto
     through the first three or four decades of the
     seventeenth century. Focuses on the form both in
     Italy and in Germany. An extended subchapter of
     thirty-six pages is devoted to the contributions of
     Monteverdi to the spiritual concerto. Especially
     valuable are chronological lists of vocal concertos
     in Italy from ca. 1538 to 1642 and in Germany from
     ca. 1600 to 1630. Also includes a chronological
     list of bicinia and tricinia from ca. 1538 to 1642.
     Bibliography; large supplement of musical examples.

20. Agazzari, Agostino. Del sonare sopra'l basso con
     tutti li stromenti e dell'uso loro nel conserto.
     Siena: Domenico Falcini, 1607; facsimile edition,
     Milan: Bollettino Bibliografico Musicale, 1933;
     reprint ed., Bologna: Forni, 1985. 11 pp. MT49
     A25 D4

     An early figured bass treatise in which the
     author divides instruments into two classes:
     instruments of foundation and instruments of
     ornamentation. Stresses the importance of the
     basso continuo in music that follows the expression
     of the text. For an English translation of a
     portion of this treatise, see Strunk, item 288.
     See also Rose, item 152.

21. Aldrich, Putnam. Rhythm in Seventeenth-Century
     Italian Monody. New York: Norton, 1966; reprint
     ed., Ann Arbor: UMI Press, 1978. 188 pp.
     ML290.2 A4

     Includes a discussion of the sinfonia to Monte-
     verdi's L'incoronazione di Poppea. Footnotes,
     bibliography, name and title index, and an anthol-
     ogy of Italian songs and dances."

*   Apel, Willi. "Anent a Ritornello in Monteverdi's
     Orfeo."

     Cited below as item 678.

22.   ———. "Probleme der Alternierung in der liturgi-
      schen Orgelmusik bis 1600." Congresso inter-
      nazionale sul tema Claudio Monteverdi (item 811),
      pp. 171-86.

      A survey of alternatim practice in liturgical
      vocal and organ music.

23.   Apfel, Ernst. "Rhythmisch-metrische und andere
      Beobachtungen an Ostinatobässen." Archiv für
      Musikwissenschaft 33 (1976): 48-68.

      Surveys the use of basso ostinato technique
      during the seventeenth century. Compares and
      discusses the works of numerous composers in regard
      to their practice of setting ground bass patterns.

24.   Arnold, Denis. "The Influence of Ornamentation on
      the Structure of Early 17th Century Church
      Music." Bericht über den siebenten inter-
      nationalen musikwissenschaftlichen Kongress Köln
      1958. Kassel: Bärenreiter, 1959, pp. 57-58.

      An extremely brief article analyzing the effect
      of ornamentation and embellishment upon the cul-
      tivation of the sectional structure common to
      seventeenth-century church music.

25.   ———. "Music at a Venetian Confraternity in the
      Renaissance." Acta musicologica 37 (1965): 62-
      72.

      Defines the role of religious confraternities,
      the scuole grandi, at Venice. Chronicles the
      musical activities of the S. Giovanni Evangelista
      based on the minute books of that confraternity.

*   ———. "Schütz in Venice."

      Cited below as item 208.

26.   ———. "The Significance of 'cori spezzati.'"
      Music and Letters 40 (1959): 4-18.

      Examines polychoral writing from the works of
      Willaert to ca. 1625, with some discussion of later
      works. Cites contrast in tone color as the most
      significant trait of this technique, which is

usually accompanied by simple rhythms, simple
harmonies, and distinct phrase shapes of varied
lengths.

27.   ————.   "The Solo Motet in Venice (1625-1775)."
       Proceedings of the Royal Musical Association 151
       (1979-80): 56-68.

       Sketches the history of the Venetian solo motet
       from the publication of Simonetti's collection
       Ghirlanda sacra to the musical decline of the
       Venetian conservatories. Contains a brief dis-
       cussion of Monteverdi's Exulta figlia.

28.   ————.   "Venice." The New Grove Dictionary of
       Music and Musicians, edited by Stanley Sadie.
       London: Macmillan, 1980. Vol. 19, pp. 614-20.

       Discusses the history of musical activities in
       Venice from the early fourteenth century to the
       present. Cites St. Mark's, the religious con-
       fraternities, the public opera houses, and the
       ospedali as important institutions where musical
       activities flourished. Contains a bibliography.

29.   Arnold, Frank T. The Art of Accompaniment from a
       Thorough-Bass as Practised in the XVIIth and
       XVIIIth Centuries. London: Oxford University
       Press, 1931; reprint ed. in 2 vols., New York:
       Dover, 1965. 918 pp. ML442 A7 1965

       A landmark study of thorough-bass techniques
       which includes translations of selected portions of
       significant seventeenth- and eighteenth-century
       thorough-bass treatises. Contains musical examples
       and an index.

30.   Arteaga, Stefano. Le rivoluzioni del teatro
       musicale italiano dalla sua origine fino al
       presente. 3 vols. Bologna: Carlo Trenti, 1783-
       88. 411, 214, 207 pp.

       A historically important survey of opera from
       its origins to the end of the eighteenth century.
       Discusses, in volume one, the nature of drama, the
       union of words and music, the origins of sacred and
       secular music, the intermezzi, and Florentine
       opera. Monteverdi's Arianna is cited as an impor-
       tant work.

31. Banchieri, Adriano. Conclusioni nel suono
     dell'organo. Bologna: Gio. Rossi, 1609;
     facsimile reprint, Milan: Bollettino Biblio-
     grafico Musicale, 1934; reprint ed., New York:
     Broude Brothers, 1975. 71 pp.

     Discusses organs, organists, organ builders,
     and performance practice. Monteverdi, cited as a
     modern composer in the service of Vincenzo Gonzaga,
     is recognized as a master at matching harmony to
     oration. For an English translation of the
     Conclusioni, see item 32 below.

32. ————. Conclusions for Playing the Organ.
     Translated by Lee R. Garrett. Colorado Springs:
     Colorado College Music Press, 1982. 60 pp.

     An English translation of item 31.

33. Baron, John H. "Secular Spanish Solo Song in
     Non-Spanish Sources, 1599-1640." Journal of the
     American Musicological Society 30 (1977): 20-42.

     Based upon a number of Italian manuscripts
     located primarily at Florence, Modena, and the
     Vatican, this article provides a thorough account
     of early seventeenth-century Spanish songs in
     Italy. One of the manuscripts examined was owned
     by Adriana Basile, a famous alto closely associated
     with Monteverdi in Mantua (see item 1). Concludes
     that there was probably a significant Spanish
     influence on music in Italy during this time.

*   Beat, Janet E. "Monteverdi and the Opera Orchestra
     of His Time."

     Cited below as item 455.

34. Berger, Karol. "Theories of Chromatic and Enhar-
     monic Music in Italy in the Second Half of the
     Sixteenth Century." Ph.D. dissertation, Yale
     University, 1975. 250 pp. UM Order No. 76-13696

     Examines the works of numerous theorists, includ-
     ing Claudio and Giulio Cesare Monteverdi, in order
     to ascertain the guiding principles of chromaticism
     in the late Renaissance.

35. Berry, Corre. "The Secular Dialogue Duet:
     1600-1900." Music Review 40 (1979): 273-84.

Traces the history of the secular dialogue over
a period of 300 years by examining specific
examples in some detail. In the discussion of the
early Italian dialogue duet, Monteverdi's A dio
florida bella, Tirsi e Clori, and Bel pastor are
examined.

36. Bertolotti, Antonio. Musici alla corte dei Gonzaga
     in Mantova dal secolo XV al XVIII. Milan, 1891;
     reprint ed., Bibliotheca musica bononiensis.
     Sezione III, n. 17. Bologna: Forni, 1969. 130
     pp. ML107 M29 B3 1969

Documents the history of composers, instrumen-
talists, and singers active in Mantua during the
fifteenth through the seventeenth centuries. Gives
an account of Monteverdi's musical activities at
Mantua and includes a facsimile of one of his
letters. Contains illustrations, a general index,
and an index of musicians. See also Canal, item
47, and Davari, item 57.

37. Bianconi, Lorenzo. Il seicento. Storia della
     musica, vol. 4. Turin: EDT, 1982; reprint ed.,
     Turin: EDT, 1985. 339 pp. ISBN 88 7063 021 8
     ML160 S886 v.4

A penetrating study of music in the seventeenth
century, with a decided emphasis on musical activities in Italy. Discusses Monteverdi's musical
style from his fourth book of madrigals through his
later collections. Includes an index and an annotated bibliography. This book appeared in an
English translation by David Bryant as Music in the
Seventeenth Century (Cambridge: Cambridge University Press, 1987).

38. Bianconi, Lorenzo, and Walker, Thomas. "Pro-
     duction, Consumption and Political Function of
     Seventeenth-Century Opera." Early Music History
     4 (1984): 209-96.

Discusses opera in the seventeenth century from a
political, social, and economic context. Compares
Chi soffre speri by Virgilio Mazzochi and Marco
Marazzoli, Antioco by Francesco Cavalli, and Il
talamo preservato dalla fedelta d'Eudossa, an opera
by an unnamed composer which was performed at
Reggio Emilia. Includes appendixes of documents
and supporting information.

39. Bland, Leland Dye. "The Instrumental Ritornello
     in Selected Vocal Works of Italian Composers ca.
     1670 to ca. 1710." Ph.D. dissertation, The
     University of Iowa, 1973. 404 pp. UM Order No.
     73-30,900

     A thorough account of the instrumental ritornello
     in the Baroque era. Special emphasis is given to
     the middle Baroque (ca. 1670 to ca. 1710) and, more
     specifically, the vocal works of Alessandro
     Stradella. The second chapter deals with the
     ritornello in selected works of Monteverdi and his
     contemporaries.

40. Bonta, Stephen. "From Violone to Violoncello: A
     Question of Strings?" Journal of the American
     Musical Instrument Society 3 (1977): 64-99.

     Attempts to clarify the rather clouded early
     history of the violoncello in seventeenth-century
     Italy. Discusses Monteverdi's use of the basso
     viola da braccio.

41. Boyer, Ferdinand. "Les Orsini et les musiciens
     d'Italie au debut du XVIIe siècle." Mélanges de
     philologie d'histoire et de littérature offerts a
     Henri Hauvette. Paris: Les presses françaises,
     1934; reprint ed., Geneva: Slatkine Reprints,
     1972, pp. 301-10.

     Examines the musical patronage of Virginio I
     Orsini, Duke of Bracciano, and his son, Paolo
     Giordano II.

42. Braun, Werner. Die Musik des 17. Jahrhunderts.
     Neus Handbuch der Musikwissenschaft, edited by
     Carl Dahlhaus, vol. 4. Wiesbaden: Akademische
     Verlagsgesellschaft Athenaion, 1981. 385 pp.
     ISBN 3 7997 0746 8 ML160 N389 Bd. 4

     Surveys the music of the period primarily through
     an examination of genres. Attractively printed
     with beautiful illustrations and numerous musical
     examples. Each chapter concludes with a listing of
     notes and bibliography. Also includes a fairly
     extensive glossary, name index, works index, term
     index, and list of musical examples.

43.   Brown, Howard M. "How Opera Began: An Introduction
      to Jacopo Peri's Euridice (1600)." The Late
      Italian Renaissance 1525-1630, edited by Eric
      Cochrane. London: Macmillan, 1970, pp. 401-43.

      Summarizes sixteenth-century attitudes toward
      Greek music and discusses Vincenzo Galilei's
      Dialogo della musica antica et della musica
      moderna. Contains a detailed introduction to
      Peri's Euridice.

44.   ———. "Madrigale." La Musica. Parte prima:
      Enciclopedia Storica, vol. 3. Turin: Unione
      Tipografico-Editrice Torinese, 1966, pp. 227-38.

      Traces the development of the madrigal throughout
      the sixteenth century into the seventeenth century
      and gives a concise description of composers'
      styles. Includes a bibliography. Translated into
      Italian by Annalisa Bersoni-Kelly.

45.   Bukofzer, Manfred F. Music in the Baroque Era:
      From Monteverdi to Bach. New York: Norton, 1947;
      reprint ed., London: J.M. Dent, 1977. 489 pp.
      ISBN 0 393 09745 5 ML193 B8 1977

      A comprehensive survey of Baroque music and
      musical style. Monteverdi's madrigals, dramatic
      works, and sacred compositions are briefly dis-
      cussed. Contains an extensive bibliography, a list
      of editions, a list of musical examples, and an
      index.

46.   Caccini, Giulio. Le nuove musiche. Florence:
      Marescotti, 1601; microfilm ed., Ann Arbor:
      University Microfilms, 1979. 39 pp. M3.1 C3

      Gives, in the introduction to this collection of
      arias and madrigals, a thorough explication of the
      art of vocal embellishment. A reprint of this
      introduction appeared in Solerti, item 166. An
      English translation is given in Strunk, item 288.

47.   Canal, Pietro. Della musica in Mantova. Notizie
      tratte principalmente dall'archivio Gonzaga
      Mantova. Venice: Presso la segreteria del R.
      Istituto, 1881; reprint ed., Bibliotheca musica
      bononiensis. Sezione III, n. 44. Bologna:
      Forni, 1977. 119 pp. ML290.8 M2 C2 1977

Discusses musical activities at Mantua under the
rule of Guglielmo Gonzaga and Vincenzo Gonzaga.
Considers Monteverdi's use of dissonance and notes
the criticism he received from the theorist Artusi.
Examines Monteverdi's involvement in the festivities for the marriage of Francesco Gonzaga and
Margherita of Savoy, quoting contemporary observations pertaining to Monteverdi's Arianna. Contains an appendix which elucidates Monteverdi's
association with the Court of Mantua after his
employment in Venice. See also Bertolotti, item
36.

48.   ————. "Della musica in Venezia." Venezia e le
sue lagune I. Venice: Antonelli, 1847, pp.
471-500.

49.   Castiglioni, Niccolò. "Significato storico del
melodramma nella prima metà del seicento."
Rassegna musicale 26 (1956): 196-203.

Considers cultural influences on the development
of opera in the first half of the seventeenth
century. Emphasizes the importance of the canzonette a ballo as evidence of a popular element in
early opera. Monteverdi's works are seen as
combining popular and courtly musical styles.

50.   Cesari, Gaetano. Die Entstehung des Madrigals im
16. Jahrhundert. Cremona: P. Fezzi, 1908.   81
pp.   ML2633 C4 m

Initially presented as a doctoral dissertation to
the University of Munich. An important, early
monograph dealing with the inception and rise of
the Italian madrigal in the sixteenth century.
Numerous footnotes, but no bibliography. Index of
titles. Subsequently published in Rivista musicale
italiana (item 51).

51.   ————. "Le origini del madrigale cinquecentesco."
Rivista musicale italiana 14 (1912): 1-34, 380-
428.

A revision of Cesari's earlier study, Die Entstehung des Madrigals im 16. Jahrhundert (item 50).

52.   Clercx, Suzanne. "L'Espagne du XVIe siècle, source
      d'inspiration du génie héroïque de Monteverdi."
      Musique et poésie au XVIe siècle. Paris:
      Editions du centre national de la recherche
      scientifique, 1954, pp. 329-43.

      Emphasizes the impact of Spanish music upon the
      style of Monteverdi. Suggests a possible influence
      from Spanish musicians active in Mantua.

53.   Collaer, Paul. "Lyrisme baroque et tradition
      populaire." Studia musicologica 7 (1965): 25-40.

      Explores the influence of popular music from the
      oral tradition on lyricism in Baroque music. Dis-
      cusses Monteverdi's Il combattimento di Tancredi e
      Clorinda.

54.   Cook, Susan C., and La May, Thomasin K. Virtuose
      in Italy, 1600-1640: A Reference Guide. New
      York: Garland, 1984. 163 pp. ISBN 0 824 09138 8
      ML2633 C66 1984

      Discusses notable sixteenth-century singers with
      emphasis on the ladies of Ferrara and the develop-
      ments which occurred after the demise of the Este
      court. Includes an essay on the musical repertory
      for the female vocal ensemble, an annotated bibli-
      ography of musical sources, and biographical
      sketches of early sixteenth-century female per-
      formers and composers.

*   Coutance, Guy. "L'Orfeo au temps de la fête
      baroque."

      Cited below as item 474.

55.   Dahlhaus, Carl. Untersuchungen über die Entstehung
      der harmonischen Tonalität. Saarbrücker Studien
      zur Musikwissenschaft II. Kassel: Bärenreiter,
      1968. 298 pp. ML3811 D39

      A thorough, detailed study of the evolution of
      harmonic tonality by one of the outstanding
      scholars in the field. Examines tonality from the
      fifteenth to the seventeenth centuries. The prin-
      cipal discussion is supported and followed by
      analyses of Josquin's motets, frottole by Cara and
      Tromboncino, and madrigals by Monteverdi. Written
      originally as the author's Habilitationsschrift at

GENERAL BACKGROUND FOR MONTEVERDI RESEARCH

Kiel University in 1966. Excellent bibliography;
extensive subject and name index.

56. ───. "Zur Geschichte des Taktschlagens im
frühen 17. Jahrhundert." Studies in Renaissance
and Baroque Music in Honor of Arthur Mendel,
edited by Robert L. Marshall. Kassel: Bärenreiter, 1974, pp. 117-23. ISBN 3 7618 0412 1
ML194 S82

A learned and provocative study. Examines the
practice of beating time (4/4 or 4/2) as discussed
in Francesco Piovesana's Misure harmoniche regolate
of 1627 and Lorenzo Penna's Li primi albori
musicali of 1679. Also contains a helpful discussion of the problematical "Vi ricorda o boschi
ombrosi" from Monteverdi's Orfeo.

57. Davari, Stefano. "La Musica a Mantova: notizie
biografiche di maestri di musica, cantori e
suonatori presso la corte di Montova nei secoli
XV, XVI, XVII, tratte dai documenti dell'
'Archivio storico Gonzaga.'" Rivista storica
Mantovana 1 (1884): 53-; reprinted in La Musica a
Mantova, edited by Gherardo Ghirardini. Mantua:
Editrice Baruffaldi, 1975. 40 pp.

A well-documented study of music in Mantua,
which centers on the activities of Bartolomeo
Tromboncino, Marchetto Cara, Carlo di Launay, and
Angelo Testagrassa. Contains an appendix written
by the editor which updates Davari's work. See
also Canal, item 47, and Bertolotti, item 36.

58. Dent, Edward J. "The Sixteenth-Century Madrigal."
The New Oxford History of Music, edited by Jack
A. Westrup, Gerald Abraham, et al., vol. 4: The
Age of Humanism, 1540-1630. London: Oxford
University Press, 1968, pp. 31-95.

A concise overview of the madrigal, with a
discussion of the frottola, villanella, and
madrigal comedy. Discusses the musical style of
Monteverdi's fourth and fifth books of madrigals.
Views Monteverdi as a composer whose own musical
style set him apart from the norms of sixteenth-
century musical style.

59.   Dixon, Graham. "Continuo Scoring in the Early
      Baroque: The Role of Bowed-Bass Instruments."
      Chelys 15 (1986): 38-53.

      Takes issue with the custom of using a bowed
      string instrument to duplicate the bass line of
      continuo parts in seventeenth-century Italian
      music. Argues, based upon contemporary evidence,
      that the bowed bass instrument was not required in
      Italian practice until the 1670s.

60.   Donà, Mariangela. "'Affetti Musicali' nel
      seicento." Studi secenteschi 8 (1967): 75-94.

      Surveys opinions held during the seventeenth
      century on the relationship between music and
      sentiments, with an emphasis on the writings of
      Athanasius Kircher. Sees the introduction to
      Monteverdi's eighth book of madrigals as an
      important seventeenth-century declaration of the
      relation of music to emotions. Also discusses the
      merits of Affektenlehre as presented by Vincenzo
      Galilei, Kircher, and, more recently, Paul Bekker.

61.   Doni, Giovanni Battista. Lyra Barberina.
      Florence, 1763; facsimile ed., Bibliotheca musica
      bononiensis. Sezione II, n. 151. Bologna:
      Forni, 1974. ML60 D68 1763a

      The second part of Doni's Lyra Barberina, called
      Trattato della musica scenica, cites Monteverdi's
      opera Arianna. In the appendix to the Trattato
      della musica, Doni compares the solo and madrigal
      versions of the Lamento d'Arianna. Doni's Lyra
      Barberina, actually compiled in 1635, was not pub-
      lished until 1763.

*   ————. Trattato della musica scenica.

      See above, item 61.

62.   Donington, Robert. The Rise of Opera. New York:
      Charles Scribner's Sons, 1981. 399 pp. ISBN 0
      684 17165 1 ML1700 D67

      A significant but somewhat uneven explication of
      early opera. Argues that the Neoplatonic view of
      art was extremely important to the rise of opera.
      Part II, "The Achievement of Opera," contains an
      extensive examination of Monteverdi's Orfeo (pp.

143-90) and concludes with a discussion of the composer's two late Venetian operas (pp. 221-35).
Includes an appendix, notes, a select bibliography
(some entries with very brief annotations), and a
name, topic, and title index.

63. ————. "The Robustness of Early Opera." Opera 21
      (1970): 16-22.

Stresses the importance of vocal power and full
instrumentation in the performance of seventeenth-
century opera. Argues that it is historically
incorrect to sing seventeenth-century opera with
small or restrained voices. Maintains that wind
instruments were commonly added to opera orches-
tras, even though they were not indicated in the
score. Praises the revivals of early Baroque
operas mounted by Raymond Leppard yet criticizes
his published editions.

64. Drummond, John D. Opera in Perspective.
      Minneapolis: University of Minnesota Press, 1980.
      383 pp. ISBN 0 8166 0848 2 ML1700 D75

Contemplates opera and its impact on Western
culture. According to the author, the book is not
intended to be a comprehensive survey of the genre.
Contains a section devoted to a discussion of
Monteverdi's Orfeo. Includes notes, bibliography,
and a name, title, and topic index.

65. Einstein, Alfred. The Italian Madrigal. 3 vols.
      Princeton: Princeton University Press, 1949;
      reprint ed., Princeton: Princeton University
      Press, 1971. 476, 432, 333 pp. ISBN 0 691 09112
      9 ML2633 E32

The fundamental study in English. Recognized
for its comprehensive coverage of the topic and for
its first-rate scholarship. Significant for its
treatment of both text and music. Contains an
index of names and places. The 1971 edition
includes an index to capoversi and titles supplied
by Joel Newman. No bibliography. Volume 3 is a
volume of music. Translated by Alexander H.
Krappe, Roger Sessions, and Oliver Strunk.

66. ————. "Orlando furioso and La Gerusalemme
     Liberata as Set to Music during the 16th and 17th
     Centuries." Music Library Association Notes 8
     (1951): 623-30.

     Supplements the listing of sixteenth- and
     seventeenth-century musical settings of Orlando
     furioso and Gerusalemme liberata found in the
     author's The Italian Madrigal (item 65). Gives
     only the earliest publication date of works, the
     number of voices, and the canto and stanza numbers.

67. Fano, Fabio; Blume, Friedrich; Arnold, Denis; and
     Messinis, Mario. "Venedig und venezianische
     Handschriften." Die Musik in Geschichte und
     Gegenwart, edited by Friedrich Blume. Kassel:
     Bärenreiter, 1949-. Vol. 13 (1966), cols.
     1371-97. ML100 M92

     Divided into two large sections (each subdivided
     into chapters), a historical survey of music in
     Venice is followed by an excellent discussion of
     Venetian manuscripts. Translations into German
     were provided by Egon Voss, Klaus Hortschansky, and
     Anna Frese.

68. Fellerer, Karl Gustav. Der Stilwandel in der
     abendländischen Musik um 1600. Rheinisch-
     Westfälische Akademie der Wissenschaften.
     Opladen: Westdeutscher Verlag, 1972. 88 pp.
     ISBN 3 531 07180 7 ML194 F44

     Provides an illuminating discourse upon the
     dramatic changes that occurred in music simul-
     taneously with the waning of polyphony and the rise
     of monody. Emphasizes the role of Monteverdi in
     this development. Numerous footnotes, but no
     bibliography.

69. Fenlon, Iain. Music and Patronage in Sixteenth-
     Century Mantua. 2 vols. Cambridge: Cambridge
     University Press, 1980. 233, 151 pp. ISBN 0 521
     22905 7 ML290 8M2 F4

     Traces the development of music and culture in
     Mantua during the sixteenth century. Emphasizes
     the fact that "Mantuan patronage is practically
     synonymous with Gonzaga patronage." Also concen-
     trates on musical activities at the ducal basilica
     of Santa Barbara. The second volume is a

collection of Mantuan music from representative
composers, including Monteverdi. Footnotes, bibliography, appendixes, and name index.

70. ————. "Music and Spectacle at the Gonzaga Court,
     c. 1580-1600." Proceedings of the Royal Musical
     Association 103 (1976-77): 90-105.

     Chronicles the record of theatrical presentations
     at the Mantuan court during the late sixteenth
     century. Recognizes the important Ferrarese and
     Florentine influence upon Mantuan theater.

71. Ferrari Barassi, Elena. "A proposito di alcuni
     bassi ostinati del periodo rinascimentale e
     barocco." Memorie e contributi alla musica dal
     medioevo all'età moderna. Offerti a Federico
     Ghisi nel settantesimo compleanno (1901-71),
     edited by Giuseppe Vecchi. Bologna: Istituto di
     Filologia Latina e Medioevale, 1971, pp. 347-64.
     ML55 G48 1973

     Not examined. Summary in RILM Abstracts, 10/3
     (September-December 1976): 327-28, states that the
     article asserts that some basso ostinatos of the
     early seventeenth century stimulated new musical
     forms.

72. Fortune, Nigel. "Continuo Instruments in Italian
     Monodies." Galpin Society Journal 6 (1953): 10-
     13.

     Based on an examination of monody collections
     published between 1602 and ca. 1630, Fortune
     presents a helpful introduction to continuo instru-
     ments used in Italy during the first half of the
     seventeenth century.

73. ————. "A Handlist of Printed Italian Secular
     Monody Books, 1602-1635." R.M.A. Research
     Chronicle 3 (1963): 27-50.

     This checklist of printed monody collections
     includes composer, title, number of songs, and some
     explanatory notes. See also Fortune's article,
     item 74.

74. ————. "Italian Secular Monody from 1600 to 1635:
     An Introductory Survey." Musical Quarterly 39
     (1953): 171-95.

Centers on the contributions made to monody by
composers active in Florence in the first third of
the seventeenth century. Points out the importance
of monody in both madrigal and aria at this time.
Also surveys poets active during this period.

75. ————. "Italian 17th-Century Singing." Music and
     Letters 35 (1954): 206-19.

An important examination of correct singing
style and technique for seventeenth-century Italian
songs. The opinions expressed are based primarily
upon prefaces to collections of secular monodies,
monodic motets, and polyphonic madrigals, as well
as prefaces to operas.

76. Galilei, Vincenzo. Dialogo della musica antica et
     della moderna. Florence: Giorgio Marescotti,
     1581; facsimile ed., New York: Broude Brothers,
     1967. 149 pp. ML171 1581a

An important treatise by a member of the Florentine Camerata. Discusses contemporary tuning
systems and compares Greek music theory with the
theory of Galilei's time. Severely criticizes
polyphonic music for its lack of expressiveness and
discusses musical instruments and notation. A
portion of this work is translated in Strunk, item
288. See also Brown, item 43.

77. Gallico, Claudio. "Assalito da briganti Monteverdi
     sulla via di Venezia." Civiltà mantovana 1/2
     (1966): 24-29.

78. ————. "Dimore mantovane di Monteverdi." Civiltà
     mantovana 1/1 (1966): 27-31.

79. ————. "Mantua." The New Grove Dictionary of
     Music and Musicians, edited by Stanley Sadie.
     London: Macmillan, 1980. Vol. 11, pp. 633-35.

Traces musical activities in the city of Mantua
from the Middle Ages to the present. Lists many
musicians active at the Gonzaga court and emphasizes the musical importance of the Basilica of
Santa Barbara in the latter sixteenth century.
Contains a bibliography.

80. Galvani, Livio Niso. I teatri musicali di Venezia
     nel secolo XVII (1637-1700): memorie storiche e
     bibliografiche. Milan, 1879; reprint ed.,
     Bibliotheca musica bononiensis. Sezione III, n.
     32. Bologna: Forni, 1984. 193 pp.

     Gives a chronology of works performed in
     sixteen Venetian theaters during the seventeenth
     century. The author prefaces the work with a brief
     history of Venetian theaters. Contains four
     indexes: a general index with comments, an index of
     drama titles, an index of poets, and an index of
     composers and their works.

81. Gárdonyi, Zsolt. "Toleranz für Texte?" Der
     Kirchenmusiker 29 (1978): 48-49.

     Confronts the controversy associated with the
     use of parody or contrafactum in church music.

82. Genova, T. "From the History of the Basso Ostinato
     in the 17th and 18th C., Monteverdi, Purcell,
     Bach, etc." Voprosy muzykal'noj formy, III,
     edited by Vladimir Protopopov. 3 vols. Moscow:
     Muzyka, 1977. 270 pp. In Russian.

     Not examined. Summary in RILM Abstracts, 11/2
     (May-August 1977): 151, translates the title of the
     article as given above.

83. George, Graham. "The Structure of Dramatic Music,
     1607-1909." Musical Quarterly 52 (1966): 465-82.

     Maintains that large-scale dramatic works are
     held together not only by the narrative but are
     unified by an overall tonal structure which may be
     of the closed or interlocking type. Observes that
     Monteverdi's Orfeo focuses on the tonal centers of
     D and G. Other dramatic works written before the
     early twentieth century are analyzed.

84. Glixon, Beth L. "Recitative in Seventeenth-Century
     Venetian Opera: Its Dramatic Function and Musical
     Language." Ph.D. dissertation, Rutgers Uni-
     versity, 1985. 462 pp. UM Order No. 85-20,360

     Concentrates on recitative and its role in
     Venetian opera from 1641 to 1684. Contains a
     discussion of L'incoronazione di Poppea.

85. Goldschmidt, Hugo. "Die Instrumentalbegleitung der
    italienischen Musikdramen in der ersten Hälfte
    des XVII. Jahrhunderts." Monatshefte für Musik-
    geschichte 27 (1895): 52-62.

    A significant study by one of the pioneers in
    early seventeenth-century music research. Examines
    the development of the basso continuo in early
    Baroque opera. Points out the importance of the
    directions concerning instrumentation given by
    Monteverdi in Orfeo. The discussion focuses on a
    comparison of Monteverdi's scores with those of
    Caccini, Peri, Cavalieri, Kapsberger, Gagliano,
    Cavalli, Cesti, and others. Also includes a tran-
    scription of an aria by Kapsberger dating from
    1612.

86. ———. Die italienische Gesangsmethode des XVII.
    Jahrhunderts und ihre Bedeutung für die Gegen-
    wart. Breslau: Schlesische, 1892; reprint ed.,
    Leipzig: Volkswacht Gera, 1978. 137 pp.
    MT823 G62 1978

    An influential study. Valuable as a source of
    information regarding Italian singing technique in
    the seventeenth and eighteenth centuries. Contains
    footnotes and an extensive supplement of musical
    examples.

87. ———. "Das Orchester der italienischen Oper im
    17. Jahrhundert." Sammelbände der Inter-
    nationalen Musik-Gesellschaft 2 (1900/01): 16-75.

    The pioneering study. Traces the development of
    the Italian opera orchestra from the use of instru-
    ments in mid-sixteenth-century vocal music to the
    operas of Cavalli and Cesti. Pays particular
    attention to Monteverdi's Orfeo and its influence.
    Concludes with instrumental selections from operas
    by Malvezzi, Rossi, Cavalli, and Pallavicino. The
    article was reprinted in Goldschmidt's Studien zur
    Geschichte der italienischen Oper im 17. Jahr-
    hundert, cited below as item 88.

88. ———. Studien zur Geschichte der italienischen
    Oper im 17. Jahrhundert. 2 vols. Leipzig:
    Breitkopf & Härtel, 1901-1904; reprint ed.,
    Hildesheim: Olms, 1967. 412, 203 pp.

The fundamental study. Traces the development
of Italian opera in the seventeenth century. The
second volume provides a thorough and detailed
examination of Monteverdi's L'incoronazione di
Poppea. Valuable for its copious supplement of
musical examples representing most of the prominent
composers of the era. Bibliography and name index.

89.   Grout, Donald Jay. "The Chorus in Early Opera."
      Festschrift Friedrich Blume zum 70. Geburtstag,
      edited by Anna Amalie Abert and Wilhelm
      Pfannkuch. Kassel: Bärenreiter, 1963, pp.
      151-61.

      Examines numerous problems associated with the
      term "chorus" in operas of the early seventeenth
      century. In addition, scrutinizes the place and
      function of the chorus in early opera. Monte-
      verdi's Orfeo is one of many works cited and
      discussed.

90.   ———. A Short History of Opera. 2nd ed. New
      York: Columbia University Press, 1965. 852 pp.
      ISBN 0 231 08978 3   ML1700 G83 1965

      Surveys the history of opera from its inception
      to the mid-twentieth century. Chapter six dis-
      cusses the musical style and symmetry of Monte-
      verdi's Orfeo. Continues, in chapter eight, with
      comments on L'incoronazione di Poppea and Il
      ritorno d'Ulisse. Grout's work, which appeared in
      its first edition in 1947, is still considered by
      many to be the finest survey of opera in the
      English language.

91.   Gutmann, Veronika. "Viola bastarda-Instrument oder
      Diminutionspraxis?" Archiv für Musikwissenschaft
      35 (1978): 178-209.

      Carefully investigates the confusion surrounding
      the sixteenth- and early seventeenth-century term
      viola bastarda. Attributes much of the misunder-
      standing associated with the term to the Syntagma
      musicum of Michael Praetorius. Concludes that
      parts designated for the viola bastarda were obvi-
      ously performed on the viola da gamba.

92. Haar, James. Essays on Italian Poetry and Music in
     the Renaissance, 1350-1600. Berkeley, Los
     Angeles, and London: University of California
     Press, 1986. 245 pp. ISBN 0520 05397 4 MS1633
     H2 1968

     Examines the relationship between text and music
     during this period of Italian culture. Contains
     several insightful comments on the madrigal style
     of Monteverdi. Concludes with a sizable appendix
     of musical examples. Footnotes, but no bibli-
     ography. Also includes an index of names, titles,
     and topics.

93. Hammerstein, Notker. "'Recreationes...Principe
     dignae.' Überlegungen zur adligen Musikpraxis an
     deutschen Höfen und ihren italienischen Vor-
     bildern." Claudio Monteverdi: Festschrift
     Reinhold Hammerstein (item 794), pp. 213-35.

     Notes the significant contribution of the Italian
     style on music at the German courts.

94. Hanning, Barbara Russano. Of Poetry and Music's
     Power: Humanism and the Creation of Opera.
     Studies in Musicology, No. 13. Ann Arbor: UMI
     Research Press, 1980. 371 pp. ISBN 0 835 71071
     8 ML1702 H36

     A careful, well-researched examination of a
     topic important to the understanding of early
     Baroque opera. Contains a reprint of Striggio's
     libretto to Orfeo. Originally published as the
     author's Ph.D. dissertation. Extensive notes,
     excellent bibliography, and appendixes. Name and
     subject index.

95. Harnoncourt, Nikolaus. Der musikalische Dialog:
     Gedanken zu Monteverdi, Bach und Mozart.
     Salzburg: Residenz Verlag, 1984. 304 pp. ISBN
     7017 0372 8 ML60 H337 1984

     A collection of short essays by one of the
     foremost authorities on early music performance.
     The five articles dealing with Monteverdi are
     entitled "'L'Orfeo'-Dichtung und Musik, Tempi";
     "Instrumentation und Bearbeitung von 'L'Orfeo'";
     "'Il Ritorno d'Ulisse in patria'"; "'L'Incoro-
     nazione di Poppea'"; and "Die Marienvesper (Vespro

della Beata Vergine)." Discography, but no
footnotes or bibliography.

96. Hausswald, Günter. Die Musik des Generalbass-
     Zeitalters. Das Musikwerk, vol. 45. Cologne:
     Volk, Gerig, 1973. 180 pp.

     Not examined. Summary in RILM Abstracts, 8/1
     (January-April 1974): 23, states that the publi-
     cation includes compositions by Monteverdi and
     other composers from the thorough-bass epoch. Also
     included is a discussion of thorough-bass notation
     and Baroque theory.

97. Heuss, Alfred. "Die venetianischen Opern-
     Sinfonien." Sammelbände der Internationalen
     Musik-Gesellschaft 4 (1902/03): 404-77.

     Traces the history of the Venetian opera sinfonia
     from its beginnings to around 1700. Divides the
     discussion into three periods: up to 1660, 1660-
     1680, and 1680-1700. Includes an extensive
     supplement of examples from works by Cavalli,
     Ziani, Pallavicino, Franceschini, Marini, and
     Cazatti. This article was extracted from the
     author's doctoral dissertation completed at the
     University of Leipzig in 1903. See also Heuss,
     item 513.

98. Hoffman, Donald. "The Chromatic Fourth." The
     Consort 26 (1970): 445-58.

     Examines the development of the chromatic fourth
     in music from the sixteenth century to the nine-
     teenth century. Identifies four musical functions
     of the chromatic fourth. Discusses numerous
     examples containing that musical figure.

99. Ivanovich, Cristoforo. Minerva al tavolino. 2
     vols. Venice: N. Pezzana, 1688.

     Not examined. Thomas Walker, in "Gli errori di
     'Minerva al tavolino'" (item 182), describes this
     work as a collection of poetry, letters, and prose
     together with an important chronology of operas
     performed in Venice between 1637 and 1681.

100.   Jung, Hermann. Die Pastorale: Studien zur
       Geschichte eines musikalischen Topos. Neue
       Heidelberger Studien zur Musikwissenschaft, vol.
       9. Bern: Francke, 1980. ISBN 3 7720 1457 7
       ML160 J8 1980

       A revision of Jung's 1976 dissertation. Traces
       the genre of the pastorale from antiquity to the
       middle of the eighteenth century. Examines Orfeo
       and several madrigal settings by Monteverdi. Con-
       tains a rather lengthy bibliography, notes, and
       name index.

101.   Kloiber, Rudolf. Handbuch der Oper. 2 vols.
       Regensburg: Gustav Bosse, 1951; reprint ed.,
       1973. 875 pp. ISBN 3 7618 0422 9 MT95 K47 197

       A handbook containing discussions of representa-
       tive works by the most important composers. In-
       cludes entries on Monteverdi's Orfeo and L'incoro-
       nazione di Poppea. Also presents a succinct essay
       tracing the development of opera from its begin-
       nings to the twentieth century.

102.   Kretzschmar, Hermann. "Die venetianische Oper und
       die Werke Cavalli's und Cesti's." Viertel-
       jahrsschrift für Musikwissenschaft 8 (1892):
       1-76.

       A valuable, early essay providing great insight
       into seventeenth-century Venetian opera. Divides
       the study into three periods: 1637-60, 1660-80, an
       1680-1700. Recognizes the importance of Monteverd
       to the development of the Venetian operatic style.

103.   Kroyer, Theodor. Die Anfänge der Chromatik im
       italienischen Madrigal des XVI. Jahrhunderts.
       Leipzig: Breitkopf & Härtel, 1902; reprint ed.,
       Farnborough: Gregg International, 1968. 160 pp.
       ML2633 K93

       A reprint of Kroyer's Ph.D. dissertation of 1897
       from the University of Munich. Following an intro
       duction, the book consists of five chapters (with
       numerous subchapters): I. The Madrigal; II. Chro-
       maticism and its Genesis; III. The First Epoch, Th
       Chromaticism of the First Madrigalists; IV. The
       Second Epoch, Chromaticism in the Golden Age of th
       Madrigal; V. The Third Epoch, The Principal Chro-
       maticist N. Vicentino and the Romantics of the

Sixteenth Century. Includes an index and a
supplement of musical examples.

*   Lecoat, Gerard George. "Music and the Rhetoric of
         the Arts During the Age of Monteverdi."

         Cited below as item 381.

104.   Lee, M. Owen. "Orpheus and Eurydice: Blueprint for
         Opera." The Canadian Music Journal 6 (1962):
         23-36.

         Emphasizes the importance of the Orpheus myth to
         drama and music from Poliziano's Favola d'Orfeo of
         1472 to several twentieth-century works. Contends
         that the Orfeos of Poliziano, Monteverdi, and Gluck
         are the three great landmark works in the history
         of opera. Recognizes Monteverdi's version of the
         myth as the first music drama.

105.   Leichtentritt, Hugo. Geschichte der Motette.
         Leipzig: Breitkopf & Härtel, 1908; reprint ed.,
         Hildesheim: Olms, 1967; also published Wiesbaden:
         Breitkopf & Härtel, 1976. 453 pp. ML3090 L52

         A monumental study. Traces the development of
         the motet from its inception in France through the
         motets of J.S. Bach. Includes a bibliography and
         an index of names and topics.

106.   Leopold, Silke. "Chiabrera und die Monodie: Die
         Entwicklung der Arie." Studi musicali 10 (1981):
         75-106.

         Investigates the influence of the poet Gabriello
         Chiabrera on the development of monody and aria.
         Compares the forewords of two contemporaneous
         works: Chiabrera's Le maniere dei versi toscani
         (1599) and Giulio Caccini's Le nuove musiche
         (1602). Eight examples of monodies by various
         composers are provided at the end of the article.

107.   ————. "Die Hierarchie Arkadiens: soziale
         Strukturen in den frühen Pastoralopern und ihre
         Ausdrucksformen." Schweizer Jahrbuch für
         Musikwissenschaft, new series 1 (1981): 71-92.

         Identifies the pastoral play as significant to
         the genesis of early opera. Examines pastoral
         operas composed between the first Florentine operas
         and the later Venetian operas.

108.   ———. "Madrigali sulle egloghe sdrucciole di
        Iacopo Sannazaro; struttura poetica e forma
        musicale." Rivista italiana di musicologia 14
        (1979): 75-127.

Considers the influence of the poetry of Iacopo
Sannazaro (1455-1530) on the sixteenth- and early
seventeenth-century madrigal with emphasis on
Sannazaro's poems in Arcadia. Analyzes works of
Ruggiero Giovanelli and Felice Anerio in respect t
the influence the poetry had on their music. Cite
settings by other composers, including Monteverdi'
setting of La pastorella mia from his Scherzi
musicali (1607). Translated into Italian by Paolc
Fabbri.

109.   ———. "Orpheus in Mantua und anderswo."
        Concerto 1 (1983): 35-42.

An investigation of the development of the
Orpheus myth in opera with emphasis on the versior
by Poliziano, Rinuccini, and Striggio.

110.   Lowinsky, Edward E. Tonality and Atonality in
        Sixteenth-Century Music. Berkeley: University c
        California Press, 1961. 101 pp. ML174 L7

Asserts that the period from ca. 1575 through tl
early seventeenth century was a time when the hor:
zontal and vertical approaches to tonality were
mixed.

111.   MacClintock, Carol. "New Sources of Mantuan
        Music." Journal of the American Musicological
        Society 22 (1969): 508-11.

Reports on two hitherto unknown sources of
Mantuan music. The bass part to the twelfth book
of madrigals by Giaches de Wert, actually an
anthology, contains two original works of
Monteverdi, Pensier aspro e crudele and Sdegno la
fiamm' estinse. The other source is a manuscript
which contains six masses and a hymn by composers
of the Mantuan provenance.

*   McGee, Timothy J. "Orfeo and Euridice, the First
        Two Operas."

Cited below as item 524.

112.   Mahling, Christoph-Hellmut. Studien zur Geschichte
       des Opernchors. Trossingen-Wolfenbüttel: Editio
       Intermusica, 1962. 360 pp. ML1700 M13 58

       A reprint of the author's doctoral dissertation
       from the University of Saarbrücken in 1962. Traces
       the evolution of the opera chorus from the six-
       teenth century to Richard Wagner. Bibliography,
       tables, and illustrations.

113.   Maniates, Maria Rika. Mannerism in Italian Music
       and Culture, 1530-1630. Chapel Hill: The Uni-
       versity of North Carolina Press, 1979. 678 pp.
       ISBN 0 8078 1319 2 ML290.2 M36

       Asserts that the period from 1530 to 1630 con-
       stitutes a unified historical epoch in Italian
       culture. Surveys mannerism in poetry, painting,
       and sculpture. Examines mannerist elements in
       music theory, composition, and performance, in-
       cluding an examination of the mannerist traits in
       Monteverdi's works. Contains an extensive bibli-
       ography, an index of names, and an index of titles.

114.   Martinotti, Sergio. "Teatralità e teatro a Venezia
       nell'età di Monteverdi." Congresso inter-
       nazionale sul tema Claudio Monteverdi (item 811),
       pp. 129-38.

       Asserts that architecture and public festivals in
       Venice contributed to Venetian enthusiasm for
       theatrical presentations in the Baroque era.
       Monteverdi reflected this enthusiasm not only in
       his operas written for Venice but also in madrigals
       of a dramatic nature.

115.   Mason, Kevin Bruce. "The Chitarrone and Its
       Repertoire in Early Seventeenth-Century Italy."
       Ph.D. dissertation, Washington University, 1983.
       169 pp. UM Order No. 83-20564

       Not examined. Summary in Dissertation Abstracts
       International, 44/5 (Nov 1983): 1237-A, indicates
       that the study emphasizes the use of the chitarrone
       in chamber music and opera orchestras.

116.   Meier, Bernhard. Die Tonarten der klassischen
       Vocalpolyphonie. Utrecht: Oosthoeck, Scheltema,
       and Holkema, 1974. 478 pp. ISBN 9 031 30009 8
       ML3811 M43

An exploration of the importance of the modes i
Renaissance vocal polyphony. Divided into two
major sections, the first is concerned with basic
information about the modes and the second studie
the modes primarily from the standpoint of sixteenth-century musical technique. Contains notes
bibliography, name index, and music supplement.

117.   Mendel, Arthur. "Pitch in the 16th and Early 17t
       Centuries." Musical Quarterly 34 (1948): 28-45
       199-221; 336-57; 575-93.

       Investigates the subject of pitch in the six-
       teenth and early seventeenth centuries through a
       careful reading of Arnold Schlick's Spiegel der
       Orgelmacher und Organisten (1511) and the second
       volume of Michael Praetorius's Syntagma musicum
       (item 137). Part three of Mendel's study conside
       the method of transposition known as "chiavette."
       Concludes with an examination of Alexander J.
       Ellis's research on pitch, based on measurements
       old organ pipes.

118.   Monterosso, Raffaello. "Claudio Monteverdi e il
       suo tempo." Congresso internazionale sul tema
       Claudio Monteverdi (item 811), pp. 17-32.

       Points out that Monteverdi has been credited wi
       such distinctions as being the creator of opera t
       being the creator of modern music. Attempts to
       place the composer's achievements in proper histo
       ical context. Reviews various Renaissance and
       early Baroque views on the concept of imitation.
       Discusses Monteverdi's concepts of theatricality
       realized in his secular and sacred works.

119.   ———. "Cremona." Die Musik in Geschichte und
       Gegenwart, edited by Friedrich Blume. Kassel:
       Bärenreiter, 1949-. Vol. 2 (1952), cols.
       1773-81.

       Summarizes the history of music in Cremona,
       emphasizing musical life of the sixteenth and
       seventeenth centuries. Translated into German by
       Anna Amalie Abert.

120.   Moore, James H. "Venezia favorita da Maria: Musi
       for the Madonna Nicopeia and Santa Maria della
       Salute." Journal of the American Musicological
       Society 37 (1984): 299-355.

Investigates the increased production of Marian
motets at Venice in the early seventeenth century.
Contends that the establishment of the altar of the
Madonna Nicopeia at St. Mark's and the founding of
the votive church Santa Maria della Salute inspired
numerous Marian compositions. Describes the importance of Marian devotion in many of Monteverdi's
works. Especially significant is the discussion of
the Selva morale e spirituale.

121.   Morrow, Michael. "The Renaissance Harp." Early
        Music 7 (1979): 499-510.

        Discusses the importance of the harp in the late
        Renaissance. Most of the information is based on
        four Spanish sources of the sixteenth century.
        Monteverdi's use of the double harp in Orfeo is
        examined.

122.   Murata, Margaret. "The Recitative Soliloquy."
        Journal of the American Musicological Society 32
        (1979): 45-73.

        Affirms the importance of the recitative mono-
        logue in early seventeenth-century Italian opera,
        particularly from 1630 to 1646.

123.   Osthoff, Wolfgang. "Maske und Musik: die
        Gestaltwerdung der Oper in Venedig." Castrum
        peregrini 65 (1964): 10-49.

        Traces the rise of Venetian opera to Monteverdi's
        L'incoronazione di Poppea.

124.   ————. "Petrarca in der Musik des Abendlandes.
        Eine Betrachtung zum Sprachethos der Musik."
        Castrum peregrini 20 (1954): 5-55.

        Examines the musical settings of four Petrarch
        poems by composers from the fourteenth century to
        the seventeenth century. Monteverdi is the last
        composer included in the discussion.

125.   ————. "Trombe sordine." Archiv für Musikwissen-
        schaft 13 (1956): 77-95.

        Surveys the use of the muted trumpet in the
        seventeenth- and eighteenth-century orchestra from
        Monteverdi to Haydn.

126. Palisca, Claude V. Baroque Music. 2nd. ed.
      Englewood Cliffs, New Jersey: Prentice-Hall,
      1981. 300 pp. ISBN 0 13 055954 7 ML193 P34
      1981

      A concise history of music in the Baroque perio(
      with emphasis on the seventeenth century. Dis-
      cusses Monteverdi's musical style and compares
      Monteverdi's Orfeo with Peri's Euridice. Contain:
      a bibliography and an index.

127. ───. Humanism in Italian Renaissance Musical
      Thought. New Haven: Yale University Press, 198!
      471 pp. ISBN 0 300 03302 8 ML290.2 P34 1985

      Documents the influence of ancient Greek musica
      thought on the Italian Renaissance. The last two
      chapters, "The Poetics of Music" and "Theory of
      Dramatic Music," are concerned with music as
      poetry, the poetics of imitation, and the musical
      theories of Girolamo Mei. Bibliography and index

*   ───. "Vincenzo Galilei's Counterpoint Treatis(
      A Code for the Seconda pratica."

      Cited below as item 672.

128. Paoli, Rodolfo. "Difesa del primo melodramma."
      Rassegna musicale 20 (1950): 93-100.

      Observes that the accomplishments of the Floren
      tine Camerata have often been judged negatively.
      Asserts that the Camerata emphasized words over
      music, while Monteverdi treated both with equal
      prominence. States that this does not justify th
      judgment of inferiority with regard to the works
      Peri, Caccini, or Cavalieri.

129. Parisi, Susan. "Virtuoso Performers at the Court
      of Mantua, 1587-1627: An Archival Study." Ph.D
      dissertation in progress, University of Illinoi

130. Pintér, Éva. "New Elements of Vocal Style in the
      First Half of the 17th Century." Studia
      musicologica 22 (1980): 205-35.

      A thorough essay examining the development of
      vocal style and form in the early seventeenth
      century. Divided into two parts, the first secti
      deals with the stylistic characteristics of Monte
      verdi's vocal concertos, while the second section

compares Monteverdi's works with the vocal chamber
music of other early Baroque composers. Argues
that, with the exception of opera, Monteverdi pre-
ferred concerto form after about 1605. Concludes
with a supplement containing transcriptions of
vocal pieces by selected seventeenth-century
composers.

131.   Pirrotta, Nino. "Early Opera and Aria." New Looks
       at Italian Opera, edited by William W. Austin.
       Ithaca: Cornell University Press, 1968, pp.
       39-107. ML1733.1 N5 1968

       An important monograph. Discusses the beginnings
       of opera and aria with specific attention given to
       the claims of Peri, Caccini, and Cavalieri and
       examines the polemics resulting from those alle-
       gations. Monteverdi's contributions to early opera
       are also examined. This monograph later appeared
       as chapter six in Pirrotta's Li due Orfei (item
       134).

*   ———————. "Early Venetian Libretti at Los Angeles."

       Cited below as item 549.

132.   ———————. "Monodia." La Musica. Parte prima:
       Enciclopedia Storica, vol. 3. Turin: Unione
       Tipografico-Editrice Torinese, 1966, pp. 363-69.

       Discusses the origins of monody, the birth of
       opera, the stile recitativo, and the basso con-
       tinuo. Compares the musical style of Peri and
       Caccini. Contains a brief bibliography.

133.   ———————. Music and Culture in Italy from the Middle
       Ages to the Baroque. Studies in the History of
       Music, vol. 1, edited by Lewis Lockwood and
       Christoph Wolff. Cambridge: Harvard University
       Press, 1984. 485 pp. ISBN 0 674 59108 9
       ML290.1 P57 1984

       Contains an outstanding collection of twenty-two
       essays. Essays pertaining to Monteverdi and his
       times are items 402, 550, 551, and 554 in this
       bibliography.

134. Pirrotta, Nino, and Povoledo, Elena. Li due Orfei
      da Poliziano a Monteverdi. Turin: EDI, 1969;
      2nd. ed., Turin: Giulio Einaudi, 1981. 472 pp.
      ML1733 P57 1981

      Identifies mythological plays of the fifteenth
      century as important forerunners of seventeenth-
      century opera. Considers the philosophical ideas
      of the Florentine Camerata to be of little impor-
      tance in the creation of early opera. The second
      half of this study, by Elena Povoledo, provides
      informative essays on the origins of Italian sce-
      nography. This book appeared, with some revisions
      in an English translation by Karen Eales, as Music
      and Theatre from Poliziano to Monteverdi (Cam-
      bridge: Cambridge University Press, 1982).

135. Pöhlmann, Egert. "Antikenverständnis und Anti-
      kenmissverständis in der Operntheorie der
      Florentiner Camerata." Die Musikforschung 22
      (1969): 11-12.

      Explores the question of how well the members of
      the Florentine Camerata understood the role of
      music in Greek and Roman tragedy.

136. Povoledo, Elena. "Una rappresentazione accademica
      a Venezia nel 1634." Studi sul teatro veneto fi
      rinascimento ed età barocca. Civiltà veneziana
      studi 24, edited by Maria Teresa Muraro.
      Florence: Olschki, 1971, pp. 119-69.

      Discusses representations produced in academies
      in Venice from the end of the sixteenth century to
      1637. Gives an in-depth description of Prospero
      Bonarelli's Tragedy il solimano, as presented by
      the Accademia degli Immobili in 1634. Contains a
      chronology of representations performed in Venice
      from 1593-1642, bibliography, and photographs of
      engravings from printed representations.

137. Praetorius, Michael. Syntagma musicum. 3 vols.
      Wolfenbüttel: Holwein, 1618-20; facsimile
      reprint, edited by Wilibald Gurlitt, Documenta
      musicologica, vols. 21, 14, 15, Kassel:
      Bärenreiter, 1958-60. 504, 278, 260 pp.

      Generally regarded as one of the most informativ
      musical treatises of its time. Especially signifi
      cant for the study of the seventeenth century are

volume 2, which deals with musical instruments, and
volume 3, which discusses genres and performance
practice in Italy, Germany, France, and England.

138.   Prunières, Henry. "The Italian Cantata of the
        XVIIth Century." Music and Letters 7 (1926):
        38-48; 120-32.

        An in-depth survey of the Italian cantata. Cites
        Monteverdi's Il combattimento di Tancredi et
        Clorinda as foreshadowing the musical construction
        of the cantatas of Carissimi and Scarlatti. Notes
        other works of Monteverdi in relation to the
        development of the solo cantata.

139.   Racek, Jan. "Die dramatisierende Funktion der
        Pause in der italienischen Vokal- und
        dramatischen Musik des 17. Jahrhunderts."
        Festschrift Karl Gustav Fellerer zum 70.
        Geburtstag am 7. Juli 1972, edited by Heinrich
        Hüschen. Cologne: Volk, 1973, pp. 463-71.

        Not examined. Summary in RILM Abstracts, 8/2-3
        (May-December 1974): 166, indicates that the essay
        emphasizes the dramatic significance of the
        Generalpause in Monteverdi's Orfeo.

*   Razzi, Fausto. "Polyphony of the seconda prattica:
        Performance Practice in Italian Vocal Music of
        the Mannerist Era."

        Cited below as item 694.

140.   Redlich, Hans F. "Early Baroque Church Music."
        The New Oxford History of Music, edited by Jack
        A. Westrup, Gerald Abraham, et al., vol. 4: The
        Age of Humanism, 1540-1630. London: Oxford
        University Press, 1968, pp. 520-49.

        A concise overview of church music in the late
        sixteenth and early seventeenth centuries centered
        on the musical activities at Rome and Venice.
        Discusses Monteverdi's Vespers of 1610.

141.   Robinson, Michael F. Opera before Mozart. New
        York: William Morrow, 1967; 3rd ed., London:
        Hutchinson, 1978. 168 pp. ISBN 0 091 36221 0
        ML1700 R6 1978

        Traces the development of opera from ca. 1600 to
        ca. 1780. Presents relevant cultural influences on

opera. Monteverdi's operas are placed in proper
historical perspective.

142.   Roche, Jerome. "Anthologies and the Disseminatic
        of Early Baroque Italian Sacred Music." Sound-
        ings 4 (1974): 6-12.

        Delineates the spread of Italian sacred music
        through anthologies published in Venice, Milan,
        Rome, Strasbourg, Leipzig, and Munich. Composi-
        tions by Monteverdi appeared in collections
        published by Bonometti, Calvi, and Simonetti in
        Venice, Sammaruco in Rome, and Profe in Leipzig.

143.   ————. "The Duet in Early Seventeenth-Century
        Italian Church Music." Proceedings of the Roya
        Musical Association 93 (1966-67): 33-50.

        Surveys the Italian practice of the church duet
        in the early Baroque. Discusses the works of
        several composers, most importantly Viadana,
        Grandi, and Monteverdi. Includes complete tran-
        scriptions of two Grandi church duets: Hodie nobi
        de caelo and Anima Christi.

144.   ————. "Liturgical Music in Italy, 1610-60." ⁻
        New Oxford History of Music, edited by Jack A.
        Westrup, Gerald Abraham, et al., vol. 5: Opera
        and Church Music, 1630-1750. London: Oxford
        University Press, 1975, pp. 350-70.

        Discusses concertato psalm settings, the
        orchestral mass, and works in the style antico
        written in Italy between 1610 and 1660. Asserts
        that Monteverdi's sacred works had a significant
        influence on his Venetian contemporaries.

145.   ————. The Madrigal. New York: Charles
        Scribner's Sons, 1972; also published London:
        Hutchinson, 1972. 167 pp. ISBN 0 684 13341 5
        (Scribner's) ISBN 0 091 13260 6 (Hutchinson)
        ML2600 R63 1972

        A concise survey of the madrigal from its
        beginnings through the early seventeenth century.
        Musical style is discussed with citations from
        important madrigals. Briefly examines Monteverdi
        madrigal books. Contains a source list of mad-
        rigals, a bibliography, and an index.

146. ————. North Italian Church Music in the Age of
      Monteverdi. Oxford: Clarendon Press, 1984. 177
      pp. ISBN 0 193 16118 4 ML2933 R6 1984

      Masterfully written and remarkably comprehensive,
      this book is a revision of the author's significant
      doctoral dissertation (item 147 below). Incorpo-
      rates recent research on the subject published
      subsequent to the original work. Valuable espe-
      cially for the chapter entitled "The Social and
      Geographical Context," which brings into sharp
      focus the important musical activity flourishing in
      cities other than Venice. Contains a selective
      bibliography, notes, a name and place index, a
      catalog of music source material, and an index of
      musical examples.

147. ————. "North Italian Liturgical Music in the
      Early Seventeenth Century." Ph.D. dissertation,
      University of Cambridge, 1968. 560 pp.

      A significant and thorough study of the subject.
      Argues that liturgical music played a central role
      in the development of the new Baroque style.
      Examines the sacred music of Giovanni Gabrieli,
      Alessandro Grandi, and Monteverdi, along with that
      of many of their contemporaries. Includes a valu-
      able chronological list (Appendix I) of source
      material containing northern Italian liturgical
      music. Appendixes and bibliography. See above,
      item 146.

148. Rodis-Lewis, Geneviève. "Musique et passions au
      XVIIe siècle (Monteverdi et Descartes)." XVIIe
      siècle 92 (1972): 81-98.

      Primarily an investigation of thought relevant
      to the influence of music on the passions as
      revealed in writings from the first half of the
      seventeenth century. Focuses chiefly on treatises
      and letters by Descartes, Mersenne, and Jan Albert
      Bannius.

149. Rolland, Romain. Les origines du théâtre lyrique
      moderne: Histoire de l'opéra en Europe avant
      Lully et Scarlatti. Paris: E. Thorin, 1895. New
      ed., Paris: E. de Boccard, 1931; reprint ed.,
      Geneva: Slatkine, 1971. 316 pp. ML1702 R75 197

Originally presented as a doctoral dissertation
to the University of Paris in 1895. Chapter 4 (pp
83-86) is devoted to a discussion of Monteverdi.
Includes a chronology (pp. 84-86) of the composer'
life and works. Contains a bibliography, table of
contents, and a short supplement of musical
examples.

150. Ronga, Luigi. "La vocalità nella musica italiana
     da Palestrina a Monteverdi." Letteratura modern
     1 (1950): 77-82.

     Briefly discusses musical expression from
     Palestrina to Monteverdi and emphasizes that by th
     time of Monteverdi's music even the madrigal ex-
     pressed the emotions of the individual.

151. Rosand, Ellen, ed. Opera I: Up to Mozart. The
     Garland Library of the History of Western Music.
     Vol. 11. New York: Garland, 1985. 354 pp. ISB
     0 8240 7460 2 ML1700.063 198

     A reprint of significant articles concerning
     opera before Mozart. Items 43 and 123 in this
     bibliography are reprinted in this collection.

152. Rose, Gloria. "Agazzari and the Improvising
     Orchestra." Journal of the American
     Musicological Society 18 (1965): 382-93.

     In his thorough-bass treatise Del sonare sopra'l
     basso con tutti li stromenti e dell'uso loro nel
     conserto (item 20), Agostino Agazzari distinguishe
     instruments designated "like a foundation" from
     those designated "like an ornament." Although it
     is not certain to what kind of music Agazzari is
     alluding in the treatise, Rose considers that the
     incomplete or missing instrumental portions in
     seventeenth-century opera scores may be music
     improvised according to Agazzari's indications.

153. Sartori, Claudio. "Mantua." Die Musik in Ge-
     schichte und Gegenwart, edited by Friedrich
     Blume. Kassel: Bärenreiter, 1949-. Vol. 8
     (1960), cols. 1602-05.

     Offers a useful survey of music in Mantua
     beginning with the piffari and trombetti of the
     fourteenth century. Translated into German by
     Friedrich Blume.

154. Schalz, Nicolas. Studien zur Komposition des
     Gloria. Musikalische Formgestaltung von der
     Gregorianik bis zu Monteverdi. Frankfurter
     Beiträge zur Musikwissenchaft, vol. 3. Tutzing:
     Schneider, 1980. 531 pp. ML3088 S

     A comprehensive investigation of monophonic and
     polyphonic musical settings of the Gloria of the
     Mass from the medieval period to Monteverdi. The
     essay on Monteverdi (pp. 432 to 459) is the second
     section of chapter VII. Originally presented to
     the Johann Wolfgang Goethe University in 1974 as
     the author's doctoral dissertation.

155. Schmitz, Eugen. Geschichte der Kantate und des
     geistlichen Konzerts: Geschichte der weltlichen
     Solokantate. Leipzig, 1914; reprint ed.,
     Hildesheim: Olms, 1966; also published Wiesbaden:
     Breitkopf & Härtel, 1966. 327 pp. ML2800 S

     A reprint of Schmitz's influential book on the
     cantata, which was the publication of his Habili-
     tationsschrift presented to the University of
     Munich in 1909. Divided into two large sections,
     the first examines the cantata in Italy and the
     second deals with the cantata in France, Germany,
     and England. Name index, but no bibliography. See
     also Schmitz, item 156.

156. ————. "Zur Frühgeschichte der lyrischen Monodie
     Italiens im 17. Jahrhundert." Jahrbuch der
     Musikbibliothek Peters 18 (1911): 35-48.

     Deplores the lack of research at the time the
     article was written on the lyric influence in
     monody. Schmitz, a scholar in the field of the
     chamber cantata, produced this article from
     material gathered while researching his book
     Geschichte der Kantate und des geistlichen
     Konzerts, item 155.

157. ————. "Zur Geschichte des italienischen
     Continuo-Madrigals im 17. Jahrhundert." Sammel-
     bände der Internationalen Musik-Gesellschaft 2
     (1909-10): 509-28.

     Establishes 1602 as the correct date for the
     beginning of the basso continuo in the madrigal,
     specifically with the collections of Salomone Rossi
     and Pompeo Signorucci. Represented among the

composers whose works are discussed are Monteverdi,
Anerio, Olivieri, Ugoni, Turini, Grandi, Mazzocchi,
and Mazzaferata. Particular attention is devoted
to the madrigals of Monteverdi, commencing with the
fifth book of 1605.

158. ————. "Zur Geschichte des italienischen Kammer-
     duetts im 17. Jahrhundert." Jahrbuch der Musik-
     bibliothek Peters 23 (1916): 43-60.

     A historically important contribution. Lauds the
     chamber duets of Agostino Steffani as the out-
     standing examples of the genre.

159. Schrade, Leo. "Sulla natura del ritmo barocco."
     Rivista musicale italiana 56 (1954): 3-27.

     Compares the use of rhythm in the Baroque with
     earlier eras. Claudio Monteverdi is heralded as
     the first Baroque composer to realize the relation-
     ship of rhythm to the affect of the text. Cavalli
     is cited as a composer who continued the use of
     rhythmic models bound closely to the dances of the
     time.

160. See, Max. "Der tragische Opernschluss. Eine
     dramaturgische Studie." Neue Zeitschrift für
     Musik 129 (October 1968): 431-41; (November
     1968): 485-93; (December 1968): 537-45.

     Considers the tragic ending in opera from the
     time of the Florentine Camerata to the twentieth-
     century operas of Alban Berg. Discusses Monte-
     verdi's Orfeo, Il combattimento di Tancredi e
     Clorinda, and L'incoronazione di Poppea.

161. Seidel, Wilhelm. "Die Rückkehr des Orpheus zur
     Musik. Die Wirkungen der Musik in Monteverdis
     erster Oper." Claudio Monteverdi: Festschrift
     Reinhold Hammerstein (item 794), pp. 409-25.

     An examination of the Orpheus myth as the subject
     for musical drama, stressing the setting by
     Monteverdi.

162. Selfridge-Field, Eleanor. <u>Venetian Instrumental</u>
      <u>Music from Gabrieli to Vivaldi</u>. Blackwell's
      Music Series, edited by Frederick W. Sternfeld.
      Oxford: Blackwell, 1975; also published New York:
      Praeger, 1975. 351 pp. ISBN 0 275 53670 X
      ML290.8 V26

      An elaboration of the author's doctoral thesis.
      Part one is a documentary history which discusses
      music at St. Mark's and at theaters, academies, and
      confraternities in Venice. Part two discusses
      musical forms and the music of specific composers
      from Gabrieli through Vivaldi and the Marcellos.
      Monteverdi's influence on instrumental music is
      considered. Includes an appendix of the Basilica
      staff at St. Mark's, a glossary of musical instru-
      ments and terms, a bibliography, and an index.

163. Smith, Patrick J. <u>The Tenth Muse: A Historical</u>
      <u>Study of the Opera Libretto</u>. New York: Alfred A.
      Knopf, 1970; reprint ed., New York: Schirmer
      Books, 1975. 417 pp. ML2110 S62 1975

      Critically reviews the relationship of librettist
      and composer in operatic masterpieces from the
      early seventeenth century through the early
      twentieth century. Cites conventions of
      seventeenth-century opera and discusses Giovanni
      Francesco Busenello's librettos, including <u>L'inco-</u>
      <u>ronazione di Poppea</u>. Busenello is recognized by
      the author as the first creative librettist.

164. Solerti, Angelo. <u>Gli albori del melodramma</u>. 3
      vols. Milan: Remo Sandron, 1904; reprint ed.,
      Hildesheim: Olms, 1969. 165, 353, 384 pp.

      A well-documented history of opera in the first
      half of the seventeenth century. Also contains
      discussion devoted to dramatic representations with
      music from the Renaissance. Praises Monteverdi's
      <u>Orfeo</u> for the composer's ability to instill into
      the music the sentiment of the poetry. Includes a
      transcription of the extant music from Monteverdi's
      <u>Arianna</u>. Volumes two and three contain a collec-
      tion of librettos by Rinuccini, Chiabrera,
      Striggio, and others.

165. ———. Musica, ballo e drammatica alla corte
      Medicea dal 1600 al 1637. Florence: R. Bemporad,
      1905; reprint ed., New York: Benjamin Blom, 1968.
      549 pp.

      Provides information found by the author in a
      diary of the Medici court at the national library
      in Florence. Includes a record of festivities from
      1600 to 1637.

166. ———. Le origini del melodramma: testimonianze
      dei contemporanei. Turin: Fratelli Bocca, 1903;
      reprint ed., Hildesheim: Olms, 1969. 262 pp.

      Contains writings on opera from the first four
      decades of the seventeenth century. Includes
      prefaces and dedications of Peri, Caccini,
      Rinuccini, and others. Reprints Pietro della
      Valle's Discorso from Giovanni Battista Doni's De'
      trattati di musica, printed in Florence in 1758, as
      well as portions of Doni's Trattato della musica
      scenica. Both the commentaries of Pietro della
      Valle and Doni cite Monteverdi. Provides an
      appendix with a bibliography of printed operas from
      1600 to 1640 and an extensive bibliography of works
      on opera.

167. ———. "Le rappresentazioni musicali di Venezia
      dal 1571 al 1605 per la prima volta descritte."
      Rivista musicale italiana 9 (1902): 503-58.

      Lists all the Venetian rappresentazioni from 1571
      to 1605, including information on their frontis-
      pieces and their versos. Gives a portion from the
      beginning and ending of their texts. Notes that we
      have little knowledge of the music which accompa-
      nied these festivities. An appendix includes the
      complete text to the Tragedia of S. Cl. Cornello
      Frangipani.

168. Sternfeld, Frederick W. "The Birth of Opera: Ovid,
      Poliziano, and the lieto fine." Analecta
      musicologica 19 (1979): 30-51.

      Contends, based primarily on the study of scores
      and librettos to eighteen dramatic works produced
      from 1589 to 1656, that early opera flourished
      because of court patronage, the happy ending which
      pleased the audience, and the libretto based on a

humanistic favola pastorale. Concludes with two
lists of scores and dramas.

169. ————. "A Note on stile recitativo." Proceedings
     of the Royal Musical Association 110 (1983-84):
     41-44.

     Searches for the origin and history of the term
     stile recitativo. Examines the appearance of the
     term in treatises by Agazzari, Bonini, and Doni.

170. Stevens, Denis. "Music in Mantua." Musical
     Times 102 (1961): 306-61.

     Recognizes the importance of music at the
     Mantuan court under the patronage of the Gonzaga
     family.

171. ————. "Two Centuries of Venice." Music and
     Musicians 16 (July 1968): 26-27.

     Gives a brief outline of the significance of
     music in Venice during the sixteenth and seven-
     teenth centuries.

172. Strainchamps, Edmond. "The Life and Death of
     Caterina Martinelli: New Light on Monteverdi's
     'Arianna.'" Early Music History 5 (1985): 155-
     86.

     Supplies new documentation on the life of
     Caterina Martinelli, the virtuoso singer who was
     under Monteverdi's tutelage in Mantua until her
     untimely death. Contains an appendix of documents
     concerning Martinelli.

173. Surian, Elvidio. "Cremona." The New Grove
     Dictionary of Music and Musicians, edited by
     Stanley Sadie. London: Macmillan, 1980. Vol. 5,
     pp. 30-31.

     Stresses the musical importance of the cathedral
     in Cremona from the twelfth century through the
     early seventeenth century. Cites academies active
     in the city and discusses Cremona's late blossoming
     theatrical life. Contains a bibliography.

174. Tagmann, Pierre M. Archivalische Studien zur
     Musikpflege am Dom von Mantua (1500-1627). Bern:
     Haupt, 1967. 99 pp. ML 3033 8 M32 T25

An essential source regarding music in Mantua during the sixteenth and early seventeenth centuries. Notes the important relationship between court and cathedral during this period. Bibliography, chronology, name index, and numerous footnotes.

175. Tarr, Edward H., and Walker, Thomas. "'Bellici carmi, festivo fragor': Die Verwendung der Trompete in der italienischen Oper des 17. Jahrhunderts." Hamburger Jahrbuch für Musik-wissenschaft 3 (1978): 143-203.

Thoroughly traces the role of the trumpet in seventeenth-century Italian opera. Contains numerous musical examples.

176. Tegen, Martin. "Den gamla och den nya stilen." Musikrevy 22 (1967): 139-43. In Swedish.

Surveys the rise of the new Baroque style.

177. Testi, Flavio. La musica italiana nel seicento. La lirica da camera, l'oratorio, la musica da chiesa, la musica per strumenti, la teoria, il costume musicale. Milan: Bramante Editrice, 1972. 501 pp. ML290.2

Continues Testi's comprehensive history of seventeenth-century Italian music. Monteverdi's madrigals, sacred works, and the Artusi-Monteverdi controversy are discussed. Includes a bibliography and name index. See also Testi, item 178.

178. ————. La musica italiana nel seicento. Il melodramma. Milan: Bramante Editrice, 1970. 493 pp. ML290.2 T5

A comprehensive history of Italian opera in the seventeenth century. The chapter "Le opere di Monteverdi" includes a discussion of the librettos and music of Monteverdi's extant operas. Includes bibliography and name index. See also Testi, item 177.

179. Towneley, Simon. "Early Italian Opera." The New Oxford History of Music, edited by Jack A. Westrup, Gerald Abraham, et al., vol. 4: The Age of Humanism, 1540-1630. London: Oxford University Press, 1986, pp. 821-44.

Examines Italian opera from its beginning to ca.
1630. Monteverdi's Orfeo is viewed as the first
opera with an appeal beyond that for the historian.

*   Uberti, Mauro, and Schindler, Oskar. "Contribution
      à la recherche d'un art vocal monteverdien: la
      couleur."

      Cited below as item 701.

180. Vecchi, Giuseppi. Le accademie musicali del primo
      seicento e Monteverdi a Bologna. Bologna:
      Antiquae Musicae Italicae Studiosi, 1969.
      210 pp. ML290.8 B68 V4

      A quatercentenary tribute to Monteverdi, in which
      all relationships between the composer and the city
      of Bologna are explored, notably that of Monte-
      verdi's visit to the city in 1619, the Artusi-
      Monteverdi controversy, and Banchieri's writings
      compared to the seconda pratica. Studies in detail
      the academies of Bologna during the late sixteenth
      and early seventeenth centuries. Contains appen-
      dixes which give portions of treatises by important
      Bolognese scholars contemporary with Monteverdi.
      These include parts of Discorso secondo musicale di
      Antonio Braccino da Todi by G.M. Artusi; Conclu-
      sioni nel suono dell'organo, Cartella musicale nel
      canto figurato fermo e contrapunto, Lettere
      armoniche, and Discorso della lingua bolognese by
      Banchieri; and La mascara by Ercole Bottrigari.

*   Vetter, Walther. "Zur Stilproblematik der
      italienischen Oper des 17. und 18. Jahrhunderts."

      Cited below as item 580.

181. Waeltner, Ernst Ludwig. "Monteverdi und die
      Entstehung der Oper." Melos, Neue Zeitschrift
      für Musik 3 (1977): 492-96.

      Intended for the general reader, Waeltner
      presents a succinct overview of the development of
      early opera.

182. Walker, Thomas. "Gli errori di 'Minerva al
      tavolino.'" Venezia e il melodramma nel
      seicento. Studi di musica veneta, vol. 5, edited
      by Maria Teresa Muraro. Florence: Olschki, 1976,
      pp. 7-20.

Points out errors in Cristoforo Ivanovich's
Minerva al tavolino (item 99), an important
chronology of operas performed in Venice between
1637 and 1681.

183. Weaver, Robert L. "The Orchestra in Early Italian
      Opera." Journal of the American Musicological
      Society 17 (1964): 83-89.

Traces the changes in instrumentation which
occurred in the opera orchestra during the
seventeenth century. Weaver contends that a
multicolored Renaissance orchestra made up of a
variety of instruments evolved into a monochrome
orchestra consisting of violins of various sizes
and continuo. Maintains that the purpose of the
orchestra is to convey the affections of the music
through rhythm, motives, melody, and harmony rather
than through tone color. See also Rose, item 152.

184. Wellesz, Egon. "Die Aussetzung des Basso Continuo
      in der italienischen Oper." Report of the Fourth
      Congress of the International Musical Society.
      London: Novello, 1912, pp. 282-85.

Acknowledges two types of basso continuo styles,
one for chamber music and one for dramatic music.
Points out the problem of the basso continuo in
early opera due to the incompleteness of the
scores. Makes a plea for stylistically correct
editions of early music.

185. ————. "Cavalli und der Stil der venetianischen
      Oper von 1640-1660." Studien zur Musikwissen-
      schaft 1 (1913): 1-103.

A seminal and copious contribution to the
history of Baroque opera in general and Cavalli
specifically. Refers to Monteverdi, Cavalli's
teacher, as the creator of Venetian opera. Organized, for the most part, in chapters devoted to the
specific musical forms of opera. Concludes with a
substantial appendix of musical examples.

186. Whenham, John. Duet and Dialogue in the Age of
      Monteverdi. 2 vols. Studies in British
      Musicology No. 7, edited by Nigel Fortune. Ann
      Arbor: UMI Research Press, 1982. 287, 469 pp.
      ISBN 0 835 71313 X   ML1633

Discusses the rise of the secular duet and recitative dialogue from 1600 to the death of Monteverdi (1643). Considers duets that appeared in madrigal books and in monody books to be equally influenced by the new stylistic musical developments. Documents Monteverdi's contributions to the duet and recitative dialogue. Volume 2 contains an analytical catalog of Italian secular duets and an anthology with all the main types of continuo duets and a selection of dialogues. Contains notes, an extensive bibliography, and an index.

187. Williams, Peter. "Figurenlehre from Monteverdi to Wagner." Musical Times 120 (1979): 816-18.

Calls attention to certain musical figures used by composers from Orfeo to Die Meistersinger von Nürnberg.

188. Winter, Paul. Der Mehrchörige Stil. Frankfurt: C.F. Peters, 1964. 114 pp. ML1500 W

A monograph tracing the growth of the polychoral style. The book is copiously footnoted and presents a fairly comprehensive bibliography. Also includes appendixes and name and topic indexes.

189. Wolff, Hellmuth Christian. "Bühnenbild und Inszenierung der italienischen Oper 1600-1700." Congresso internazionale sul tema Claudio Monteverdi (item 811), pp. 109-15.

A valuable essay maintaining that seventeenth-century Italian stage design for opera originated from two sources: the Renaissance theater and the intermedio. Describes the sets of stage designers such as Francesco Guitti, Ferdinando Tacca, Lorenzo Bernini, and others. Stresses the importance of the use of perspective in the sets of Italian opera during this epoch and the influence of Italian set design in other European countries.

190. ———. "Italian Opera from the Later Monteverdi to Scarlatti." The New Oxford History of Music, edited by Jack A. Westrup, Gerald Abraham, et al., vol. 5: Opera and Church Music, 1630-1750. London: Oxford University Press, 1975, pp. 1-72. ISBN 0 19 316305

Continues the survey of Italian opera from volume
four of The New Oxford History of Music. Discusses
Monteverdi's Venetian operas. Asserts the importance of recurring stylization in the opera
libretto of the latter seventeenth century.

191. ———. The Opera I: 17th Century. Translated by
Robert Kolben. Anthology of Music, vol. 38.
Cologne: Arno Volk, 1971. 124 pp. M2 M945 vol.
38

A collection of musical examples from seventeenth-century operas. The anthology of music is
prefaced by a historical introduction and informative notes on each entry. Includes excerpts from
Monteverdi's Orfeo and Il ritorno d'Ulisse. Also
contains source references, a bibliography, and
English translations of the texts.

192. Worsthorne, Simon Towneley. Venetian Opera in the
Seventeenth Century. Oxford: Clarendon Press,
1954; reprint ed., New York: Da Capo, 1984.
194 pp. ISBN 0 306 76227 7 ML1733.8 V4 W77 19

Discusses the history of Venetian opera in the
seventeenth century with emphasis on Venetian
theaters. Examines the importance of the aria, the
chorus, and the orchestra in Venetian opera.
Asserts that there is little indication that Monteverdi's Il ritorno d'Ulisse or L'incoronazione di
Poppea were known by later seventeenth-century
composers. Includes twenty-three plates, reproductions from manuscripts, musical examples,
appendixes of Venetian opera documentation, a
bibliography, and an index.

193. Zanetti, Emilia. "Ancora sul catalogo
dell'archivio musicale dei Gonzaga." Nuova
rivista musicale italiana 3 (1974): 377-78.

Gives background and history of the collection
cataloged in Guglielmo Barblan's Musiche della
cappella di S. Barbara in Mantova (see item 860).
Evaluates the format of the above-mentioned
catalog.

194. Zarlino, Gioseffo. Le istitutioni harmoniche.
Venice, 1558; facsimile ed., New York: Broude
Brothers, 1965. 347 pp. ML171 Z35 155a

One of the most influential theoretical dis-
courses of the sixteenth century. Examines, in
part one, mathematical aspects of music and, in
part two, discusses Greek music. Parts three and
four give an exhaustive treatment of the art of
counterpoint and the use of modes from the perspective of a practicing musician. Part three of
Zarlino's Istitutioni appeared in an English
translation by Guy A. Marco and Claude V. Palisca
as The Art of Counterpoint, published by Yale University Press in 1968. Part four was published by
Yale University Press in 1983 under the title On
the Modes. A portion of the third part of
Zarlino's Istitutioni is translated in Strunk, item
288.

195. Zimmerman, Franklin B. "Purcell and Monteverdi."
      Musical Times 99 (1958): 368-69.

      Associates Monteverdi with Purcell through a
      fragment of an instrumental transcription of
      Monteverdi's madrigal Cruda Amarilli attached to
      the autograph copy of Purcell's Benedicite in
      B-flat (Bodlean ms. mus. A.1). Contends that
      Purcell's well-known enthusiasm for Italian
      composers must have included Monteverdi.

196. Zingerle, Hans. Die Harmonik Monteverdis und
      seiner Zeit. Innsbruck: Edition Helbling, 1951,
      32 pp. M781 Z77 1951

      Considers the harmonic procedures of Monteverdi
      and his contemporaries. Includes an extensive
      appendix of musical examples by Monteverdi, Cesti,
      Cavalli, Carissimi, and Scarlatti. Footnotes, but
      no bibliography.

3. Studies of Monteverdi's Contemporaries

197. Abert, Anna Amalie. Die stilistischen Grundlagen
      der 'Cantiones sacrae' von Heinrich Schütz.
      Berlin: Druck der Salesianischen Offizin, 1935.
      235 pp.

      Identical with item 198 below.

198.   ————. Die stilistischen Voraussetzungen der
        'Cantiones Sacrae' von Heinrich Schütz. Kieler
        Schriften zur Musikwissenschaft, vol. 29.
        Wolfenbüttel: Kallmeyer, 1935; reprint ed.,
        Kassel: Bärenreiter, 1986. 238 pp. ISBN 3 7618
        0773 2   ML410 S35 A3 1986

        A thorough study of Schütz's collection of
        concertato motets. Notes influences from numerous
        German and Italian composers, including Monteverdi.
        Contains footnotes, bibliography, and a name index.
        Identical with item 197, cited above.

199.   Ademollo, Alessandro. La bell'Adriana ed altre
        virtuose del suo tempo alla corte di Montova.
        Città di Castello: S. Lapi, 1888. 359 pp. ML420
        B8 A2

        Adriana Basile, known as "La bell'Adriana," was
        one of the most famous singers of the early
        seventeenth century (see item 1). Ademollo
        documents the life of this singer as well as many
        other virtuosos of the time. Adriana was active at
        Mantua and was well known to Monteverdi. Contains
        a helpful index for locating citations of important
        persons.

200.   Adrio, Adam. "Ambrosius Profe (1589-1661) als
        Herausgeber italienischer Musik seiner Zeit."
        Festschrift Karl Gustav Fellerer zum sechzigsten
        Geburtstag, edited by Heinrich Hüschen.
        Regensburg: Gustav Bosse Verlag, 1962, pp. 20-27.

        Evaluates the importance and contributions of
        Profe, a minor organist and composer in Breslau, as
        a music editor and publisher. Examines Profe's
        chief work, the four volumes of Geistliche
        Concerten und Harmonien produced from 1641 to 1646,
        in which Monteverdi and many other Italian
        composers are well represented. Devotes an entire
        section to a discussion of Monteverdi's use of
        contrafactum.

201.   Arkwright, G.E.P. "An English Pupil of
        Monteverdi." The Musical Antiquary 4 (1912-13):
        236-57.

        The earliest article identifying the English
        composer Walter Porter as a student of Monteverdi.
        In addition to presenting numerous biographical

details, three selections from Porter's Madrigales
and Ayres of 1632 are printed.

202. Armstrong, James. "The 'Antiphonae, Seu Sacrae
      Cantiones' (1613) of Giovanni Francesco Anerio: A
      Liturgical Study." Analecta musicologica 14
      (1974): 89-150.

      Contains a thorough discussion of Anerio's
      Antiphonae, seu sacrae cantiones (published in 3
      volumes in 1613), a collection of antiphons for
      Vespers. Volume 2 also includes three antiphons
      for Compline. Points out similarities between the
      Vespers of Monteverdi and Anerio.

203. Arnold, Denis. "Alessandro Grandi, a Disciple of
      Monteverdi." Musical Quarterly 43 (1957):
      171-86.

      Discusses the influence of Monteverdi on
      Alessandro Grandi who, in 1620, became Monteverdi's
      assistant at Venice. Grandi, an advocate of the
      concertato style, made a distinction between
      melodic writing for chorus and for solo voice. It
      is the mature style of Monteverdi which is most
      evident in Grandi's Masses and psalms.

204. ————. "Cavalli at St. Marks." Early Music 4
      (1976): 266-74.

      Compares the sacred music of Francesco Cavalli
      with that of his alleged teacher, Monteverdi.
      Gives a critical evaluation of selected works from
      Cavalli's Musiche sacre concernenti messa, e salmi
      concertati con istromenti, imni, antifone et
      sonate, a due, 3, 4, 5, 6, 8, 10 & 12 voci of 1656.

205. ————. Giovanni Gabrieli and the Music of the
      Venetian High Renaissance. London: Oxford
      University Press, 1979. 322 pp. ISBN 0 19
      315232 0 ML410 G11 A8

      An excellent account of Gabrieli's life and
      works. Numerous references are made to composi-
      tions by Monteverdi. Briefly assesses the influ-
      ence of Monteverdi's style in Venice.

206. ————. "Monteverdi and His Teachers." The New
      Monteverdi Companion (item 780), pp. 91-106.

Stresses the influence of various composers upon
Monteverdi's musical style. Notes characteristics
learned from Ingegneri and Wert. This article
first appeared in The Monteverdi Companion (item
779).

207.   ————. "Monteverdi: Some Colleagues and Pupils."
        The New Monteverdi Companion (item 780), pp.
        107-24.

Identifies numerous musical similarities in the
works of Monteverdi and other late sixteenth- and
seventeenth-century composers. Points out, for
example, Michelangelo Rossi's use of Monteverdi's
stile concitato idea in the opera Erminia sul Gior-
dano. Suggests that Amante Franzoni was probably
one of the first composers to be influenced by
Monteverdi. This article first appeared in The
Monteverdi Companion (item 779).

208.   ————. "Schütz in Venice." Music and Musicians
        21 (1972): 30-35.

Investigates the Venetian influence on the music
of Heinrich Schütz, with emphasis on that of
Giovanni Gabrieli and Monteverdi. Concludes that
although Schütz was an experienced composer when he
returned to Venice in 1628, his musical style did
change as a result of this second Venetian expe-
rience. Emphasizes the influence of Monteverdi's
musical expression of poetic images on Schütz.

209.   ————. "Schütz's 'Venetian' Psalms." Musical
        Times 113 (1972): 1071-73.

Discusses the Psalmen Davids in light of the
Venetian practice of Giovanni Gabrieli and, to a
lesser extent, Monteverdi. Believes that Schütz's
use of falsobordone in psalms was modeled after
Monteverdi's Vespers music.

210.   ————. "The Second Venetian Visit of Heinrich
        Schütz." Musical Quarterly 71 (1985): 359-74.

Notes Italian influences upon the music of Schütz
stemming from the composer's trip to Venice in
1628. Contends that Monteverdi's stile concitato
was the most important new element learned by
Schütz.

211. Barblan, Guglielmo. "Un ignoto 'Lamento d'Arianna'
      Mantovano." Rivista italiana di musicologia
      (item 838), pp. 217-28.

      Compares the five-voice setting of Rinuccini's
      Lamento d'Arianna by the obscure Mantuan composer
      Giulio Cesare Antonelli with Monteverdi's five-
      voice version, giving musical examples from
      Antonelli's setting. Points out that although
      Antonelli set a number of texts also used by
      Monteverdi (including Cruda Amarilli and O
      Mirtillo), his works were more in the style of
      Gastoldi than in the style of Monteverdi. Cites
      other settings of the famous Arianna lament.

212. Bianconi, Lorenzo. "Struttura poetica e struttura
      musicale nei madrigali di Monteverdi." Congresso
      internazionale sul tema Claudio Monteverdi (item
      811), pp. 335-48.

      Compares Monteverdi's Luci serene e chiare from
      his fourth book of madrigals (1603) to a setting of
      the same text by Gesualdo (1596). Reveals that
      Monteverdi articulates the syntax of the poem
      musically, whereas Gesualdo distinguishes portions
      of the poem with contrasting musical procedures.
      Analyzes Monteverdi's musical rhetoric in his
      seventh and eighth books of madrigals and distin-
      guishes a change in style from that in the fourth
      and fifth books.

213. Bussi, Francesco. "La produzione sacra di Cavalli
      e i suoi rapporti con quella di Monteverdi."
      Rivista italiana di musicologia (item 838), pp.
      229-54.

      Re-evaluates Francesco Cavalli's standing as a
      composer of sacred works. Compares Cavalli's
      dichotomy of musical style with that of his
      teacher, Monteverdi.

214. Carapezza, Paolo Emilio. "Schützens italienische
      Madrigale: Textwahl und stilistiche Beziehungen."
      Schütz-Jahrbuch 1 (1979): 44-62.

      Contends that the madrigals of Schütz were
      modeled after similar works by Monteverdi and
      Marenzio.

215. ———. "L'ultimo oltramontano o vero l'anti-
      monteverdi (un esempio di musica reservata tra
      manierismo e barocco)." Nuova rivista musicale
      italiana 4 (1970): 213-43; 411-44.

      Although principally a study of the oltramontano
      Claudio Pari, a composer active in Palermo during
      the early seventeenth century, the author also
      compares Pari's madrigals to Monteverdi's works.
      Demonstrates that Pari's madrigal Lasciatemi
      morire, from his fourth book of madrigals, contains
      strong influences from Monteverdi's setting of the
      same text. Presents numerous examples of Pari's
      use of dissonance and reveals a highly organized
      musical structure in these works. Illustrates
      examples from Pari's works and includes a
      contemporary comment on Pari's works by G.B.
      Ajello.

*   Clercx, Suzanne. "L'Espagne du XVIe siècle, source
      d'inspiration du génie héroïque de Monteverdi."

      Cited above as item 52.

216. Crain, Gordon F. "Francesco Cavalli and the
      Venetian Opera." Opera 18 (1967): 446-51.

      Surveys the early history of Venetian opera
      with emphasis on the contributions of Francesco
      Cavalli. Briefly compares the musical style of
      Cavalli with that of Monteverdi and includes a plot
      outline of Cavalli's L'Ormindo.

217. Dubrovskaja, Tat'jana. Rol' madrigala v tvorčestv
      G. Šjutca. Moscow: Moskovskaja Konservatorija,
      1973. 30 pp. In Russian.

      Not examined. Summary in RILM Abstracts, 8/2-3
      (May-December 1974): 160, indicates that the essay
      shows that Schütz's Italian madrigals clearly
      demonstrate his association with Monteverdi.

218. Fellerer, Karl Gustav. "Claudio Monteverdi e la
      musica del suo tempo." Rivista italiana di
      musicologia (item 838), pp. 270-81.

      Gives an account of the numerous influences on
      the musical style of Monteverdi, including the
      works of Viadana, the balletti, the canzonette, the
      airs de cour, and the music of the Florentine
      school. Cites composers contemporary with

Monteverdi and gives a clear picture of the musical
atmosphere of the times. Suggests a strong
influence from Monteverdi and other Italian
composers on German composers of the seventeenth
century.

219. Forsythe, Holly S. "A Modern Performance Edition
      of Selected Madrigals by Benedetto Pallavicino
      (1551?-1601)." 2 vols. M.M. thesis, Converse
      College, 1974. 122 pp.

      Not examined. Summary in RILM Abstracts, 8/2-3
      (May-December 1974): 148, indicates that the thesis
      examines and edits representative examples of the
      madrigals of Pallavicino, Monteverdi's predecessor
      as maestro di capella at the Mantuan court.

220. Ghisi, Federico. "Alcuni aspetti stilistici della
      musica sacra monteverdiana in Giacomo Carissimi."
      Congresso internazionale sul tema Claudio
      Monteverdi (item 811), pp. 305-12.

      Considers Monteverdi's three great sacred collec-
      tions to have had an influence on Carissimi. Also
      notes that some of Monteverdi's secular works, such
      as Chiome d'oro from his seventh book of madrigals,
      influenced Carissimi.

221. Glover, Jane. Cavalli. New York: St. Martin's
      Press, 1978. 191 pp. ISBN 0 312 12546 1 ML410
      C3913 G6 1978

      A major study of one of Monteverdi's most sig-
      nificant successors. Contains end notes for each
      chapter, a bibliography, appendixes, and an index.

222. Hammerstein, Irmgard. "Zur Monteverdi-Rezeption in
      Deutschland. Johann Hermann Scheins 'Fontana
      d'Israel.'" Claudio Monteverdi: Festschrift
      Reinhold Hammerstein (item 794), pp. 175-212.

      Notes the influence of Monteverdi upon German
      composers in the early seventeenth century.
      Advocates that madrigals from Monteverdi's third,
      fourth, and fifth madrigal books provided paradigms
      for Schein's Fontana d'Israel and other later
      works.

223. Hammond, Frederick. Girolamo Frescobaldi.
      Cambridge: Harvard University Press, 1983. 408
      pp. ISBN 0 674 35438 9 ML410 F85 H35 1983

      A comprehensive study of the life and works of
      one of Monteverdi's most important contemporaries.
      Provides a catalog of works, extensive notes, a
      substantial bibliography, and an index of names,
      topics, and places.

224. Heller, Adalbert. "Heinrich Schütz in seinen
      italienischen Madrigalen." Gustav Becking zum
      Gedächtnis. Eine Auswahl seiner Schriften und
      Beiträge seiner Schüler, edited by Walter
      Kramolisch. Tutzing: Hans Schneider, 1975, pp.
      373-412. ISBN 3 7952 0124 1 ML55 B33 1975

      A comparative study that considers the Italian
      madrigals of Schütz in light of the works of
      selected contemporaneous composers. Discusses
      settings of O primavera by Schütz, Marenzio, and
      Monteverdi.

225. Hucke, Helmut. "Palestrina als Autorität und
      Vorbild im 17. Jahrhundert." Congresso
      internazionale sul tema Claudio Monteverdi (item
      811), pp. 253-61.

      Attempts to assess the recognition and influence
      of Palestrina's style in the seventeenth century,
      particularly in Italy and Germany. Sources cited
      for authority include treatises by Agazzari,
      Praetorius, Banchieri, Landi, Bernhard, and others

226. Hughes, Charles W. "Porter, Pupil of Monteverdi."
      Musical Quarterly 20 (1934): 278-88.

      Discusses the music of the English composer
      Walter Porter (ca. 1587 or ca. 1595-1659), who
      allegedly studied with Monteverdi sometime prior t
      1616. The presence of diverse techniques such as
      monody and the concertato style in Porter's first
      publication, Madrigales and Ayres of 1639, seems t
      support Porter's claim of being a student of
      Monteverdi. Hughes compares and contrasts Porter'
      works with those of Monteverdi, as well as with
      another important pupil of Monteverdi, Heinrich
      Schütz.

227. Jung, Hermann. "Schütz und Monteverdi. Einige
      Aspekte ihrer historischen und stilistischen
      Beziehungen." Claudio Monteverdi: Festschrift
      Reinhold Hammerstein (item 794), pp. 271-95.

      Explores the relationship between Schütz and
      Monteverdi. Begins with a quotation from a 1672
      memorial address in honor of Schütz by the Dresden
      poet David Schirmer, which notes a connection
      between the two composers. Contains quotes and
      opinions by other authorities ranging from Spitta
      to Stravinsky.

228. Kast, Paul. "Tracce monteverdiane e influssi
      romani nella musica sacra del Kapsberger."
      Rivista italiana di musicologia (item 838), pp.
      288-93.

      Asserts that the declamation, text repetition,
      and homorhythmic musical style found in Johann
      Hieronymus Kapsberger's Cantiones sacrae (1628) and
      Modulatus sacri (1630) show an influence of the
      musical style of Claudio Monteverdi. Kapsberger
      was a German composer who traveled to Rome in
      1604-1605.

229. Kenton, Egon F. "The Late Style of Giovanni
      Gabrieli." Musical Quarterly 48 (1962): 427-43.

      Succinctly compares Monteverdi's Sonata sopra
      Sancta Maria ora pro nobis with Gabrieli's Dulcis
      Jesu, patris imago. Maintains that certain sty-
      listic features of Gabrieli's music were adopted by
      Monteverdi, even though no reference to Gabrieli is
      made in Monteverdi's letters.

230. ————. Life and Works of Giovanni Gabrieli.
      Musicological Studies and Documents, vol. 16.
      Rome: American Institute of Musicology, 1967.
      557 pp. ML410 G11 K4

      Kenton's study, which, in an opening chapter,
      translates the first two chapters of Winterfeld's
      landmark work (item 255) on Gabrieli, presents a
      thorough, analytical examination of the composer's
      work. Maintains that Gabrieli provided a model for
      Monteverdi in the exchange of instruments and
      voices.

231. Kinkeldey, Otto. "Luzzasco Luzzaschi's Solo-
      Madrigale mit Klavierbegleitung." Sammelbände
      der Internationalen Musik-Gesellschaft 9
      (1907-1908): 538-65.

      Compares Luzzaschi's madrigals for one voice and
      cembalo accompaniment to madrigals by Monteverdi
      and others.

232. Kirkendale, Warren. "Zur Biographie des ersten
      Orfeo, Francesco Rasi." Claudio Monteverdi:
      Festschrift Reinhold Hammerstein (item 794), pp.
      297-329.

      Chronicles the career of Francesco Rasi, the
      composer and musician who originated the title role
      in Monteverdi's first opera.

233. Komoda, Haruko. "Francesco Cavalli no opera."
      Ongaku gaku 21 (1975): 185-98. In Japanese.

      Not examined. Summary in RILM Abstracts, 9/3
      (September-December 1975): 251, notes that this is
      a summary of the author's M.A. thesis from Tokyo
      National University. Shows the influence of
      Monteverdi in Cavalli's operas.

234. Kreidler, Walter. Heinrich Schütz und der Stile
      Concitato von Claudio Monteverdi. Stuttgart:
      Fackel and Klein, 1934; also published Kassel:
      Bärenreiter, 1934. 146 pp. ML410 S35 K7

      Originally Kreidler's doctoral dissertation from
      the University of Bern. Divided into three chap-
      ters, the first assesses the expressive role of the
      stile concitato, particularly emphasizing the con-
      nection between that style and the text. Monte-
      verdi's use of the style is the subject of the
      second chapter and Schütz's treatment of the style
      is the topic of the third chapter. Musical exam-
      ples and bibliography.

*   Kretzschmar, Hermann. "Die venetianische Oper und
      die Werke Cavalli's und Cesti's."

      Cited above as item 102.

235. Kunze, Stefan. "Instrumentalität und Sprach-
      vertonung in der Musik von Heinrich Schütz
      (Erster Teil)." Schütz-Jahrbuch 1 (1979): 9-43.

Attempts to show a correlation between text
setting and instrumental style in both Venetian
music and in monody. Discusses Monteverdi's
Lamento d'Arianna.

236. Kurtzman, Jeffrey G. "Giovanni Francesco Capello,
      an Avant-Gardist of the Early Seventeenth
      Century." Musica disciplina 31 (1977): 155-82.

      Sheds light on the sacred music of the progres-
      sive Italian composer Capello, a contemporary of
      Monteverdi. Makes numerous comparisons between the
      music of the two. Regards Capello as one of the
      first composers of dialogues and solo motets.

237. Luisi, Leila Galleni. "Il Lamento d'Arianna di
      Severo Bonini (1613)." Congresso internazionale
      sul tema Claudio Monteverdi (item 811), pp.
      573-82.

      Analyzes the musical style of Severo Bonini's
      setting of Rinuccini's Lamento d'Arianna, which the
      author contends was influenced by the style of
      Monteverdi. Bonini's earlier style followed that
      of Caccini. However, by the time of his Lamento
      d'Arianna of 1613, Bonini's style enabled him to
      express the psychological situation of his char-
      acters musically. Cites excerpts from Bonini's
      Lamento.

238. MacClintock, Carol. Giaches de Wert (1535-1596):
      Life and Works. Musicological Studies and
      Documents, vol. 17, edited by Armen Carapetyan.
      N.p.: American Institute of Musicology, 1966.
      285 pp.

      Examines the life and works of a contemporary of
      Claudio Monteverdi who was at the court of Mantua
      when Monteverdi assumed his position there ca.
      1589. Asserts that the influence of Wert's later
      madrigal style can be seen in Monteverdi's third
      book of madrigals published in 1592. Includes an
      appendix of Wert's dedications, a list of works
      (printed and manuscript sources), a bibliography,
      and an index.

239. Meister, Hubert. Untersuchungen zum Verhältnis von
      Text und Vertonung in den Madrigalen Carlo
      Gesualdos. Regensburg: Gustav Bosse, 1973. 205
      pp. ISBN 3 7649 2098 X ML410 G29 M4

A comprehensive treatise investigating the six
madrigal books of Gesualdo. Compares Gesualdo's
settings to madrigals by Monteverdi and Marenzio.
Originally presented as a doctoral dissertation tc
the University of Cologne. Extensively footnoted,
with a bibliography of about 120 items.

240. Moore, James H. Vespers at St. Mark's: Music of
      Alessandro Grandi, Giovanni Rovetta and Francesc
      Cavalli. 2 vols. Ann Arbor: UMI Research Press
      1981. 388, 264 pp. ISBN 0 835 71143 9 ML290.8
      V26 M66

      A comprehensive examination of music composed fc
      Vespers services at St. Mark's in Venice during tl
      seventeenth century. Concentrates, in light of tl
      influence of Monteverdi, upon the contributions of
      three composers: Grandi, Rovetta, and Cavalli.
      Volume 2 is an anthology of music. Includes
      appendixes, notes, bibliography, and a name and
      topic index. Originally published as the author's
      Ph.D. dissertation.

241. Moser, Hans Joachim. Heinrich Schütz. His Life
      and Work. Translated by Carl F. Pfatteicher.
      St. Louis: Concordia, 1959. 740 pp. ML410 S35
      M62 1959

      The first edition in the original German was pul
      lished by Bärenreiter in 1936; a second edition
      appeared in 1954. The outstanding study of
      Schütz's life and works. Particularly helpful to
      students of Monteverdi is the chapter entitled "Tl
      Venice of Monteverdi." Footnotes, but no bibli-
      ography. Also appendixes, name index, and topic
      index.

242. Newcomb, Anthony. "Alfonso Fontanelli and the
      Ancestry of the Seconda Pratica Madrigal."
      Studies in Renaissance and Baroque Music in Hon
      of Arthur Mendel, edited by Robert L. Marshall.
      Kassel: Bärenreiter, 1974, pp. 47-70. ISBN 3
      7618 0412 1 ML55 M415 57

      Contends that the Ferarrese musical style of th
      1590s foreshadows the seconda pratica of Monte-
      verdi, especially the madrigals of Luzzaschi,
      Gesualdo, and Alfonso Fontanelli. Includes
      excerpts from important letters written by
      Fontanelli to Ridolfo Arlotti.

243.   Osthoff, Wolfgang. Heinrich Schütz: l'incontro
       storico fra lingua tedesca e poetica musicale
       italiana nel seicento. Centro Tedesco di Studi
       Veneziani, Quaderni, vol. 1. Venice: Centro
       Tedesco di Studi Veneziani, 1974. 24 pp. ML410
       S358

       A short monograph which attempts to place in
       perspective Italian influence upon the works of
       Schütz. Monteverdi is one of the composers
       considered. Footnotes and musical examples.

244.   ————. "Monteverdis Combattimento in deutscher
       Sprache und Heinrich Schütz." Festschrift
       Helmuth Osthoff zum 65. Geburtstage, edited by
       Lothar Hoffmann-Erbrecht and Helmut Hucke.
       Tutzing: Hans Schneider, 1961, pp. 195-227.

       Attributes a German language version of
       Monteverdi's Il combattimento di Tancredi e
       Clorinda to Heinrich Schütz or to one of his
       contemporaries. Includes a facsimile edition of
       the work.

245.   Petrobelli, Pierluigi. "L' 'Ermiona' di Pio Enea
       degli Obizzi ed i primi spettacoli d'opera
       veneziani." Quaderni della rassegna musicale 3
       (1965): 125-37.

       Asserts that Ermiona by Pio Enea was the first
       dramma per musica of Venice, as had been claimed by
       Cristoforo Ivanovich in his early inventory of
       Venetian operas, Minerva al tavolino (item 99).
       Contends that the genre was transmitted to Venice
       from Parma and Ferrara. Although the music by
       Felice Sances for the production is probably lost,
       the 1638 printing of the libretto contains a
       detailed description of the spectacle and a
       valuable narration by S. Nicolò Enea Bartolini.
       The list of performers given for the Venetian
       performance includes Francesco Monteverdi, Claudio
       Monteverdi's son.

246.   Roche, Jerome. "Giovanni Antonio Rigatti and the
       Development of Venetian Church Music in the
       1640's." Music and Letters (1976): 256-67.

An examination of the sacred music of Giovanni
Antonio Rigatti, one of the important church
musicians active in Venice during the first half
the seventeenth century. Compares Rigatti's Miss
e salmi of 1640 with Monteverdi's Selva morale e
spirituale, also composed in the same year.
Suggests the possibility that Rigatti may have
exerted some influence upon Monteverdi.

247. Rorke, Margaret Ann. "Sacred Contrafacta of
      Monteverdi Madrigals and Cardinal Borromeo's
      Milan." Music and Letters 65 (1984): 168-75.

Describes three books of contrafacta set to
sacred texts by Aquilino Coppini with music borrowed primarily from Monteverdi's middle books (4
and 5) of madrigals. Published in Milan, these
motets were produced by Coppini under the patrona
of Cardinal Federico Borromeo. Suggests that the
music was used with Monteverdi's consent.

248. Seelkopf, Martin Rudolf. Das geistliche Schaffen
      von Alessandro Grandi. 2 vols. N.p., 1973.
      329, 365 pp. ML410 G7635 S4 1973

Ph.D. dissertation, Julius-Maximilian Universit
Würzburg. Surveys the sacred works of Grandi,
stressing the connection between words and music.
Especially helpful to Monteverdi research are the
sections entitled "Grandis Solomotetten und
Monteverdi" and "Grandis Psalmen und Monteverdi."
Includes footnotes, bibliography, and a list of
modern editions. Volume 2 is a collection of
musical examples.

249. Selfridge-Field, Eleanor. "Bassano and the
      Orchestra of St. Mark's." Early Music 4 (1975)
      153-58.

A useful study of the orchestra at St. Mark's i
Venice during the time of Giovanni Gabrieli.
Focuses on the career of Giovanni Bassano, maestr
de' concerti at St. Mark's from 1601 until his
death in 1617. Identifies Bassano as among the
first to employ a basso continuo.

250. ————. "Dario Castello: A Non-Existent Biog-
      raphy." Music and Letters (1972): 179-90.

Attempts to reconstruct the clouded career of the obscure Venetian composer Dario Castello, best known for his instrumental works. Compares Castello's musical style with that of other contemporary composers.

251. Siegmund-Schultze, Walther. "Monteverdi und Schütz." Händel-Festspiele Halle 1967. Händel Festschrift, edited by Walther Siegmund-Schultze. Halle: n.p., 1967, pp. 37-44.

* Sørensen, Søren. "Monteverdi-Förster-Buxtehude." Cited below as item 641.

252. Teo, Kian-Seng. "John Wilbye's Second Set of Madrigals (1609) and the Influence of Marenzio and Monteverdi." Studies in Music 20 (1986): 1-11.

Claims to be one of the first studies to recognize influences from Monteverdi in the madrigals of Wilbye. Concludes with musical examples by Wilbye, Monteverdi, and Marenzio.

253. Tomlinson, Gary A. "Rinuccini, Peri, Monteverdi, and the Humanist Heritage of Opera." Ph.D. dissertation, University of California at Berkeley, 1979. 368 pp. UM Order No. 8014907

Not examined. Summary in Dissertation Abstracts International, 41 (July 1980): 17-A, indicates that this study examines humanistic expression in the librettos of Rinuccini, the music of Peri, and in the collaboration of Rinuccini and Monteverdi in Arianna.

* Wellesz, Egon. "Cavalli und der Stil der venetianischen Oper von 1640-1660." Cited above as item 185.

254. Willetts, Pamela J. The Henry Lawes Manuscript. London: The Trustees of the British Museum, 1969. 83 pp. ML410 L33 W5

Catalogs the contents of the Henry Lawes manuscript. Compares, in the introduction, Monteverdi's Arianna with Lawes's Ariadne Lament, a setting of a poem by William Cartwright. Correlates Monteverdi's setting of Guarini's Cruda

Amarilli to that of Lawes in order to further
substantiate the influence of Monteverdi on Henry
Lawes's later works. Contains photographs of
Lawes's manuscripts and printed works and works o:
other contemporary composers, including an early
seventeenth-century copy of the opening of
Monteverdi's Lamento d'Arianna, Add MS. 30491,
f.39.

255. Winterfeld, Carl von. Johannes Gabrieli und sein
      Zeitalter. 3 vols. in 2. Berlin: Schlesinger,
      1834; reprint ed., Hildesheim: Olms, 1965.   202
      228, 157 pp. ML290.2 V4 W7

      Winterfeld's landmark work, important both for
its biography of Gabrieli and its musical history
of Venice, paved the way for the rediscovery of
Monteverdi. Volume 2 contains a lengthy essay on
the music of Monteverdi (pp. 28-59) and volume 3,
an anthology of music, presents four compositions
by Monteverdi. Footnotes, but no bibliography.

MONTEVERDI'S LIFE

1. Letters, Documents, and Pictures

256. Arnold, Denis, and Fortune, Nigel. "The Man As
      Seen through His Letters." The Monteverdi
      Companion (item 779), pp. 19-87.

      A translation and commentary of 39 Monteverdi
      letters based on those published in Gian Francesco
      Malipiero's Claudio Monteverdi (item 271). These
      letters reveal the composer's ideas, methods, and
      approach to composition. Cites the date of the
      letters and gives the numbers assigned to the
      letters in the Malipiero source.

257. Banchieri, Adriano. Lettere armoniche. Bologna:
      Girolamo Mascheroni, 1628; Lettere scritte à
      diversi patroni, & amici. Bologna: Nicolò
      Tebaldini, 1630; facsimile ed., Bibliotheca
      musica bononiensis Sezione V, n. 21, with an
      introduction by Giuseppe Vecchi. Bologna: Forni,
      1968. 160, 47 pp. ML194 A2 B2 1968

      A publication of letters written by Banchieri
      to musicians and persons of other disciplines. One
      letter from the 1628 publication and one from the
      1630 collection is addressed to Monteverdi. The
      reprint edition has an index.

258. ————. Lettere scritte à diversi patroni, &
      amici. Bologna: Nicolò Tebaldini, 1630. 47 pp.

      See Banchieri, item 257.

259. Biba, Otto. "Neues aus dem Archiv der Gesellscha
     der Musikfreunde in Wien." Österreichische
     Musikzeitschrift 32 (1977): 90-92.

     Reports on the acquisition of a Bernardo Strozz
     (1581-1644) portrait of Monteverdi by the
     Gesellschaft der Musikfreunde in Vienna.

260. Bonafini, Umberto, ed. Catologo delle lettere
     autografe di Claudio Monteverdi conservate pres
     l'archivio di stato gonzaghesco di Mantova.
     Mantua: CITEM, 1968? 10 pp.

*   Caffi, Francesco. Storia della musica sacra nell
     già cappella ducale di San Marco in Venezia dal
     1318 al 1797.

     Cited below as item 298.

261. de Logu, Giuseppe. "An Unknown Portrait of
     Monteverdi by Domenico Feti." The Burlington
     Magazine 109 (1967): 706-709.

     Identifies for the first time a painting by
     Domenico Feti in the Hermitage at Leningrad as a
     portrait of Monteverdi. The subject of the
     portrait had been erroneously identified as
     Giovanni Gabrielli, called Sivel, an actor at the
     Mantuan Court. A replica of the painting hangs a
     the Accademia in Venice.

*   de' Paoli, Domenico, ed. Claudio Monteverdi:
     Lettere, dediche e prefazioni.

     Cited below as item 272.

262. Einstein, Alfred. "Abbot Angelo Grillo's Letters
     As a Source Material for Music History." Essay
     on Music. New York: Norton, 1956, pp. 153-73.

     Discusses the correspondence of the poet Abbot
     Don Angelo Grillo with several musicians, includi
     Monteverdi. Grillo indicates in his letters that
     Monteverdi had set some of his poems, but they ar
     not identified. This study gives a revealing
     portrait of the relationship between poet and
     musician.

263. Fabbri, Paolo. "Inediti monteverdiani." Rivista
     italiana di musicologia 15 (1980): 71-85.

Clarifies Monteverdi's relationship with the court at Modena. Reproduces letters written to Monteverdi and those which mention Monteverdi.

264. Fortune, Nigel. "Monteverdi through His Letters." Music and Musicians 15 (1967): 20-23.

A superficial view of Monteverdi via his letters. Excerpts from the letters, extracted from the translations in The Monteverdi Companion (item 779), illustrate Monteverdi's opinions on matters ranging from his family and working conditions to singers and librettos.

265. Gallico, Claudio. "Contra Claudium Montiuiridum." Rivista italiana di musicologia 10 (1975): 346-59.

Documents the litigation over the ownership of the Santo Tomaso, the former residence of Monteverdi's father-in-law, Giacomo Cattaneo. Monteverdi became involved in the dispute between 1624 and 1625, a legal battle which he lost. Gallico provides the necessary quotes from relevant records, including letters of Monteverdi.

266. ———. "Monteverdi e i dazi di Viadana." Rivista italiana di musicologia 1 (1966): 242-45.

Clarifies a statement made by Monteverdi in a letter to the Duke of Mantua of October 27, 1604, that referred to the municipality of Viadana, which has been confused with the composer Lodovico Viadana. Also cites a letter of Claudia Cattaneo to Annibale Chieppio, which asked that Monteverdi's salary might be paid from the taxes of Viadana. Gallico emphasizes that the musical interaction of Monteverdi and Lodovico Viadana was of little significance.

267. ———. "Newly Discovered Documents Concerning Monteverdi." Musical Quarterly 48 (1962): 68-72.

Clarification of Monteverdi's biography is advanced in this article by the discovery of documents from the Parochial Archives of St. Peter's Cathedral in Mantua, which indicate the baptism of his daughter, Leonora Camilla, in 1603, and a son, Massimiliamo Giacomo, born in 1604. Other documents cited are from the Parochial

Archives of S. Andres, formerly at Santi Simone e
Giuda. These records consist of Monteverdi's
marriage record (1599) and the baptismal record of
another son, Francesco Baldassare, born in 1601.

268. Lesure, François, ed. Exposiçao comemorativa do 4
      centenario do nascimento de Claudio Monteverdi
      (catalogo). Lisbon: Fundaçao C. Gulbenkian,
      1967. In Portuguese.

      Not examined. Summary in RILM Abstracts, 1/2
      (May-August 1967): 16, describes this book as a
      catalog of Monteverdi documents exhibited from
      various countries compiled for the 1967 expositior
      in Lisbon honoring the birth of the composer.

269. ———. "Un nouveau portrait de Monteverdi."
      Revue de musicologie 53 (1967): 60.

      Briefly describes an anonymous portrait of
      Monteverdi acquired by the André Meyer Collection.
      Provides a succinct background of Monteverdi
      iconography. Compares the painting with the famou
      portrait of the composer located in the
      Ferdinandeum, Innsbruck.

270. Lunelli, Renato. "Iconografia monteverdiana."
      Rivista musicale italiana 47 (1943): 38-45.

      An iconographic study of a portrait of a compose
      in the Ferdinandeum Museum at Innsbruck. At the
      time of the article this portrait was thought by
      many to be of Giovanni Pierluigi da Palestrina,
      based on a handwritten note on the back of the
      portrait. Comparison with the only certain por-
      trait of Monteverdi in Marinoni's Fiori poetici of
      1644 reveals the Ferdinandeum portrait to be of
      Monteverdi. Lunelli, however, rejects Bernardo
      Strozzi as the painter of this portrait.

271. Malipiero, G. Francesco. Claudio Monteverdi.
      Milan: Fratelli Treves, 1929. 297 pp. ML410 M7
      M16

      An early study, now superseded by de' Paoli's
      work (item 272), by the editor of the first col-
      lected edition of Monteverdi's works. Contains
      prefaces, dedications of works, title pages of
      works, and 119 Monteverdi letters. The intro-
      duction consists of a brief overview of the

composer from the viewpoint of one involved in
editing the Monteverdi complete edition.

272. Monteverdi, Claudio. Lettere, dediche e
      prefazioni: edizione critica con note a cura da
      Domenico de' Paoli. Rome: Edizioni di Santis,
      1973. 426 pp. ML410 M77 A4 1973

      An outstanding collection of 124 Monteverdi
      letters with commentaries by Domenico de' Paoli.
      Includes a list of recipients, with comments on
      their identity and a citation of letters in which
      they are mentioned. Has an index of works with
      letters cited and an index of letters with place,
      date, and recipient. The remainder of this work
      contains prefaces and dedications with commentaries
      by de' Paoli.

273. ————. The Letters of Claudio Monteverdi.
      Translated and introduced by Denis Stevens.
      London: Faber and Faber, 1980. 443 pp. ISBN 0
      571 11551 9 ML410 M77 1980

      This edition is the first complete translation
      into English of Monteverdi's extant letters. In
      addition to providing thorough bibliographical
      information for each letter, Stevens includes an
      important commentary before every item. The
      outstanding introduction covers the following
      topics: handwriting and literary style, range of
      topics, problems of identification, and location
      and state of the letters.

274. Mortari, Luisa. Bernardo Strozzi. Rome: De
      Santis, 1966. 519 pp. ND623.S7 M6

      A comprehensive study of the works of the artist
      Bernardo Strozzi, who is credited with painting the
      portrait of Monteverdi in the Ferdinandeum at
      Innsbruck. Reproduces the famous painting and
      briefly discusses this work.

275. ————. "Il ritratto di Claudio Monteverdi di
      Bernardo Strozzi." Arte veneta 31 (1977):
      205-207.

110   MONTEVERDI'S LIF

276.   Osthoff, Helmuth. "Gedichte von Tomaso Stigliani
       auf Giulio Caccini, Claudio Monteverdi, Santino
       Garsi da Parma und Claudio Merulo." Miscelánea
       en homenaje a Monseñor Higinio Anglès, II.
       Barcelona, 1961, pp. 615-21.

       Reprints and discusses poems by the Italian poet
       Tomaso Stigliani (1573-1651) and contains valuable
       information pertaining to several important
       composers.

277.   Pereyra, M.L. Explication de la lettre qui est
       imprimée dans le cinquième livre de madrigaux de
       Claudio Monteverde. Paris: Schola Cantorum,
       1911. 20 pp.

       Translates into French both Monteverdi's letter
       printed in the fifth book of madrigals that replie
       to Artusi's polemical essay and the well-known
       Dichiaratione, Giulio Cesare Monteverdi's expli-
       cation of his brother's letter and musical style,
       published in the Scherzi musicali of 1607.

278.   Pontiroli, Giuseppe. "Della famiglia di Claudio
       Monteverdi: parentele e relazioni." Bollettino
       storico cremonese 25 (1970-71): 45-68.

       Includes seventy-four documents from state
       archives which give additional information on
       Monteverdi's genealogy and his immediate family.
       This article amplifies the author's earlier mono-
       graph Notizie sui Monteverdi su personaggi ed
       artisti del loro ambiente (item 279).

279.   ———. Notizie sui Monteverdi su personaggi ed
       artisti del loro ambiente. La casa natale di
       Claudio Monteverdi. Biblioteca storica
       cremonese, vol. 17, Collana storica, vol. 15.
       Cremona: Bollettino Storico Cremonese, 1968. 67
       pp.

       Part one contains contributions to the history c
       the Monteverdi family based on unpublished docu-
       ments. Part two is a Monteverdi genealogy. Part
       three reproduces documents in the state archives c
       Cremona, the Biblioteca Governativa, and various
       parochial archives.

280. Rosenthal, Albi. "A Hitherto Unpublished Letter of
      Claudio Monteverdi." Essays Presented to Egon
      Wellesz, edited by Jack A. Westrup. Oxford:
      Clarendon Press, 1966, pp. 103-07.

      Publishes and discusses for the first time a
      letter written by Monteverdi in Venice on September
      18, 1627. Intended for the Marchese Enzo Benti-
      voglio, the letter discusses an intermedio, no
      longer extant, that Monteverdi was composing for
      the approaching wedding of Cosimo de Medici's
      daughter at Parma.

*   Santoro, Elia. La famiglia e la formazione di
      Claudio Monteverdi: note biografiche con
      documenti inediti.

      Cited below as item 336.

281. ————. Iconografia monteverdiana: comitato
      cremonese per le celebrazioni monteverdiane nel
      IV centenario della nascita. Annali della
      Biblioteca governativa e libreria civica di
      Cremona, volume 19, edited by A. Daccò. Cremona:
      Athenaeum Cremonese, 1968. 49 pp. Z933 C73 v.19
      fasc.1

      The definitive study of Monteverdi iconography.
      Santoro has discovered evidence that the Greven-
      broch miniature is a likeness of Monteverdi and
      that it was probably based on the same painting as
      the Decini engraving of the composer in the Fiori
      poetici. Also devotes chapters to the portraits of
      Monteverdi by Domenico Feti and Bernardo Strozzi.
      Although this work does not contain a bibliography,
      it is well documented; the footnotes provide an
      extensive bibliography of Monteverdi iconography,
      including studies on Bernardo Strozzi. Reproduces
      all of the portraits and engravings discussed.

282. Sartori, Claudio. "La cappella musicale del Duomo
      de Salò. Notizie inedite su Orazio Vecchi,
      Tiburzio Massaino, Orazio Scaletta e Giulio
      Monteverdi tratte dall'Archivio del Comune di
      Salò." Il Lago de Garda. Atti del Congresso
      Internazionale dell'Ateneo di Salò II. Vincenza:
      Arti Grafiche, 1969, pp. 171-82.

      Not examined. Summary in RILM Abstracts, 4/1
      (January-April 1970): 22, indicates that Sartori

has discovered documents which shed new light on
the history of musical activities at the Cathedral
of Salò.

283.   ———. "Giulio Cesare Monteverde a Salò: nuovi
          documenti inediti." Nuova rivista musicale
          italiana 1 (1967): 685-96.

          Documents Giulio Cesare Monteverdi's appointment
          as maestro di cappella at the Cathedral of Salò on
          April 10, 1622. Notes that records from the munic-
          ipality of Salò indicate that Giulio Cesare's
          financial circumstances were not good. Speculates
          that Giulio Cesare died in 1630.

284.   ———. "Monteverdiana." Musical Quarterly 38
          (1952): 399-413.

          Several minor documents referring to Monteverdi
          are cited in this study. Documents concerning
          Monteverdi's Milanese friends Padre Cherubino
          Ferrari and Aquilino Coppino are cited, in additio
          to information about the composer's connection wit
          Milan before and after departing for Venice.

285.   ———. "Nuovo volto di Monteverdi." La Scala 4
          (1952): 46-48.

          Comments on Monteverdi's countenance in three
          portraits of the composer. Speculates that the
          unidentified portrait in Einstein's The Italian
          Madrigal (item 65), page 724, may be of Monteverdi
          Contains illustrations.

286.   Sommi Picenardi, Guido. "D'Alcuni documenti
          concernenti Claudio Monteverde." Archivio
          storico lombardo, serie terza, 4 (1895): 154-62.

          Reproduces several documents concerning
          Monteverdi or written by Monteverdi which are
          located in the State Archives in Venice. Among
          these are two statements from the procurators at
          St. Mark's, one announcing Monteverdi's appointmen
          as maestro di cappella and the other confirming
          this appointment for an additional ten years. Als
          includes two letters penned by Monteverdi, one of
          which contains the composer's denunciation of the
          singer Domenico Aldegati.

*   Stevens, Denis, ed. The Letters of Claudio
        Monteverdi.

        Cited above as item 273.

287.   ————. "Selected Letters of Monteverdi Translated
        and with Commentaries." The New Monteverdi
        Companion (item 780), pp. 15-88.

        Offers forty translated letters of Monteverdi
        which are intended to reveal more about the
        composer within the context of his social and
        musical environment. The letters are cross-
        referenced with letters in Stevens's complete
        edition of the Monteverdi letters (item 273).

288.   Strunk, Oliver. Source Readings in Music History.
        New York: Norton, 1950; reprint ed., 5 paperback
        vols., New York: Norton, 1965. 192, 175, 218,
        170, 167 pp. ML160 S89

        Contains an English translation of a portion of
        the second part of L'Artusi, overo delle imper-
        fezioni della moderna musica (1600), Giulio Cesare
        Monteverdi's Declaratione from Claudio Monteverdi's
        Scherzi musicali (1607), and the foreword to
        Monteverdi's Madrigali guerrieri, et amorosi
        (1638).

289.   Vitali, Carlo. "Far filologia col grimaldello:
        ancora un epistolario 'definitivo' di Claudio
        Monteverdi." Nuova rivista musicale italiana 16
        (1982): 73-75.

        Discusses the ways in which Denis Stevens and
        Domenico de' Paoli have dealt with the problem of
        identifying the recipients of Monteverdi's letters.
        Argues that relying too heavily on the wording of a
        letter's salutation may lead to faulty assumptions.
        Maintains that Monteverdi's letter of February 23,
        1630, was probably sent to the same recipient, Enzo
        Bentivoglio, as his letter of March 9, 1630.

290.   ————. "Una lettera vivaldiana perduta e
        ritrovata, un inedito monteverdiano del 1630 e
        altri carteggi di musicisti celebri, ovvero
        splendori e nefandezze del collezionismo di
        autografi." Nuova rivista musicale italiana 14
        (1980): 404-12.

Among the letters of composers discovered in the
Biblioteca Communal at Forlì, the author quotes a
letter from Monteverdi to the Marquis Enzo
Bentivoglio (March 9, 1630) which concerns a
canzonetta promised by the composer. Bentivoglio
supervised the marriage festivities of Odoardo
Farnese and Margherita de' Medici, which took place
in Parma and included works by Monteverdi.

2. Biographical Studies

291.   Ambros, August Wilhelm. "Claudio Monteverdi und
       seine Schule." Geschichte der Musik. 3rd ed.
       Leipzig: Leuckart, 1909; reprint ed., Hildesheim:
       Olms, 1968. Vol. 4, pp. 533-624.

       One of the most important nineteenth-century
       histories of music. The essay devoted to Monte-
       verdi, Chapter 7, contains a lengthy discussion of
       the composer's life and works. The last section of
       the essay emphasizes Monteverdi's importance to the
       development of Venetian opera.

292.   Antonicek, Theophil. "Claudio Monteverdi und
       Österreich." Österreichische Musikzeitschrift 26
       (1971): 266-71.

       Chronicles the travels of Monteverdi to Austria
       and notes the numerous contacts made by the
       composer in that country throughout his career.
       Reports on the activities of other Italian musi-
       cians in Austria, such as the composers Giovanni
       Battista Buonamente and Francesco Campagnolo, a
       student of Monteverdi, and the singers Virginia
       Andreini and Margherita Basile. Points out that
       Basile was very likely a relative of Monteverdi's
       wife.

293.   Arnold, Denis. "Claudio Monteverdi." The New
       Grove Italian Baroque Masters, edited by Stanley
       Sadie. New York: Norton, 1984, pp. 1-79. ISBN C
       393 01690 0   ML102 I5 N48 1984

       Presents a slight revision of Arnold's article in
       The New Grove Dictionary of Music and Musicians,
       cited below as item 294. Contains a list of

Monteverdi's works (compiled by Elsie M. Arnold)
and a first-rate bibliography. No footnotes.

294. ————. "Claudio Monteverdi." The New Grove
      Dictionary of Music and Musicians, edited by
      Stanley Sadie. London: Macmillan, 1980. Vol.
      12, pp. 514-34. ISBN 0 333 23111 2 ML100 N48

Views Monteverdi as a composer who refined the
musical techniques of his day. Summarizes the
important events of the composer's life and
includes an in-depth discussion of Monteverdi's
works and the theoretical basis of those works.
Includes a list of his works and a bibliography.
See item 293 for an updated revision of this
article.

295. ————. Monteverdi. The Master Musicians Series.
      London: J.M. Dent, 1963; revised ed., London:
      J.M. Dent, 1975. 212 pp. ISBN 0 460 03155 4
      ML410 M77 A8 1975

Evaluates Monteverdi in light of the modern
research published about other composers of his
era. Sees Monteverdi not as the creator of modern
music but as a "moderate and progressive composer."
This thorough study of the life and works of Monteverdi concludes with a chapter on Monteverdi's
influence, which considers the composer's aesthetic
philosophy as his most influential legacy. Includes a calendar of events in the composer's life
and a complete list of Monteverdi's works.
Bibliography is selective.

296. ————. "The Monteverdian Succession at St.
      Mark's." Music and Letters 42 (1961): 205-11.

Describes the events surrounding the selection
of Monteverdi to the post of maestro di cappella at
St. Mark's in Venice, as well as the appointment of
his successor. Monteverdi's predecessor, Giulio
Cesare Martinengo, was a little-known composer
heavily plagued by debts until his death in 1613.
Rovetta, Monteverdi's successor, was promoted to
the position only after an extensive search for a
more eminent musician.

116   MONTEVERDI'S LIFE

297. Barblan, Guglielmo; Gallico, Claudio; and Pannain,
      Guido. Claudio Monteverdi, nel quarto centenario
      della nascita. Turin: Edizioni RAI Radio-
      televisione Italiana, 1967. 366 pp. ML410 M77
      B4

      Three noted Monteverdi scholars contribute major
      sections in this tribute to the Monteverdi quater-
      centenary. Barblan offers a biographical study of
      the composer which includes an annotated bibliog-
      raphy of Monteverdi biographies. Gallico supplies
      a portion given to the stage works with a chapter
      devoted to Orfeo. In Pannain's part, discussion is
      centered on the madrigal books of the composer with
      some discussion of sacred works. Contains numerous
      musical examples, some from Monteverdi manuscripts.
      Gallico's and Pannain's sections also contain
      bibliographies.

298. Caffi, Francesco. Storia della musica sacra nella
      già cappella ducale di San Marco in Venezia dal
      1318 al 1797. 2 vols. Venice: G. Antonelli,
      1854; reprint ed., Milan: Bollettino Biografico
      Musicale, 1931; reprint ed., 2 vols. in 1,
      Florence: Olschki, 1987. 577 pp. ISBN 8 822
      23479 0 ML2933.8 V5 C2 1987

      This history of choral musicians and organists
      contains one of the earliest accounts of Claudio
      Monteverdi. Recognizes Monteverdi as a Venetian
      composer of madrigals, sacred works, and dramatic
      works. Notes briefly the composer's biography
      prior to his appointment at St. Mark's, including
      the famous Artusi-Monteverdi controversy. Cites
      Padre Martini as recognizing Monteverdi's genius.
      Volume 2 of Caffi's work includes three supple-
      mentary entries on the composer and reproduces
      three of Monteverdi's letters.

299. Davari, Stefano. "Notizie biografiche del distinto
      maestro di musica Claudio Monteverdi, desunte dai
      documenti dell'Archivio storico Gonzaga." Atti e
      memorie della R. accademia virgiliana di Mantova
      10 (1884-85): 79-183.

300. de' Paoli, Domenico. "Claudio Monteverdi."
      Bollettino bibliografico musicale 4 (1929): 1-16.

A brief, biographical sketch of Monteverdi
which has been superseded by the author's later
biographies of the composer (items 301 and 302).
Includes a list of Monteverdi's printed works and
their reprints, a bibliography, and a list of
available modern editions.

301.   ————. Claudio Monteverdi. Milan: Ulrico Hoepl,
        1945. 357 pp. ML410 M77 P3

A well-documented biography, with additional
background on such topics as the Italian madrigal,
Florentine Camerata, Guglielmo and Vincenzo
Gonzaga, and the basilica of St. Mark's. Includes
considerable Monteverdi correspondence. Discusses
the composer's works and includes three ariettas in
an appendix in facsimile as well as transcribed
into modern notation. Contains a brief bibliography and is well illustrated with reproductions
of historical maps, paintings, and photographs of
historic locations. See also de' Paoli, item 302.

302.   ————. Monteverdi. Milan: Rusconi, 1979.
        592 pp. ML410 M77 P35

An expanded edition of the author's Claudio
Monteverdi (item 301). Updated with documents
recently brought to light and a list of works now
considered lost. Includes a chronology of
Monteverdi's life and a list of the composer's
works with dates of first performances and
manuscript sources. Bibliography, discography,
index of works, and an index of names.

303.   Fabbri, Paolo. Monteverdi. Turin: E.D.T. Edizione
        di Torino, 1985. 460 pp. ISBN 88 7063 035 8
        ML410 M77 F2 1985

A well-documented study of the life and works of
the composer. Organized into three large chapters:
The Years of Youth in Cremona, At the Court of the
Gonzaga, and The Venetian Period. Identifies the
poets of several madrigals for the first time.
Includes a catalog of works, extensive bibliography, and an index of names.

304. Fétis, François-Joseph. "Monteverde." Biographie
      universelle des musiciens et bibliographie
      générale de la musique. 2nd ed. Paris: Firmin
      Didot Frères, 1866-70; reprint ed., Brussels:
      Culture et Civilisation, 1972. Vol. 6, pp. 180-
      86.

      Provides an overview of Monteverdi's life and
      works. Presents Monteverdi as the composer most
      responsible for the stylistic transformation that
      occurred in music around 1600.

305. Ficker, Rudolf von. "Alte Meister: Claudio
      Monteverdi." Neues Musikblatt 16 (1937): 7-9.

      An appraisal of Monteverdi's life and works
      intended more for the general reader than for the
      musical scholar.

306. Gerber, Ernst Ludwig. Historisch-biographisches
      Lexikon der Tonkünstler. Edited by Othmar
      Wessely. Graz: Akademische Druck- u.
      Verlagsanstalt, 1977. 516 pp. ML105 G38

      A brief discussion (cols. 452-54) of Monteverdi's
      life and works is presented in this historically
      significant biographical dictionary. Refers to
      Monteverdi as "the Mozart of his time." Originally
      published in Leipzig by J.G.I. Breitkopf in 1790-
      92. See below, item 307.

307. ————. Neues historisch-biographisches Lexikon
      der Tonkünstler. Edited by Othmar Wessely. 2
      vols. Graz: Akademische Druck- u. Verlag-
      sanstalt, 1966. 412, 422 pp.

      Published initially by A. Kühnel in Leipzig in
      1812-14, this edition supplements Gerber's
      Historisch-biographisches Lexikon der Tonkünstler
      (item 306).

308. Goldschmidt, Harry. Um die Sache der Musik. Reden
      und Aufsätze (Reclams Universal-Bibliothek 446).
      Leipzig: Reclam, 1970. 334 pp.

      A collection of essays on various composers.
      Includes an assessment of Monteverdi intended for
      the general reader.

309. Horton, John. Monteverdi. Sevenoaks: Novello,
      1975. 20 pp. ML410 M77 H6

A superficial account of Monteverdi's life and works. Published as part of the Novello Short Biographies series. Concludes with a brief list of Monteverdi's major works and a select bibliography of only nine items.

310. Konen, Valentina. Claudio Monteverdi. Moscow: Sovetskij Kompozitor, 1971. 323 pp. In Russian.

Not examined. Summary in RILM Abstracts, 5/2 (May-August 1971): 160, indicates that this book is the first Russian biographical study of Monteverdi.

311. ————. "Monteverdi's Creative Path." Klassice-skoe iskusstvo Zapadna (1973): 172-210. In Russian.

Not examined. Summary in RILM Abstracts, 7/3 (September-December 1973): 254, discloses that the article discusses Monteverdi's life and works.

312. Konold, Wulf. Claudio Monteverdi. Hamburg: Rowohlt, 1986. 142 pp. ISBN 3 499 50348 4 ML 410 M77 K66 1986

A guide to Monteverdi's life and works written for the general reader rather than the musical scholar. Includes a chronology, notes, list of works, bibliography, and name index.

313. Lange, Martin. "Claudio Monteverdi in der Zeitwende um 1600." Musik und Gesellschaft 17 (May 1967): 289-94.

A cursory examination of Monteverdi's life and works. Notes his role in the musical style change that occurred around 1600.

314. Le Roux, Maurice. Claudio Monteverdi. Paris: Editions du Coudrier, 1951. 191 pp. ML410 M78 L62

A survey of Monteverdi's life and works intended more for the general reader than for the music specialist. Organized broadly by genre. Includes a list of works, a list of modern editions, a discography, and a woefully inadequate bibliography.

315. Leonhardt, Gustav. "Hoe revolutionair was Claudio
      Monteverdi." Opera journaal 4 (1973-74): 9. In
      Dutch.

      Considers Monteverdi the most important composer
      to bridge the Renaissance and Baroque musical
      styles.

316. Leopold, Silke. Claudio Monteverdi und seine Zeit.
      Laaber: Laaber-Verlag, 1982. 368 pp. ISBN 3
      9215 1872 5 ML410 M77 L5

      An excellent contribution to Monteverdi litera-
      ture concentrating on important aspects of his
      music. Noteworthy for an extensive chronology of
      his life and times. Contains a chronological list
      of works, an index of text incipits, a name index,
      a discography, and a sizable bibliography.

317. Malipiero, G. Francesco. "Claudio Monteverdi of
      Cremona." Musical Quarterly 18 (1932): 383-96.

      Duplicates, to a large extent, the introduction
      to the author's Claudio Monteverdi (item 271).
      This concise survey of the composer's life and
      works cites Francesco Caffi's Storia della musica
      sacra nella già cappella ducale di San Marco in
      Venezia (item 298) as being the first work in the
      nineteenth century to recognize Monteverdi.

318. Marinoni, Giovanni. Fiori poetici raccolti nel
      funerale del' signor Claudio Monteverde maestro
      di cappella della ducale di S. Marco. Consecrati
      da d. Gio: Battista Marinoni, detto Giove...all'
      illustrissimi & eccellentissimi sig. procuratori
      di chiesa di S. Marco. Venice: F. Miloco, 1644.
      70 pp. ML410 M77 M18

      Comprises a collection of prose and poetry writ-
      ten as a tribute to Monteverdi after his death in
      1643. The necrology by Matteo Caberlotti is the
      first biographical sketch of the composer. Con-
      tains an engraving of a portrait of Monteverdi by
      Biacolo Decini.

319. Osthoff, Wolfgang. "Monteverdi, Claudio." Riemann
      Musik-Lexikon. 12th ed. Edited by Wilibald Gur-
      litt and Hans Heinrich Eggebrecht. Personenteil:
      Ergänzungsband, II. Edited by Carl Dahlhaus.
      Mainz: B. Schott, 1975, pp. 217-19.

Contains a much briefer entry than the Monteverdi article cited as item 340, but the bibliography is expanded.

320. Pannain, Guido. "Claudio Monteverdi." La Musica. Parte prima: Enciclopedia storica, vol. 3. Turin: Unione Tipografico-Editrice Torinese, 1966, pp. 370-95.

An overview of the life and works of Claudio Monteverdi, with emphasis on the gradual evolution of musical style in the composer's works. Contains a list of works and a bibliography.

321. Passuth, László. "Claudio Monteverdi az 'opera atya.'" Élet és tudomány 22 (12 May 1967): 866-70. In Hungarian.

Not examined. Summary in RILM Abstracts, 1/2 (May-August 1967): 16, describes the article as an account of Monteverdi's trip to Hungary in 1595 as part of the entourage of Vincenzo Gonzaga.

322. ———. A mantuai herceg muzsikusa: Claudio Monteverdi korának regényes története. Budapest: Zeneműkiadó Vállalat, 1959. 573 pp.

A biography written in the style of a romantic novel. The German translation is cited as item 323.

323. ———. Monteverdi, Der Roman eines grossen Musikers. Vienna: Paul Neff, 1959; 2nd ed., Leipzig: VEB Deutscher Verlag für Musik, 1982. 549 pp. ML3925 M55 P4

This is a German translation of item 322. The second edition was published under the title Divino Claudio: ein Monteverdi-Roman.

324. Pontiroli, Giuseppe. "Casa natale di Claudio Monteverdi e ampliamento dell'albero genealogico della famiglia Monteverdi." Archivio storico lombardo 9/5-6 (1966-67): 248-58.

325. ———. "Nuove ricerche sui Monteverdi. Filippo, fratello del musico Claudio, chirurgo maggiore dell'ospedale 'S. Maria di Pietà' in Cremona." Bollettino storico cremonese 24 (1969): 267-77.

Asserts that Monteverdi's brother, Filippo, was a
surgeon at the S. Maria di Pietà in Cremona.
Includes genealogical research on the Monteverdi
family.

326.   Prunières, Henry. <u>Claudio Monteverdi</u>. Paris:
       Alcan, 1924; reprint ed., 1931; reprint ed.,
       Paris: Editions d'Aujourd'hui, 1977. 177 pp.
       ML410 M77 P77

       Published as a volume in <u>Les maîtres de la
       musique</u> series, this is the author's initial
       biography of the composer. Combines a complete
       account of Monteverdi's life with a discussion of
       his works. Contains a list of works and a brief
       bibliography.

327.   ————. "Monteverdi à la chapelle de Saint-Marc."
       <u>Revue musicale</u> 7 (1926): 260-78.

       Extracted, with some minor deletions, from two
       chapters ("The Chapel of San Marco" and "Monte-
       verdi's Sacred Music") of the author's biography of
       Monteverdi, which appears as item 328, published
       later in the same year as this article. Recounts
       the circumstances surrounding the appointment of
       Monteverdi to St. Mark's in 1613. Presents an
       overview of the composer's duties as <u>maestro di
       cappella</u>. Surveys his sacred works and points out
       the relationship between Monteverdi's sacred and
       secular compositions.

328.   ————. <u>Monteverdi, His Life and Work</u>. Translated
       by Marie D. Mackie. London: Dent, 1926; reprint
       ed., New York: Dover, 1972; reprint ed., West-
       port: Greenwood Press, 1973. 293 pp. ISBN 0 837
       13996 1 ML410 M77 P771

       A translation of <u>La vie et l'oeuvre de Claudio
       Monteverdi</u>, cited as item 329, with some minor
       alterations of the text.

329.   ————. <u>La vie et l'oeuvre de Claudio Monteverdi</u>.
       Paris: Librairie de France, 1926. 315 pp.
       ML410 M77 P772

       An expanded version of Prunières's original study
       (item 326). Also adds an appendix containing
       reprints of selected letters, a table of

illustrations, name and work index, and notes. For
an English translation of the work, see item 328.

330. Pulver, Jeffrey. "Claudio Monteverde." The Strad
      25-26 (1915-16).

      An extended article providing a survey of Monte-
      verdi's life and works. Valuable for its time
      because the author locates the original sources of
      the works.

331. Redlich, Hans F. Claudio Monteverdi: Leben und
      Werk. Olten: Otto Walter, 1949. 232 pp. ML410
      M77 R43

      A major achievement by a prolific Monteverdi
      scholar. Provides an authoritative account of the
      composer's life and works. Offers suggestions for
      proper performance practice and for preparing
      modern editions. Concludes with the following:
      table of works, chronology, bibliography, notes,
      list of abbreviations, name index, and table of
      illustrations. For an English translation of this
      work, see item 332.

332. ————. Claudio Monteverdi: Life and Works.
      Translated by Kathleen Dale. London: Oxford,
      1952; reprint ed., Westport: Greenwood Press,
      1970. 204 pp. ISBN 0 8371 4003 x ML410 M77
      R432 1970

      A translation of item 331. Expands the original
      volume by the addition of several new chapters,
      plus added excerpts from Monteverdi's letters,
      rewritten footnotes, additional musical examples, a
      glossary of terms, and other minor revisions. Also
      new in this volume is material revised and trans-
      lated from Claudio Monteverdi: Das Madrigalwerk
      (item 408).

333. ————. "Monteverdi, Claudio." Die Musik in
      Geschichte und Gegenwart, edited by Friedrich
      Blume. Kassel: Bärenreiter, 1949-. Vol. 9
      (1961), cols. 511-32.

      Redlich's article presents a concise introduction
      to Monteverdi's life and works and includes a list
      of works by genre, a list of editions, and an
      extensive bibliography. Concludes with a brief

discussion of the composer's brother, Giulio
Cesare.

334. Roche, Maurice. <u>Monteverdi</u>. Paris: Editions du
      Seuil, 1960. 192 pp. ML410 M77 R6

      A biographical study intended more for the
      general reader than for the scholar. Contains a
      very brief bibliography of only 25 items. Also
      includes a list of works, discography, chronology,
      and index of names and works.

335. Santoro, Elia. "La casa natale dei Monteverdi nel
      quartiere Piazano." <u>Colloqui cremonesi</u> 1 (1968):
      35-47.

336. ————. <u>La famiglia e la formazione di Claudio
      Monteverdi: note biografiche con documenti
      inediti: comitato cremonese per le celebrazioni
      monteverdiane nel IV centenario della nascita</u>
      (Annali della Biblioteca governativa e libreria
      civica di Cremona, volume 18: 1967 Fasc. I),
      edited by Angelo Daccò. Cremona: Athenaeum
      Cremonense, 1967. 89 pp. ML410 M78 S237

      Documents the life of Monteverdi with emphasis on
      his early years in Cremona. Discusses the musical
      atmosphere at Cremona and gives an in-depth look at
      Marc Antonio Ingegneri. Confirms that Monteverdi's
      mother was Madalena Zignani, daughter of a gold-
      smith. Denies that Baldassarre Monteverdi,
      Claudio's father, was a physician. Identifies
      Filippo as being one of Claudio's two brothers.
      Examines Monteverdi's early works with a chapter
      devoted to the composition of <u>Orfeo</u>. Contains
      photographs of places, letters, and printed works.

337. Sartori, Claudio. <u>Monteverdi</u>. Brescia: La Scuola,
      1953. 236 pp. ML410 M7 S3

      Chronicles the life and works of the composer
      with many quotations from Monteverdi's letters.
      The bibliography lists only books and monographs.
      Gives a chronological but incomplete list of works.

338. Schneider, Louis. <u>Un précurseur de la musique
      italienne aux XVIe et XVIIe siècles. Claudio
      Monteverdi. L'homme et son temps.</u> Paris:
      Perrin, 1921. 366 pp. ML410 M77 S3

An extended account of Monteverdi's life and
works written by one of the earliest French specialists on the composer. Contains an expansive
catalog of Monteverdi's works. Also includes a
rather complete bibliography for its day. Index of
names and works.

339. Schrade, Leo. "Claudio Monteverdi--ein
      Revolutionär der Musikgeschichte." Neue
      Zeitschrift für Musik 123 (1962): 153-57.

      Contends that Monteverdi was one of those un-
      common composers responsible for the creation of a
      new musical epoch. Discusses numerous aspects of
      the composer's style. Cites Monteverdi as a prede-
      cessor of both Schütz and Bach in the setting of
      sacred texts.

340. ―――――. "Monteverdi, Claudio." Riemann Musik-
      Lexikon. 12th ed. Edited by Wilibald Gurlitt
      and Hans Heinrich Eggebrecht. Personenteil, vol.
      2. Mainz: B. Schott, 1961, pp. 244-49.

      A synoptic account of Monteverdi's biography.
      Provides a list of modern editions and a basic
      bibliography. See also the Ergänzungsband, item
      319.

341. ―――――. Monteverdi: Creator of Modern Music. New
      York: Norton, 1950; reprint ed., New York: Da
      Capo, 1979. 384 pp. ISBN 0 306 79565 5   ML410
      M77 S35

      The first definitive biography in the English
      language. Schrade's coverage of Monteverdi has
      been supplemented by other authors but not sur-
      passed. The first two chapters summarize the
      musical environment in the second half of the
      sixteenth century, including a brief survey of
      musical anthologies published. Monteverdi's works
      are discussed somewhat chronologically with
      numerous citations from his music. The author
      based this musical study in large part on the 1942
      Malipiero edition of the composer's compositions.

342. Sommi Picenardi, Guido. Claudio Monteverdi a
      Cremona. Milan, 1895.

343.   Stevens, Denis. "Claudio Monteverdi." Enciclopedia
       della musica. Milan: Ricordi, 1964. Vol. 3, pp.
       205-08.

       Gives a concise account of Monteverdi's life and
       works. Asserts that Monteverdi was one of the most
       original and innovative composers of his day.
       Includes an excellent reproduction of the Monte-
       verdi portrait attributed to Strozzi and a close-up
       of the frontispiece to the Fiori poetici of 1644.
       Includes a list of works and a bibliography.

344.   ————. "Monteverdi, Petratti, and the Duke of
       Bracciano." Musical Quarterly 64 (1978): 275-94.

       Recounts in great detail, based on letters origi-
       nally brought to light by Ferdinand Boyer and Henry
       Prunières, a brief episode in the career of Monte-
       verdi which took place from December 1619 to
       February 1620. Acting upon a request from Paolo
       Giordano II, Duke of Bracciano, Monteverdi super-
       vised the printing of a collection of arias for one
       or two voices composed by the obscure Cremonese
       musician Francesco Petratti. This article first
       appeared in Italian as "Monteverdi, Petratti e il
       duca di Bracciano" in Studi musicali 6 (1977): 69-
       85.

345.   ————. "Monteverdi's Necklace." Musical
       Quarterly 59 (1973): 370-81.

       Recounts the events chronicled by Monteverdi in
       his letters surrounding the publication and
       subsequent dedication of the seventh book of
       madrigals to Caterina Medici Gonzaga, Duchess of
       Mantua. As was the custom of the period, a neck-
       lace was given to Monteverdi by the duchess in
       appreciation for the dedication. This article
       first appeared in Memorie e contributi alla musica
       dal medioevo all'età moderna offerti a F. Ghisi nel
       settantesimo compleanno (1901-1971), edited by G.
       Vecchi. Bologna: AMIS, 1971, pp. 33-47.

346.   Tellart, Roger. Claudio Monteverdi: l'homme et son
       oeuvre. Paris: Seghers, 1964; reprint ed.,
       Lausanne: La Guilde du Livre, 1970. 191 pp.
       ML410 M77 T44

Divided into two parts (with four chapters in
each), the first is a biographical account while
the second is a survey of Monteverdi's music.
Provides a catalog of works, a discography, a list
of modern editions, and a sparse bibliography.

347. Tiby, Ottavio. Claudio Monteverdi. Collezione i
      Maestri della musica n. 30. Turin: Arione, 1944.
      43 pp.

      An introductory monograph containing a biography
      which emphasizes events surrounding Monteverdi's
      compositions. Contains reproductions of frontis-
      pieces to Monteverdi's music.

348. Tiepolo, Maria Francesca. "Minima monteverdiana."
      Rassegna degli archivi di stato 29 (1969):
      135-43.

349. Vogel, Emil. "Claudio Monteverdi." Viertel-
      jahrsschrift für Musikwissenschaft 3 (1887):
      315-450.

      The basic study regarding biographical infor-
      mation about Monteverdi. Originally presented as a
      doctoral dissertation to the University of Berlin
      in 1887. Organized into three chapters (with
      numerous subchapters) by locale: Cremona, Mantua,
      and Venice. Also contains explanatory footnotes,
      chronological and alphabetical lists of works,
      selected letters, and the score of the Lamento
      d'Arianna.

350. Walther, Johann Gottfried. Musikalisches Lexikon
      oder musikalische Bibliothek. Leipzig: Wolffgang
      Deer, 1732; facsimile reprint, edited by Richard
      Schaal, Kassel: Bärenreiter, 1953. 670 pp.
      ML100 W21 1953

      Provides only scant information (pp. 420-21)
      concerning Monteverdi's life and works.

351. Westrup, Jack A. "Claudio Monteverdi." The
      Heritage of Music, edited by Hubert Foss, vol. 3.
      London: Oxford University Press, 1951, pp. 1-14.

      A concise, useful introduction to the music of
      Monteverdi. Published as part of a three-volume
      work devoted to essays on the music of great
      composers.

352. Witold, Jean. "Claudio Monteverdi." Musique de
      tous les temps 14 (1961): 19-24.

IV

STUDIES OF MONTEVERDI'S MUSIC

1. Madrigals, Canzonette, and Scherzi Musicali

* Allorto, Riccardo. "Il prologo dell'Orfeo. Note
  sulla formazione del recitativo monteverdiano."
  Cited below as item 443.

* Anfuso, Nella, and Gianuario, Annibale. Le tre
  Arianne di Claudio Monteverdi.
  Cited below as item 446.

353. Arnold, Denis. Monteverdi Madrigals. BBC Music
  Guides. London: British Broadcasting Corpo-
  ration, 1967; reprint ed., Seattle: University of
  Washington Press, 1969; reprint ed., London:
  British Broadcasting Corporation, 1975. 61 pp.
  ISBN 0 295 95021 8   MT115 M7 A7

  Examines Monteverdi's madrigals, with emphasis on
  influences which affected the composer's musical
  style. Briefly comments on Monteverdi's Canzonette
  and Scherzi musicali. Contains musical examples
  and footnotes, but no bibliography or index.

* ———. "'Seconda pratica': A Background to Monteverdi's Madrigals."
  Cited below as item 656.

*   Barblan, Guglielmo. "Un ignoto 'Lamento d'Arianna
        Mantovano."

        Cited above as item 211.

*   Barblan, Guglielmo; Gallico, Claudio; and Pannain,
        Guido. Claudio Monteverdi, nel quarto centenari
        della nascita.

        Cited above as item 297.

354.   Beaudoin, Russell Martin. "Seconda Pratica of
        Claudio Monteverdi as Used in His Quinto Libro d
        Madrigali a cinque voci (1605)." M.M. thesis,
        Michigan State University, 1984. 109 pp.

*   Berry, Corre. "The Secular Dialogue Duet:
        1600-1900."

        Cited above as item 35.

*   Bianconi, Lorenzo. "Struttura poetica e struttura
        musicale nei madrigali di Monteverdi."

        Cited above as item 212.

355.   Bielitz, Mathias. "Zum Verhältnis von Form und
        Semantik in der Musik von Monteverdi." Claudio
        Monteverdi: Festschrift Reinhold Hammerstein
        (item 794), pp. 53-121.

        A perceptive essay dealing with Monteverdi's
        treatment of text and structure. Emphasizes the
        close relationship of words to music found in the
        composer's works.

356.   Bonino, MaryAnn Teresa. "Monteverdi's Use of
        Musical and Dramatic Expression in His First Fou
        Books of Madrigals." M.A. thesis, University o
        Southern California, 1963. 103 pp.

        Maintains that the first four madrigal books
        foreshadow the musical style and technique of
        Monteverdi's later works. Reviews madrigal poetry
        of the sixteenth century in Italy. Contains an
        appendix of musical examples and a bibliography.

357.   Burney, Charles. A General History of Music from
        the Earliest Ages to the Present Period. 4 vol
        London, 1776-89; reprint ed., 2 vols., New York
        Dover, 1957. 817, 1098 pp. ML159 B96 1957

Recognizes Monteverdi as one of the most eminent
composers of his era. Summarizes Monteverdi's
accomplishments and points out that he had
opponents who regarded him as a corrupter (Artusi).
Describes Monteverdi's harmonic innovations and
mentions his importance as a composer of opera,
primarily with reference to Arianna. Offers a
transcription of Stracciami pur il core from the
third book of madrigals.

358.   Cavicchi, Adriano. "Teatro monteverdiano e
       tradizione teatrale ferrarese." Congresso
       internazionale sul tema Claudio Monteverdi (item
       811), pp. 139-56.

Observes the expanded interest in theater at the
court of Mantua with the rise to power of Vincenzo
Gonzaga. Considers the staging of Guarini's Il
pastor fido as an important theatrical event which
had an influence on Monteverdi. This production,
which took place in Mantua in 1598, had its scenery
and stage mechanisms overseen by the Ferrarese G.B.
Aleotti. Speculates that Monteverdi probably
supplied some music for this representation and
that some madrigals set to Guarini's texts in
Monteverdi's fourth and fifth books of madrigals
were derived from music he wrote for Il pastor
fido. Believes that the Mantuan Il pastor fido had
an influence on Monteverdi's later Mantuan production of Orfeo. Emphasizes a reciprocal relationship between the Court of Ferrara and that of
Mantua in the area of dramatic presentations.

359.   Cesari, Gaetano. "Die Entwicklung der Montever-
       dischen Kammermusik." Haydn-Zentenarfeier: III.
       Kongress der internationalen Musikgesellschaft:
       Bericht. Vienna: Artaria & Co.; Leipzig:
       Breitkopf & Härtel, 1909, pp. 153-56.

Briefly discusses the madrigal books of Monteverdi.

360.   Charter, James. "'Cruda Amarilli': A Cross-section
       of the Italian Madrigal." Musical Times 116
       (1975): 231-34.

Notes the differences between the musical
settings of Guarini's poem Cruda Amarilli by Wert,
Marenzio, and Pallavicino. Comments briefly on
settings of this text by Monteverdi and d'India.

361. Chiereghin, Salvino. "Claudio Monteverdi."
      Rivista musicale italiana 47 (1943): 212-19.

      Emphasizes the importance of music among the
      arts during the seventeenth century. Recaps
      Monteverdi's accomplishments as a composer, with
      emphasis on his eighth book of madrigals and his
      operatic works.

362. Cimbro, Attilio. "I madrigali di Claudio
      Monteverdi." _Musica II_ (item 813), pp. 4-34.

      An overview of Monteverdi's madrigal style, in
      which he is compared to Marenzio and other madri-
      galists of the sixteenth century. The author doe$
      not proceed chronologically with a discussion of
      the works but instead considers different aspects
      of the madrigals, such as rhythm, text, harmony,
      and mode. Refers to specific locations of the
      madrigals in Malipiero's edition of Monteverdi's
      works.

363. Dahlhaus, Carl. "_Ecco mormorar l'onde_: Versuch,
      ein Monteverdi-Madrigal zu interpretieren."
      Chormusik und Analyse, edited by Heinrich Poos.
      2 vols. Mainz: B. Schott, 1983, pp. 139-54.

      Dedicated to Anna Amalie Abert for her seventy-
      fifth birthday, this article presents an in-depth
      discussion of Monteverdi's madrigals from the
      second madrigal book of 1590. Following pre-
      liminary remarks, Dahlhaus focuses on the pro-
      gressive features of the work.

364. Danckwardt, Marianne. "Das Lamento d'Olimpia
      'Voglio voglio morir'--eine Komposition Claudio
      Monteverdis?" _Archiv für Musikwissenschaft_ 41
      (1984): 149-75.

      Rejects Monteverdi as the composer of the _Lamen_
      d'Olimpia. Osthoff (item 817) declares Monteverd
      to be the composer.

*   Dent, Edward J. "The Sixteenth-Century Madrigal.
      Cited above as item 58.

*   Einstein, Alfred. _The Italian Madrigal_.
      Cited above as item 65.

365. Fabbri, Paolo. "Concordanze letterarie e
      divergenze musicali intorno ai 'Madrigali a
      cinque voci...Libro primo' di Claudio Monte-
      verdi." Musica e filologia. Contributi in
      occasione del festival 'Musica filologia.'
      Verona, 30 settembre-18 ottobre 1982, edited by
      M. Di Pasquale. Verona: Edizioni della Società
      letteraria, 1983, pp. 53-83.

366. Fano, Fabio. "Il Combattimento di Tancredi e
      Clorinda e L'Incoronazione di Poppea di Claudio
      Monteverdi." Studi sul teatro veneto fra
      rinascimento ed età barocca. Civiltà veneziana
      studi 24, edited by Maria Teresa Muraro.
      Florence: Olschki, 1971, pp. 345-71.

      Notes that even though scholars have classified
      Monteverdi's Il combattimento as a species of
      oratorio, the work was composed before the Roman
      oratorio flourished. Observes that the narrative
      style of Il combattimento can be found in later
      works of Carissimi, Schütz, and others. Praises
      the characterization in Monteverdi's Poppea.
      Considers Il combattimento and Poppea the two
      finest works of Monteverdi's Venetian period.

367. Firca, Gheorghe. "Patru sute de ani dela nasterea
      lui Claudio Monteverdi." Muzica 17 (September
      1967): 22-27. In Rumanian.

      Not examined. Summary in RILM Abstracts, 1/3
      (September-December 1967): 17, mentions that the
      article discusses Monteverdi's "role in the
      development of polyphony and the madrigal style,
      and his continuing popularity in Rumania."

*   Fortune, Nigel. "Monteverdi and the seconda
      prattica: From Madrigal to Duet."

      Cited below as item 663.

368. Gallico, Claudio. "Emblemi strumentali negli
      'Scherzi' di Monteverdi." Rivista italiana di
      musicologia (item 838), pp. 54-73.

      Re-examines the significance of Monteverdi's
      Scherzi musicali a tre voci (1607) in light of the
      contribution made to the Italian instrumental style
      by the ritornellos in these works. Expressiveness
      of writing, idiomatic violin writing, and a texture

anticipating the sonata da camera are cited as
contributions made by Monteverdi toward an evolvi
instrumental style. Includes a thematic index of
the ritornellos in the Scherzi musicali.

369. ————. "La 'Lettera Amorosa' di Monteverdi e lo
stile rappresentativo." Nuova rivista musicale
italiana 1 (1967): 287-302.

Identifies Claudio Achillini as the poet of the
Lettera amorosa (Se i languidi miei sguardi) from
Monteverdi's seventh book of madrigals. Asserts
that the term stile rappresentativo refers to a
musical style in which the meaning of the text is
followed consistently by the music. Looks at oth
works of Monteverdi which the composer identified
as in genere rappresentativo.

370. ————. Monteverdi: poesia musicale, teatro e
musica sacra. Turin: Giulio Einaudi, 1979. 19
pp. ML410 M77 G28

An analytical view of the works of Monteverdi.
Divides the works into three categories: poetry s
to music, theater music, and sacred music. The
first chapter surveys the madrigals with emphasis
on the relationship between music and text. The
second chapter analyzes the operas and includes
significant historical background. The final
chapter, which makes up a third of this study,
traces the influences on Monteverdi's sacred styl
Devotes a sizable portion to the Vespers of 1610,
which the author considers to be unified liturgi-
cally and musically. Looks at the Selva morale
(1640) and the posthumous Missa a quattro voci..
(1650). Contains a chronology of Monteverdi's li
and works.

371. ————. "Strutture strumentali nella musica da
camera di Monteverdi." Rivista italiana di
musicologia (item 838), pp. 282-87.

Emphasizes that a harmonic plan often determine
the structure of the instrumental ritornellos in
Monteverdi's Scherzi musicali a tre voci of 1607.

372. Gianturco, Carolyn. Claudio Monteverdi: stile e
struttura. Pisa: Editrice Tecnico Scientifica,
1978. 132 pp. ML410 M77 G5

Defines the individual musical style of Monteverdi. After an introductory chapter containing a
brief biographical summary, the second chapter
illustrates recurring musical traits in Monteverdi's second book of madrigals (1590). Chapter
three describes the highly organized structure of
Act II of Orfeo. Compares Monteverdi's three
masses in chapter four and discusses the lament
from Arianna, with emphasis on its thematic structure, in chapter five. Asserts that the objectionable dissonances cited by Artusi as errors in
counterpoint are an important aspect of Monteverdi's musical style. Contains a bibliography.

373. Griffiths, David. A Catalogue of the Printed Music
Published before 1850 in York Minster Library.
York: University of York Library, 1977. 118 pp.
ML136 Y72 Y7

Included in this listing of music printed before
1850 is a copy of Monteverdi's Madrigali guerrieri,
et amorosi of 1638.

* Haar, James. Essays on Italian Poetry and Music in
the Renaissance, 1350-1600.

Cited above as item 92.

* Hammerstein, Irmgard. "Zur Monteverdi-Rezeption in
Deutschland. Johann Hermann Scheins Fontana
d'Israel."

Cited above as item 222.

374. Hammerstein, Reinhold. "Versuch über die Form im
Madrigal Monteverdis." Claudio Monteverdi:
Festschrift Reinhold Hammerstein (item 794), pp.
9-34.

The initial essay in a Festschrift honoring the
author. A reprint of an article (item 375) first
published in 1975.

375. ————. "Versuch über die Form im Madrigal
Monteverdis." Sprachen der Lyrik. Festschrift
für Hugo Friedrich zum 70. Geburtstage, edited by
Erich Köhler. Frankfurt am Main: Vittorio
Klostermann, 1975, pp. 220-41.

Stresses the relationship of text and music upon
form in the madrigals of Monteverdi. The article

was later reprinted in a Festschrift honoring
Hammerstein, cited as item 374.

376. Hermelink, Siegfried. "Das rhythmische Gefüge in
      Monteverdis Ciaccona 'Zefiro Torna.'" Congress
      internazionale sul tema Claudio Monteverdi (ite
      811), pp. 323-34.

      A detailed study of the ostinato structure
      adopted by Monteverdi in the well-known Zefiro
      torna from the Scherzi musicali of 1632.

377. Heuss, Alfred. "Ein Beitrag zu dem Thema:
      Monteverdi als Charakteristiker in seinen
      Madrigalen." Festschrift zum 90. Geburtstage S
      Excellenz des Wirklichen Geheimen Rates Rochus
      Freiherrn von Liliencron überreicht von Ver-
      tretern deutscher Musikwissenschaft, edited by
      Hermann Kretzschmar. Leipzig: 1910, pp. 93-109

      Praises the contribution to Monteverdi research
      made by Hugo Leichtentritt regarding the madrigal
      Attempts to ascertain, through the study of
      madrigals from Leichtentritt's edition, Monte-
      verdi's artistic intentions. See Leichtentritt,
      item 382.

378. Holmes, Michael. "Problemen van de barokdans."
      Opera journaal 4 (1973-74): 10. In Dutch.

      Briefly discusses Baroque dance and Monteverdi
      Il ballo delle ingrate.

379. Horsley, Imogene. "Monteverdi's Use of Borrowed
      Material in 'Sfogava con le stelle.'" Music a
      Letters 59 (1978): 316-28.

      Compares the style of Monteverdi's madrigal
      Sfogava con le stelle with the precepts stated i
      Caccini's Le nuove musiche (1602). Believes tha
      the madrigal is based on Caccini's setting of th
      same text and that it represents a reply to
      Caccini's criticism of the polyphonic madrigal.

380. Kurtzman, Jeffrey G. "An Early 17th-Century
      Manuscript of Canzonette e Madrigaletti
      Spirituali." Studi musicali 8 (1979): 149-71.

      Describes the contents of MS. L.IV.99 in the
      Biblioteca Queriniana in Brescia. This collecti
      of canzonette and madrigaletti spirituali contai

five works by Monteverdi, three of which are also
found in the Scherzi musicali of 1607 and two
works, Fuggi fuggi, cor and Se d'un angel il bel
viso, which are found only in this collection.

381. Lecoat, Gerard George. "Music and the Rhetoric of
      the Arts During the Age of Monteverdi." Ph.D.
      dissertation, University of Washington, 1973.
      313 pp. UM Order No. 73-22,584

      Not examined. Summary in Dissertation Abstracts
      International, 34 (October 1973): 1953-A, indicates
      that this study examines the link between music,
      poetry, and painting during the age of Monteverdi
      and includes a rhetorical analysis of Marino's poem
      Le strage de gl'innocenti, Poussin's painting
      Massacre des innocents, and Monteverdi's Il
      combattimento di Tancredi e Clorinda.

382. Leichtentritt, Hugo. "Claudio Monteverdi als
      Madrigalkomponist." Sammelbände der Inter-
      nationalen Musik-Gesellschaft 11 (1909-10):
      255-91.

      Among the earliest essays to emphasize the
      importance of Monteverdi as a madrigal composer.
      Discusses each of the eight madrigal books.

383. McClary, Susan Kaye. "The Transition from Modal to
      Tonal Organization in the Works of Monteverdi."
      Ph.D. dissertation, Harvard University, 1976.
      291 pp. UM Order No. 77-11,168

      Not examined. Summary in Dissertation Abstracts
      International, 37 (May 1977): 6830-A, indicates
      that this study examines the evolution of tonality
      in Monteverdi's works from ca. 1600 to ca. 1640.

384. Mace, Dean T. "Tasso, La Gerusalemme Liberata, and
      Monteverdi." Studies in the History of Music,
      vol. 1. New York: Broude, 1983, pp. 118-56.
      ISBN 0 8450 7401 6   ML3849 M87 1983

      Emphasizes the role of text in shaping the
      rhythm, harmony, and melody of the music. Ex-
      amines settings from Monteverdi's madrigal books.

385. Maione, Italo. "Tasso-Monteverdi: Il combattimento
      di Tancredi e Clorinda." Rassegna musicale 3
      (1930): 206-15.

Describes how Il combattimento fits the mood of
Tasso's Gerusalemme liberata. Sketches the actior
of Tasso's text and describes how Monteverdi's
musical setting of this text, with its shifting
tempos and fluctuating tonal centers, brings out
the dramatic content of the poem.

386. Malin, Don. "Madrigali Spirituali." Choral
      Journal 8 (January-February 1968): 7-9.

      Provides an introduction to the madrigali
      spirituali and cites Petrarch, Pietro Bembo, Bish(
      Gabriel Fiamma, and Vittoria Colona as important
      poets of madrigali spirituali texts. Mentions
      Monteverdi as a composer in this genre.

387. Martini, Giovanni Battista. Esemplare o sia sagg
      fondamentale di contrappunto. 2 vols. Bologna
      1774; facsimile ed., New Jersey: Gregg Press,
      1965. 300, 328 pp. MT55 A2 M38

      This eighteenth-century counterpoint treatise
      discusses three works by Monteverdi. In a sectior
      of volume 1 dealing with the five-voice fugue,
      Martini analyzes Stracciami pur il core and Cruda
      Amarilli. In regard to the six-voice fugue,
      Martini examines the Agnus Dei from Monteverdi's
      Missa In illo tempore. Before the analysis of
      Stracciami pur il core, Martini gives a brief
      statement on Monteverdi's accomplishments.

388. Moses, Gavriel Josef. "Literary Genre in
      Monteverdi." Ph.D. dissertation, Brown
      University, 1974. 142 pp. UM Order No. 75-921

      Not examined. Summary in Dissertation Abstract
      International, 35 (May 1975): 7262-A, indicates
      that this study investigates Monteverdi's use of
      literary genre and how the composer's literary
      awareness affected his music.

389. Newman, Joel. "Communications." Journal of the
      American Musicological Society 14 (1961): 418-1

      Reveals the poets of three madrigals by Monte-
      verdi: Filli cara e amata (book one, 1587) is by
      Alberto Parma; Crudel, perché mi fuggi (book two,
      1590) is by Guarini; and Si ch'io vorei morire
      (book four, 1603) is a setting of a poem by
      Maurizio Moro.

390. Ossi, Massimo Michele. "Claudio Monteverdi and the
      Concertato Principle: A Study of His Concertato
      Madrigals." Ph.D. dissertation in progress,
      Harvard University.

*   Osthoff, Wolfgang. "Monteverdis Combattimento in
      deutscher Sprache und Heinrich Schütz."

      Cited above as item 244.

*   ———. "Petrarca in der Musik des Abendlandes.
      Eine Betrachtung zum Sprachethos der Musik."

      Cited above as item 124.

391. Pannain, Guido. "Studi monteverdiani I." Rassegna
      musicale 28 (1958): 7-15.

      This is the first of a fifteen-part study con-
      cerning the music of Monteverdi. In this intro-
      ductory essay the author describes the different
      approaches that Redlich, Leichtentritt, Einstein,
      and Schrade have taken in studying Monteverdi's
      madrigals. Agrees with Redlich's argument that the
      madrigals of Monteverdi are not divided into two
      opposite stylistic groups. Argues that the effect
      of Monteverdi's personality on the individuali-
      zation of form is important in considering his
      works.

392. ———. "Studi monteverdiani II." Rassegna
      musicale 28 (1958): 97-108.

      Assesses the views of Schrade, Leichtentritt, and
      Einstein concerning Monteverdi's third book of
      madrigals. Discusses Padre Martini's opinions on
      Monteverdi's use of dissonance and quotes portions
      of Martini's Esemplare o sia saggio fondamentale di
      contrappunto (item 387). Remarks that Artusi and
      Monteverdi had opposite musical conceptions.

393. ———. "Studi monteverdiani III." Rassegna
      musicale 28 (1958): 187-95.

      Examines the musical style in Monteverdi's fifth
      and sixth books of madrigals. Believes that the
      fifth book does not represent a break in the
      composer's musical style. Asserts that the birth
      of opera originated in the works of the lyric
      madrigalists and not in the literary philosophies
      of the Florentine masters.

394. ———. "Studi monteverdiani IX." *Rassegna
      musicale* 30 (1960): 24-32.

Examines the madrigal version of the *Lamento d'
Arianna* and other works in Monteverdi's sixth book
of madrigals in light of comments made by Doni,
Einstein, and Redlich.

395. ———. "Studi monteverdiani X." *Rassegna
      musicale* 30 (1960): 230-40.

Continues the author's previous discussion from
"Studi monteverdiani IX" concerning Monteverdi's
sixth book of madrigals. *Qui rise o Tirsi*, *Zefirc
torna*, *Ohimè il bel viso*, *Misero Alceo*, and *Batto*,
qui pianse are considered.

396. ———. "Studi monteverdiani XI." *Rassegna
      musicale* 30 (1960): 312-24.

Discusses the musical style in Monteverdi's
seventh book of madrigals. *Tempro la cetra*, *O con
sei gentile*, and *O viva fiamma* are considered in
some detail. Critical comments by several authors
are cited concerning the *Lettera amorosa* and
Partenza amorosa.

397. ———. "Studi monteverdiani XII." *Rassegna
      musicale* 31 (1961): 14-26.

Examines the musical structure of Monteverdi's
seventh book of madrigals, concentrating on the
duets in this collection. Draws attention to the
tripartite structure of these duets and Monteverdi's combination of homophonic and polyphonic
texture. Discusses views on the origin and use o:
the term "Romanesca."

398. ———. "Studi monteverdiani XIII, XIV." *Rasseg*
      musicale 32 (1962): 1-20.

Examines works in Monteverdi's eighth book of
madrigals in light of observations made by contemporary Monteverdi scholars. Discusses the
composer's use of *stile concertato* and the use of
instruments with emphasis on Monteverdi's *Il
combattimento di Tancredi e Clorinda*.

399. ———. "Studi monteverdiani XV." *Quaderni dell
      rassegna musicale* 3 (1965): 13-24.

Examines the use of basso ostinato in Monteverdi's eighth book of madrigals and posthumous
ninth book of madrigals.

400. Pestelli, Giorgio. "Le poesie per la musica
      monteverdiana. Il gusto poetico di Monteverdi."
      Congresso internazionale sul tema Claudio
      Monteverdi (item 811), pp. 349-60.

      Surveys Monteverdi's choice of texts for his
      madrigals with many references to Pirrotta's
      article on the same subject (item 403). Recog-
      nizes that Monteverdi chose poetry for his early
      madrigals and librettos for his late madrigals.

401. Petrobelli, Pierluigi. "'Ah, dolente partita':
      Marenzio, Wert, Monteverdi." Congresso
      internazionale sul tema Claudio Monteverdi (item
      811), pp. 361-76.

      Compares three settings of Ah, dolente partita
      from Guarini's Il pastor fido composed by Luca
      Marenzio (1594), Giaches de Wert (1595), and
      Claudio Monteverdi (1597). Marenzio's setting is
      concerned with the proper declamation of the text
      while Wert's version creates a mosaic of con-
      trasting sections corresponding to single verses.
      Monteverdi, whom the author believes was influenced
      by Wert, created a texture in which each voice
      moves independently of the others, resulting in an
      autonomous enunciation of each voice.

402. Pirrotta, Nino. "Monteverdi's Poetic Choices."
      Music and Culture in Italy from the Middle Ages
      to the Baroque. Studies in the History of Music,
      vol. 1, edited by Lewis Lockwood and Christoph
      Wolff. Cambridge: Harvard University Press,
      1984, pp. 271-316. ISBN 0 674 59108 9 ML290.1
      P57 1984

      An English translation by David Morgenstern of
      Pirrotta's article "Scelte poetiche di Monteverdi"
      (item 403).

403. ————. "Scelte poetiche di Monteverdi." Nuova
      rivista musicale italiana 2 (1968): 10-42,
      266-54.

      In addition to being a study of Monteverdi's
      poetic choices, this is an in-depth examination of

the way in which the composer set both madrigal ar
opera texts. Identifies some of Monteverdi's pre-
viously unidentified texts and corrects frequent
mistakes of attribution. Changes in the composer'
musical style are considered in light of the poetr
Monteverdi set to music. This article appeared ir
an English translation by David Morgenstern as
"Monteverdi's Poetic Choices" (item 402).

404. Poos, H. "Anmerkungen zum Monteverdis Madrigal
      Schaffen." Quinto congresso europeo sul canto
      corale. Problemi di tecnica e di didattica dell
      vocalità corale nel madrigali cinquecentesco...
      atte e documentazioni. Gorizia, 1974.

405. Prunières, Henry. "Monteverdi and French Music."
      The Sackbut 3 (1922): 98-110.

      Advocates that Giulio Cesare Monteverdi's
      statement crediting Claudio with transmitting the
      French canto francese and using it in motets,
      madrigals, songs, and airs has been interpreted
      incorrectly. Maintains that it was not the style
      of Janequin or Lassus that Monteverdi introduced t
      Italy but the ancient rhythm of the air de cour
      which the composer heard on his journey to Spa wit
      the Duke of Mantua in 1599. Notices similarities
      between metric patterns found in works of Le Jeune
      Mauduit, Du Caurroy, and Monteverdi.

406. ————. "Monteverdi e la musica francese del suo
      tempo." Rassegna musicale (item 819), pp.
      483-93.

      Supports the premise that Monteverdi's style,
      especially his use of certain rhythmic patterns,
      was influenced by the French style of composition
      which Monteverdi probably heard on his visit to
      Spa. This article recaps much of what was given :
      Prunières's earlier article, item 405.

407. Rastelli, Dario. "Tancredi e Clorinda 'al
      paragone': due eminenti pagine di ispirazione
      drammatico-patetico-religiosa fra Cinque e
      Seicento nell'Italia settentrionale." Congress
      internazionale sul tema Claudio Monteverdi (ite
      811), pp. 557-69.

      Compares Tasso's Tancredi e Clorinda to
      Monteverdi's musical setting of that text and

observes indications of architectural balance as
evidenced in the appearance of the Golden Section
in these works. Draws on G. Getto's Nel mondo
della Gerusalemme (Florence, 1968) for support
concerning the analysis of Tasso. Uses only a
recording (Vedette, VST, 6011 "Madrigalisti di
Venezia") as the source for the musical analysis.

408. Redlich, Hans F. Claudio Monteverdi. Das
      Madrigalwerk: ein formengeschichtlicher Versuch.
      Berlin: Adler, 1932; reprint ed., Hildesheim:
      Olms, 1976. 273 pp. ML410 M765 R43 1976

      A revision of Redlich's Ph.D. dissertation, Das
      Problem des Stilwandels in Monteverdis Madrigal-
      werk, presented to the University of Frankfurt am
      Main in 1931. The major portion of the study is
      devoted to an examination of individual madrigals
      in order of appearance from book to book. Surveys
      in general terms some of the main elements of
      Monteverdi's style, including text setting, melody,
      harmony, polyphony, and form. Framing the prin-
      cipal discussion is an opening essay on the devel-
      opment of the madrigal and a concluding essay on
      the madrigal idea in opera and church music. An
      influential study. Numerous footnotes and a bib-
      liography.

409. ————. "Das Orchester Claudio Monteverdis. I.
      Instrumentalpraxis in Monteverdis Madrigalwerk."
      Musica viva 1 (1936): 55-64.

      Stresses the use of instruments in the madrigal
      books of Monteverdi. Argues that the works of the
      first four books, though published without any
      indication of instruments, require their addition
      in some cases. Contends that the madrigals of
      Monteverdi adumbrate the Baroque cantata style.
      Translated summaries of the article appear along-
      side the German text (which concludes with a
      summary) in English, French, and Italian.

410. Reiner, Stuart. "La vag'Angioletta (and others)."
      Analecta musicologica 14 (1974): 26-88. In
      English.

      Speculates on the identity of the singer iden-
      tified as Angioletta in Monteverdi's madrigal
      Mentre vaga Angioletta from his eighth book of
      madrigals. Documents the political circumstances

surrounding the marriage of Francesco Gonzaga to
Margherita of Savoy.

411. Riemann, Hugo. "Eine siebensätzige Tanzsuite von
      Monteverdi v.J. 1607." Sammelbände der Inter-
      nationalen Musik-Gesellschaft 14 (1912-13):
      26-33.

      A controversial article dealing with the seven
      dances comprising the "Balletto" from the Scherzi
      musicali of 1607. Redlich (item 408) refutes
      Riemann's contention that variation technique
      creates a cyclic design in this work. Concludes
      with an edition of the music.

*   Roche, Jerome. The Madrigal.

      Cited above as item 145.

412. Ronga, Luigi. "Tasso e Monteverdi." Poesia 1
      (1945): 272-80.

      Considers the combination of Tasso's lyric poetry
      and Monteverdi's music an ideal meeting of poet and
      composer. Discusses, without specific musical ci-
      tations, Monteverdi's settings of Tasso's works in
      his first three madrigal books and Tancredi e
      Clorinda.

413. Rossi, Luigi. "E la 'nobil danza.'" Opera 3
      (1967): 118-20.

      Underscores the importance of choreographed
      spectacles in music composed by Monteverdi.
      Briefly discusses Monteverdi's ballets.

414. Salzer, Felix. "Heinrich Schenker and Historical
      Research: Monteverdi's Madrigal Oimè, se tanto
      amate." Aspects of Schenkerian Theory, edited by
      David Beach. New Haven: Yale University Press,
      1983, pp. 135-52. ISBN 0 300 02800 8 MT6 A766
      1983

      Applies Schenkerian concepts to a detailed
      analysis of Monteverdi's composition from the
      fourth book of madrigals.

415. Schwartz, Rudolf. "Zu den Texten der ersten fünf
      Bücher der Madrigale Monteverdis." Festschrift
      Hermann Kretzschmar zum siebzigsten Geburtstage.
      Leipzig: C.F. Peters, 1918, pp. 147-48.

An extremely succinct article providing a list
of the poets whose texts were set by Monteverdi in
his first five madrigal books.

*   Sirch, Licia. "'Violini piccoli alla francese' e
      'canto alla francese' nell'Orfeo (1607) e negli
      'Scherzi musicali' (1607) di Monteverdi."

      Cited below as item 572.

416. Solerti, Angelo. "Un balletto musicato da Claudio
      Monteverde sconosciuto a' suoi biografi."
      Rivista musicale italiana 11 (1904): 24-34.

Reports evidence of an unknown ballet by Monteverdi, Vittoria d'Amore, written for Duke Odoardo
of Parma and Piacenza. Reproduces Bernardo
Marando's text to the ballet, dated 1641.

417. Sopart, Andreas. "Claudio Monteverdis 'Scherzi
      musicali' (1607) und ihre Beziehungen zum
      'Scherzo'-Begriff in der italienischen
      Barocklyrik." Archiv für Musikwissenschaft 38
      (1981): 227-34.

Offers a careful investigation of the frivolous
poetic text set by Monteverdi in the Scherzi
musicali (1607). Reviews the historical background
of the Italian scherzo poem during the sixteenth
and seventeenth centuries and suggests that the
genre was derived from the fifteenth-century
canzonetta.

418. Stevens, Denis. "Claudio Monteverdi: Dramatic
      Madrigals and Dialogues." Music Review 40
      (1979): 1-13.

Describes the wide variety of stylistic features
found in Monteverdi's dramatic madrigals and
dialogues. Following a brief introduction and
chronological listing of Monteverdi's secular vocal
works, individual pieces are discussed from both
categories.

419. ————. "Claudio Unclouded: A Ballet in Five
      Parts." Musical Times 101 (1960): 23.

Reports the finding of a fifth instrumental
part, hitherto unknown, to the dances in Il ballo
delle ingrate located in the fifth partbook to the
1638 edition of the composer's Madrigali guerrieri,

et amorosi. This part, apparently not titled, fits
well into the harmony of these dances.

420.   ————. "Letters to the Editor: Ravished but not
         Lost." Musical Times 119 (1978): 1013.

An appeal in the form of a letter to the editor
for scholars to search for undiscovered Monteverdi
compositions. Identifies the text of the madrigal
Come dolce hoggi l'auretta as being from Strozzi's
Proserpina rapita.

421.   ————. "Madrigali Guerrieri, et Amorosi." The
         Monteverdi Companion (item 779), pp. 227-54.

Attempts to provide a general chronology for
works in the eighth book of madrigals. Defends
Monteverdi's use of the term "madrigal" for the
collection. This article is a slight revision of
item 422.

422.   ————. "Madrigali Guerrieri, et Amorosi: A
         Reappraisal for the Quatercentenary." Musical
         Quarterly 53 (1967): 161-87.

The principal concern of this study is to date
the works of Monteverdi's eighth book of madrigals
by the implications found in their texts. Implies
that this is only a hypothesis and invites further
investigation into this area.

423.   ————. Monteverdi: Sacred, Secular, and
         Occasional Music. Cranbury, N.J.: Fairleigh
         Dickinson University Press, 1978. 147 pp. ISBN
         0 838 61937 1 ML410 M77 S8

Provides a brief, critical study of Monteverdi's
music both extant and lost. Identifies the poets
of a number of madrigal texts and presents several
hypotheses about performances of Monteverdi's
secular and sacred works.

424.   ————. "Monteverdi's Earliest Extant Ballet."
         Anuario musical 37 (1982): 39-54.

Identifies De la ballezza le dovute lodi, the
finale of the Scherzi musicali, as Monteverdi's
first extant ballet. Contains a survey of researc
about the ballet from a Hugo Riemann article of

1912 to Stevens's own book, Monteverdi: Sacred, Secular, and Occasional Music of 1978 (item 423). Offers an analysis for the seven movements of the work. See also item 425.

425. ————. "Monteverdi's Earliest Extant Ballet." Early Music 14 (1986): 358-66.

A revision of Stevens's earlier article in Anuario musical (item 424).

426. Strohm, Reinhard. "Osservazioni su 'Tempro la cetra.'" Rivista italiana di musicologia (item 838), pp. 357-64.

Examines in depth the musical structure of the madrigal Tempro la cetra from Monteverdi's seventh book of madrigals. Compares this work with the composer's Il ballo delle ingrate, portions of Orfeo, and other works of Monteverdi. Concludes that the work is not a madrigal but a ballet probably composed for a dramatic representation.

427. Szweykowski, Zygmunt. "'Ah dolente partita': Monteverdi-Sacchi." Quadrivium 12/2 (1971): 59-76. In English.

Compares Marco Sacchi's setting of Guarini's A dolente partita with that of Monteverdi. Sacchi's madrigal, which is in four parts with continuo, is similar to Monteverdi's work in the manner in which the text is interpreted musically. Includes a transcription of Sacchi's madrigal. This article also appeared in Memorie e contributi alla musica dal medioevo all'età moderna offerti a F. Ghisi nel settantesimo compleanno. Vol. 2. Bologna: A.M.I.S., 1971, pp. 59-76.

*   Tegen, Martin. "Monteverdi."

Cited below as item 577.

428. Tomlinson, Gary A. "Giambattista Guarini and Monteverdi's Epigrammatic Style." Claudio Monteverdi: Festschrift Reinhold Hammerstein (item 794), pp. 435-52.

Traces the development of the epigrammatic madrigal exemplified in Monteverdi's settings of poetry by Guarini. Concludes that Monteverdi's

epigrammatic style represents a synthesis of the
composer's earlier techniques.

429.   ———. Monteverdi and the End of the Renaissance.
        Berkeley: University of California Press, 1987.
        280 pp. ISBN 0 520 05348 6 ML410 M77 T7

        Stresses the relationship between text and music.
        The central portion of the study (chapters 2-9)
        presents a chronological investigation of the com-
        poser's secular works. This principal discussion
        is preceded by a significant opening chapter which,
        after a brief discussion of sixteenth-century
        Italian culture, examines the polemics of Galilei,
        Guarini, and Monteverdi and is concluded by an
        important closing chapter which evaluates Monte-
        verdi against the culture of his time. Includes an
        extensive list of works cited, an index of works
        and their texts, and a general index.

430.   ———. "Music and the Claims of Text: Monteverdi,
        Rinuccini, and Marino." Critical Inquiry 8
        (1982): 565-89.

        A cogent essay concerning the relationship
        between text and music. Compares the dissimilar
        poetic styles of Marino and Rinuccini and discusses
        their significance in musical settings by Monte-
        verdi.

431.   Trede, Hilmar. "Manirismus und Barock im
        italienischen Madrigal des 16. Jahrhunderts.
        Dargestellt an den Frühwerken Claudio
        Monteverdis." Ph.D. dissertation, University of
        Erlangen, 1928.

432.   Watkins, Glenn E., and La May, Thomasin.
        "'Imitatio' and 'Emulatio': Changing Concepts of
        Originality in the Madrigals of Gesualdo and
        Monteverdi in the 1590s." Claudio Monteverdi:
        Festschrift Reinhold Hammerstein (item 794), pp.
        451-87.

        A study of musical models. Examines similarities
        and differences in the madrigals of Gesualdo and
        Monteverdi. Compares the madrigals of each com-
        poser to settings of the same text by other
        composers. Observes that the works of Gesualdo and
        Monteverdi represent the apogee of the Italian
        madrigal tradition.

433.   Weismann, Wilhelm. "Ein verkannter Madrigal-Zyklus
       Monteverdis." Deutsches Jahrbuch der
       Musikwissenschaft für 1957 (1958): 37-51.

       Contends that the madrigal cycle Ecco Silvio,
       found in Monteverdi's fifth book of madrigals, has
       not received adequate consideration in Monteverdi
       research. Particularly praises the cycle for its
       union of poetry and music.

434.   Westrup, Jack A. "Monteverdi and the Madrigal."
       The Score 1 (1949): 33-40.

       Presents a general discussion, including numerous
       examples, of Monteverdi's madrigals. Describes
       stylistic characteristics recurring frequently in
       these works. Stresses the change in character
       evolving from the early madrigals through the late
       madrigals.

*   Whenham, John. Duet and Dialogue in the Age of
       Monteverdi.

       Cited above as item 186.

435.   ———. "The Later Madrigals and Madrigal-books."
       The New Monteverdi Companion (item 780), pp. 216-
       47.

       Re-evaluates Monteverdi's seventh and eighth
       books of madrigals and his late canzonettas.
       Speculates that some of the works in the seventh
       book were written while Monteverdi was in Mantua.
       Discusses Monteverdi's use of the walking bass line
       and the meaning of the designation canto alla
       francese as it applies to the composer's Scherzi
       musicali and the madrigals Dolcissimo uscignolo and
       Chi vuol haver felice e lieto il core in his eighth
       book of madrigals.

436.   Willetts, Pamela J. "A Neglected Source of Monody
       and Madrigal." Music and Letters 43 (1962):
       329-39.

       Brings to light important new information
       regarding a manuscript, British Museum Add. 31,
       440, erroneously attributed to Pietro Reggio.
       Although most of the music in the manuscript
       remains unidentified, Monteverdi is recognized as
       the composer of twenty-eight selections. Walter
       Porter is suggested as the possible compiler of

Add. 31,440. Includes a complete list of the
contents of the manuscript.

437. Wolters, Gottfried. "Monteverdis Madrigal Kunst."
      Kontakte 1 (1967): 3-5.

                          2. Operas

438. Abert, Anna Amalie. Claudio Monteverdi und das
      musikalische Drama. Lippstadt: Kistner & Siegel,
      1954. 354 pp. ML410 M77 A3

      Recognized as the fundamental study. Organized
      into three major chapters: the first deals with
      Monteverdi as an opera composer, the second con-
      siders the opera libretto, and the third, which is
      the largest of the three, traces the development of
      opera to the middle of the seventeenth century.
      Music, bibliography, notes, and an index of names.

439. ————. Claudio Monteverdis Bedeutung für die
      Entstehung des musikalischen Dramas. Darmstadt:
      Wissenschaftliche Buchgesellschaft, 1979. 103
      pp. ISBN 3 534 07614 1 ML410 M77 A65

      Provides a comprehensive survey of research on
      Monteverdi's operas. Particularly noteworthy is
      the penultimate chapter, which is concerned with
      the problems and objectives of Monteverdi research.
      The final chapter is a brief catalog of editions
      and recordings. Notes, bibliography, and an index
      of names.

440. ————. "Monteverdi e lo sviluppo dell'opera."
      Rivista italiana di musicologia (item 838), pp.
      207-16.

      Asserts that the balance between the emphasis
      on text and music in Monteverdi's Orfeo put a new
      stress on music not found in the Florentine operas
      preceding it. Sees Monteverdi's later operas as
      representing an opera reform with their expressive
      realization of text. Translated into Italian by
      Giulio Cogni.

441. ————. "Monteverdis 'Orfeo' einst und jetzt."
      Musica 12 (1958): 255-59.

Recognizes Monteverdi's indebtedness to the
members of the Florentine Camerata and acknowledges
Monteverdi's superior genius. Contends that Orfeo
is both a progressive and regressive work of art.
Addresses numerous issues associated with the
revival of Orfeo and other early operas.

442. Adams, Stan R. "A Survey of the Use of Trombones
      to Depict Infernal and Horrendous Scenes in
      Three Representative Operas." Journal of the
      International Trombone Association 9 (March
      1981): 16-20.

      A brief examination of the role of the trombone
      in opera ombra scenes with a discussion of Monte-
      verdi's Orfeo, Mozart's Don Giovanni, and Strauss's
      Salome. Includes a comparison of the sackbut with
      modern trombones.

443. Allorto, Riccardo. "Il prologo dell'Orfeo. Nota
      sulla formazione del recitativo monteverdiano."
      Congresso internazionale sul tema Claudio
      Monteverdi (item 811), pp. 157-68.

      Discusses the prologue to Monteverdi's Orfeo
      and compares it to the prologues in Peri's and
      Caccini's Euridice. Observes that the structure of
      Monteverdi's prologue, with its melodic writing
      based on a limited number of melodic paradigms, is
      similar to madrigals found in his fourth and fifth
      madrigal books.

444. Altenburg, Detlef. "Die Toccata zu Monteverdis
      'Orfeo.'" Bericht über den internationalen
      musikwissenschaftlichen Kongress Berlin 1974,
      edited by Hellmut Kühn and Peter Nitsche.
      Kassel: Bärenreiter, 1980, pp. 271-74.

      Points out that the toccata to Orfeo stems from
      the tradition of the ceremonial trumpet piece.

445. Anfuso, Nella, and Gianuario, Annibale. Claudio
      Monteverdi: Lamento d'Arianna. Studio e
      interpretazione sulla edizione a stampa del
      Gardano-Venezia 1623. Florence: Otos, 1969.
      26 pp.

      A critical study of the famous Lamento based on
      the 1623 printing of the work. The authors believe
      that the accidentals in the printing apply only to

those notes to which they are prefixed. Editorial
procedures are defended by quotes from Agazzari,
Doni, and others. Includes two transcriptions of
the Lamento d'Arianna, one based on the 1623
printing and the other on the Magliabechiana
manuscript. The conclusion compares Monteverdi's
interpretation of oratione to that of Artusi.

446. ————. Le tre Arianne di Claudio Monteverdi.
      Florence: Centro studi Rinascimento musicale,
      1975. 37 pp. ML410 M77 A76

A comparative study of the monodic version of the
Lamento d'Arianna (1623), the polyphonic version
(1614), and the Pianto della Madonna based on the
lament (1640). Analyzes in detail how Monteverdi
realized vowels and consonants of the text harmon-
ically. Recognizes that although two different
texts were set in the monodic Lamento and the
Pianto, Monteverdi gave both texts appropriate
musical settings. Speculates that Monteverdi may
have been the author of the Pianto text.

*   Apel, Willi. "Anent a Ritornello in Monteverdi's
      Orfeo."

      Cited below as item 678.

447. Arlt, Wulf. "Der Prolog des 'Orfeo' als Lehrstück
      der Aufführungspraxis." Claudio Monteverdi:
      Festschrift Reinhold Hammerstein (item 794), pp.
      36-51.

Suggests that the musical style of the prologue
to Monteverdi's first opera demonstrates important
elements of the style change that occurred around
1600.

448. Arnold, Denis. "'L'Incoronazione di Poppea' and
      Its Orchestral Requirements." Musical Times 104
      (1963): 176-78.

Looks at the problematic, unspecified orchestral
parts of Monteverdi's last opera, drawing on information in the Venetian State Archives dated just
after Poppea's appearance. Records revealing pay-
ments to musicians by the impresario Marco Faustini
indicate an orchestra of violins, violetta, and two
theorbos. Argues that this is probably an incom-
plete list and maintains that Poppea should not be

performed by the same size orchestra as Monteverdi's Orfeo.

449.   ———. "Monteverdi the Instrumentalist."
        Recorder and Music Magazine 2 (1967): 130-32.

        Praises Monteverdi for his grasp of instrumental
        idioms and for his knowledge of the techniques of
        various instruments. Cites Orfeo and the Vespers
        of 1610 as examples of his idiomatic writing for
        specific instruments.

450.   ———. "Il Ritorno d'Ulisse and the Chamber
        Duet." Musical Times 106 (1965): 183-85.

        Praises Monteverdi's use of the duet in Il
        ritorno d'Ulisse and maintains that the incor-
        poration of this genre into this opera begins a new
        path for opera composition. Points out a funda-
        mental difference between the ensemble writing of
        Monteverdi and that of Mozart and Verdi: Monte-
        verdi's ensembles never express conflict of
        personality.

451.   Azouvi, François. "Analyse structurale acte par
        acte." L'Orfeo (item 816), pp. 20-22.

        An analysis of Orfeo with emphasis on the
        importance of the chorus and orchestra.

452.   ———. "Orphée au nom fameux: du mythe à la
        légende." L'Orfeo (item 816), pp. 8-11.

        Traces the history of the Orpheus myth. Compares
        the character of Orpheus to the god Dionysus.

453.   ———. "Remarques sur les trois versions du mythe
        d'Orphée." L'Orfeo (item 816), pp. 12-14.

        Compares versions of the Orpheus myth by Virgil,
        Ovid, and Monteverdi.

454.   Bacchelli, Riccardo. Rossini e saggi musicali:
        Verdi, Beethoven, Monteverdi. Milan: Mondadori,
        1968. 589 pp. ML60 B128

        Devotes forty-four pages to six essays on Claudio
        Monteverdi. Of these, "Commenti," "Sulla 'Gran
        Fatica' dell Arianna," and "A lumi spenti," are in-
        depth essays. In his "Commenti," the author
        compares Vincenzo Gonzaga, Monteverdi's patron at

Mantua, with the character Nerone from L'incoronazione di Poppea. "Sulla 'Gran Fatica...'"
discusses Monteverdi's Arianna in light of statements made by the composer in a letter dated
October 22, 1633. "A lumi spenti" discusses
characterization in Monteverdi's Il combattimento
di Tancredi e Clorinda.

*   Barblan, Guglielmo; Gallico, Claudio; and Pannain,
      Guido. Claudio Monteverdi, nel quarto centenario
      della nascita.

      Cited above as item 297.

455. Beat, Janet E. "Monteverdi and the Opera Orchestra
      of His Time." The Monteverdi Companion (item
      779), pp. 277-301.

      Surveys the role of the orchestra in seventeenth-
      century dramatic works by Monteverdi and other
      composers. Based largely on an examination of
      scores and contemporary treatises. A much
      criticized article.

*   Bedford, Steuart. "The Problems of Poppea."

      Cited below as item 784.

456. Benvenuti, Giacomo. "Il manoscritto veneziano
      della 'Incoronazione di Poppea.'" Rivista
      musicale italiana 41 (1937): 176-84.

      Criticizes Malipiero's edition of Poppea for its
      use of material from the manuscript of the conser-
      vatory of S. Pietro a Majella in Naples. Cites the
      Venetian manuscript in the Marciana library as
      being the most accurate source for this work.
      Argues that portions of the Venetian manuscript,
      which Malipiero contends were made by a copyist,
      match the handwriting in Monteverdi's letters.

457. Borren, Charles van den. "'Il Ritorno d'Ulisse in
      Patria' de Claudio Monteverdi." Revue de l'Uni-
      versité de Bruxelles 3 (1925): 353-87.

      Ascribes, based upon the research of Hugo
      Goldschmidt, the authorship of Il ritorno d'Ulisse
      to Monteverdi. In addition to a lengthy discussion
      of the opera, the author provides a brief survey of
      the composer's Venetian operas. Discusses,

somewhat unfavorably, the 1922 edition of Ulisse by
Robert Haas. Concludes with a comparison of
Monteverdi's Ulisse and L'incoronazione di Poppea.

458.   Bossarelli, Anna Mondolfi. "Ancora intorno al
       codice napoletano della Incoronazione di Poppea."
       Rivista italiana di musicologia (item 838), pp.
       294-313.

       Reviews the literature on the Venetian and
       Neapolitan manuscripts of Monteverdi's Poppea by
       Giacomo Benvenuti and Wolfgang Osthoff, summarizing
       much of the work of the latter. Speculates that
       the Neapolitan manuscript, which the author
       believes preceded the Venetian copy, was greatly
       altered by the organist Pietro Andrea Ziani.

459.   Boyden, David D. "Monteverdi's violini piccoli
       alla francese and viole da brazzo." Annales
       musicologiques 6 (1958-63): 387-401.

       Investigates the string instruments violini
       piccoli alla francese and violini ordinari da
       braccio designated in the opening scene of Act II
       of Monteverdi's Orfeo. Contends that the former
       instruments were pochettes and that the latter
       instruments were the usual violins, citing
       Zacconi's Prattica di musica and Praetorius's
       Syntagma musicum, volume 2, as evidence.

460.   Bragard, Anne-Marie. "Deux portraits de femmes
       dans l'oeuvre de Monteverdi: Ariane et Poppée."
       Bulletin de société liègeoise de musicologie 24
       (1979): 1-14.

       Not examined. Summary in RILM Abstracts, 13/1
       (January-April 1979): 115, indicates that the
       article examines "two opposing views of Baroque
       aesthetics through the characters of Ariadne and
       Poppea."

461.   Braun, Werner. "Monteverdis grosse Bassmonodien."
       Claudio Monteverdi: Festschrift Reinhold
       Hammerstein (item 794), pp. 123-39.

       Divided into seven sections plus an introduction,
       the article carefully examines Monteverdi's monodic
       structure and style. Concludes with a comparison
       of Schütz and Monteverdi.

462.   Brizi, Bruno. "Teoria e prassi melodrammatica di
       G.F. Busenello e 'L'incoronazione di Poppea.'"
       Venezia e il melodramma nel seicento. Studi di
       musica veneta 5, edited by Maria Teresa Muraro.
       Florence: Olschki, 1976, pp. 51-74.

       Draws on prefaces and prologues of Busenello's
       works to better clarify the librettist's theory of
       what a libretto should be. Busenello contends that
       the libretto should closely follow the requirements
       of the music. Contains a metric/linguistic
       analysis of portions of Monteverdi's L'incorona-
       zione di Poppea.

463.   Bucchi, Valentino. L'Orfeo di Claudio Monteverdi.
       Florence: Fussi, 1949. 37 pp. ML410 M78 B91

       An introductory monograph on Monteverdi's Orfeo.
       Includes an opening chapter assessing the value of
       the opera and praising its recitatives. The second
       chapter discusses the libretto in relation to the
       music. A descriptive analysis of the music,
       complete with musical examples, is provided in the
       third chapter. The final two chapters note the
       first performances of Orfeo, as well as problems
       incurred in modern transcriptions and presentations
       of the work. Cites modern editions of this master-
       piece, as well as early twentieth-century
       performances.

464.   Budden, Julian. "Orpheus, or the Sound of Music."
       Opera 18 (1967): 622-30.

       Recognizes the importance of the Orpheus myth
       to opera and compares three settings of the legend
       by Monteverdi, Gluck, and Haydn.

465.   Cammarota, Lionello. "L'orchestrazione dell'
       'Orfeo' di Monteverdi." Venezia e il melodramma
       nel seicento. Studi di musica veneta 5, edited
       by Maria Teresa Muraro. Florence: Olschki, 1976,
       pp. 21-40.

       Evaluates the instrumentation specified in modern
       editions of Orfeo. Calls for a more authentic
       performance of Orfeo based on Monteverdi's indi-
       cations. Contains an appendix in which Wolfgang
       Osthoff's views on the effect of the trumpet mute
       during the time of Monteverdi are given.

466. Carter, Tim, and Butchart, David. "Letters to the
      Editor: The Original Orpheus." Musical Times 118
      (1977): 393.

      Corroborates Nigel Fortune's hypothesis (see item
      499) that the tenor Francesco Rasi probably sang
      the title role in the 1607 performance of Monte-
      verdi's Orfeo. This evidence is based on infor-
      mation found in an anthology of verse by members of
      the Mantuan Accademia degli Invaghiti.

467. Cattini, U. "'Arianna' fra il sei-settecento."
      Rassegna musicale curci 34 (1981): 48-49.

      Briefly compares Monteverdi's Arianna with the
      Arianna of Benedetto Marcello.

468. Celletti, Rodolfo. "La vocalità di Monteverdi."
      Opera 6 (January-March 1967): 11-17.

      Not examined. Summary in RILM Abstracts, 2/3
      (September-December 1968): 259, notes that the
      article is concerned with analysis of Monteverdi's
      vocal writing.

*   Cesari, Gaetano. "L' 'Orfeo' di Cl. Monteverdi
      all' 'Associazione di amici della musica' di
      Milano."

      Cited below as item 786.

469. Chevaillier, Lucien. "Le récit chez Monteverdi."
      Revue d'histoire et de critique musicales 10
      (1910): 284-94.

      An examination of recitative in Orfeo and
      L'incoronazione di Poppea. The article is based on
      the performing editions in French translation of
      both operas produced by Vincent d'Indy.

470. Chiarelli, Alessandra. "L'incoronazione di Poppea
      o Il Nerone: problemi di filologia testuale."
      Rivista italiana di musicologia 9 (1974): 117-51.

      Considers the extant versions of the text of
      Monteverdi's L'incoronazione di Poppea and, from
      the variant spellings and wordings, establishes a
      genealogy for the Venetian and Neapolitan manu-
      scripts. In addition to these scores, Chiarelli
      mentions four librettos in manuscript and two

printed librettos. Gives considerable information
on each of these sources.

471. Collaer, Paul. "Notes concernant l'instrumentation
      de L'Orfeo de Claudio Monteverdi." Congresso
      internazionale sul tema Claudio Monteverdi (item
      811), pp. 69-73.

      Examines performance practice questions arising
      from the inexactness of Monteverdi's directions
      concerning instrumentation in the score of the
      opera, particularly those regarding the choice and
      number of instruments. Recommends, for example,
      that the clarino trumpet, designated only in the
      opening toccata, be employed again in the closing
      moresca. Implores performers to become acquainted
      with the customs and conventions of the period.
      Cautions against the overuse of embellishment.

472. Corboz, Michel. "Michel Corboz: A propos de
      L'Orfeo." L'Orfeo (item 816), pp. 72-74.

      Discusses Orfeo from a conductor's point of view.

473. Courville, Xavier de. "L'Ariane de Monteverdi."
      Revue musicale 3 (1921-22): 23-37.

      Voices hope for the discovery of the lost score
      to Arianna. Offers a detailed description of the
      circumstances surrounding the composition of the
      opera. Prints portions of the libretto.

474. Coutance, Guy. "L'Orfeo au temps de la fête
      baroque." L'Orfeo (item 816), pp. 75-77.

      Examines some of the forerunners of opera and
      describes their influence upon the new genre.

475. Covell, Roger David. "Monteverdi's L'Incoronazione
      di Poppea: The Musical and Dramatic Structure."
      Ph.D. dissertation, University of New South
      Wales, 1977.

      Argues that spectacle plays a greater role in
      the opera than is generally accepted by most
      scholars. Prefers the Neapolitan copy of the score
      over the Venetian copy.

476. Day, Christine J. "The Theater of SS. Giovanni e
      Paolo and Monteverdi's L'Incoronazione di
      Poppea." Current Musicology 25 (1978): 22-38.

Describes in detail the theater of SS. Giovanni
e Paolo in Venice, where Monteverdi's L'incoronazione di Poppea was given its premiere in 1642
and revived in 1646. Contains information on the
use of the flying machine and on the sets for
Poppea.

477. de' Paoli, Domenico. "'Orfeo' and 'Pellèas.'"
     Music and Letters 20 (1939): 381-98.

     Recognizes both Monteverdi's Orfeo and Debussy's
     Pelléas et Mélisande as being isolated masterpieces
     without immediate predecessors. Contends that both
     of these works were created and developed from the
     text. Draws parallels between Monteverdi's and
     Debussy's harmonic vocabulary, orchestration, and
     overall formal design.

478. de Van, Gilles. "Métamorphoses d'Orphée."
     L'Orfeo (item 816), pp. 62-68.

     Considers the transformation of the Orpheus myth
     in its different versions.

479. Degrada, Francesco. "Gian Francesco Busenello e il
     libretto della Incoronazione di Poppea." Con-
     gresso internazionale sul tema Claudio Monteverdi
     (item 811), pp. 81-102.

     Supplies biographical and cultural background on
     Busenello in order to better understand the motives
     and expressive character of the libretto to Poppea.
     Reveals that the characters of Seneca and Ottavia
     were altered by Monteverdi to reflect a Christian
     perspective. Busenello describes a universe devoid
     of light, and Monteverdi interjects a sense of
     Christian piety, creating an expressive ambiguity
     considered by the author to be a distinctive and
     realistic element in the opera. Includes Buse-
     nello's poem Lamento d'Arianna from the manuscript
     in the Biblioteca Bertoliana at Vicenza.

480. Della Corte, Andrea. "Aspetti del 'comico' nella
     vocalità teatrale di Monteverdi." Rivista
     italiana di musicologia (item 838), pp. 255-63.

     Compares the comic character Iro from Monte-
     verdi's Il ritorno d'Ulisse with the characters
     Marzio and Curzio in Landi's Sant' Alessio.

Discusses the rise of the comic figure in
seventeenth-century opera.

481. Donington, Robert. "Communications." Journal of
the American Musicological Society 24 (1971):
140-41.

Donington's response to Stuart Reiner's review
(item 837) of Donington's article on Orfeo in The
Monteverdi Companion. Donington does concede to
some of Reiner's observations.

482. ————. "Monteverdi's First Opera." The Monteverdi Companion (item 779), pp. 257-76.

Points out aspects of musical unity in Monteverdi's Orfeo. Observes a motivic relationship
between the opening toccata and other portions of
the work. Notes the recurrence of the tritone in
music related to Euridice. Contains some Jungian
analyses of characters and situations.

*   ————. The Rise of Opera.

Cited above as item 62.

*   Drummond, John D. Opera in Perspective.

Cited above as item 64.

483. Dufflocq, Enrico M. L'Orfeo di Claudio Monteverd:
Edizioni sonore musiche italiane antiche. Milan
Giuseppe Casati, 1940. 51 pp. ML50 M789 O72
1940

Consists of a brief introduction to Monteverdi
with comments on the development of monody, notes
on the character of Orfeo, a descriptive musical
analysis of the opera, and a copy of the libretto
keyed to the previous analysis. Includes a sectic
on the original printings of Orfeo and modern
editions.

484. Dürr, Walther. "Sprachliche und musikalische
Determinanten in der Monodie. Beobachtungen an
Monteverdis 'Orfeo.'" Claudio Monteverdi:
Festschrift Reinhold Hammerstein (item 794), pp
151-62.

Stresses the relationship between text and musi
in the monodic style of Monteverdi. Recognizes t

connection between text setting and instrumental
style.

485. Epstein, Peter. "Dichtung und Musik in Monteverdis
      'Lamento d'Arianna.'" Zeitschrift für Musik-
      wissenschaft 10 (1927-38): 216-22.

      Carefully analyzes the relationship of text to
      music in the celebrated Lamento d'Arianna. Pays
      particular attention, with the aid of many examples
      and tables, to the rhythmic structure.

486. ————. "Zur Rhythmisierung eines Ritornells von
      Monteverdi." Archiv für Musikwissenschaft 8
      (1926): 416-19.

      A pithy article dealing with the rhythmic
      structure and notation of the ritornello to Orfeo's
      aria Vi ricorda o boschi ombrosi from the second
      act of Monteverdi's opera. Compares transcriptions
      by Eitner, Heuss, Riemann, and Leichtentritt.
      Argues that the correct solution, due to the dance
      character of the ritornello, alternates 6/8 and 3/4
      meter.

487. Fabbri, Paolo. "Striggio e l'Orfeo." Musicacitta,
      edited by Luciano Berio. Rome: Laterza, 1984,
      pp. 203-13.

488. ————. "Tasso, Guarini e il 'divino Claudio.'
      Componenti manieristiche nella poetica di Monte-
      verdi." Studi musicali 3 (1974): 233-54.

      Compares Guarini's Il pastor fido, Torquato
      Tasso's Aminta, and Dante's Inferno with Striggio's
      libretto to Monteverdi's Orfeo. Identifies
      mannerist elements in the text and music of Orfeo
      as well as in Monteverdi's later works.

*   Fano, Fabio. "Il Combattimento di Tancredi e
      Clorinda e L'Incoronazione di Poppea di Claudio
      Monteverdi."

      Cited above as item 366.

489. Fenlon, Iain. "Mantua, Monteverdi and the History
      of 'Andromeda.'" Claudio Monteverdi: Festschrift
      Reinhold Hammerstein (item 794), pp. 163-73.

      Based upon the recently discovered libretto,
      Fenlon's article recounts the events surrounding

Andromeda. Discusses the relationship between
Monteverdi and the librettist, Ercole Marigliani.
Speculates on the composer's apparent difficulty
with the composition of Andromeda. Provides a
brief history of dramatic works based upon the
Andromeda legend.

490.   ————. "The Mantuan 'Orfeo.'" Claudio
        Monteverdi: Orfeo (item 588), pp. 1-19.

        A revision of Fenlon's Early Music article (item
        492). Reproduces and translates the Gonzaga
        letters in Appendix 1 of the Whenham volume.

491.   ————. "The Mantuan Stage Works." The New
        Monteverdi Companion (item 780), pp. 251-87.

        Notes influences from Florence and Ferrara upon
        the development of Monteverdi's musical style at
        Mantua. Bases this significant study of Orfeo on
        the series of letters between Francesco and
        Ferdinando Gonzaga. Among other works discussed
        are Arianna, Tirsi e Clori, Il ballo delle ingrate
        Le nozze di Tetide, and Licori finta pazza
        innamorata d'Aminta. See also Fenlon, items 490
        and 492.

492.   ————. "Monteverdi's Mantuan Orfeo: Some New
        Documentation." Early Music 12 (1984): 163-72.

        Reconstructs, based primarily on the correspon-
        dence between Francesco and Ferdinando Gonzaga, the
        circumstances surrounding the first performance of
        Monteverdi's opera. For additional information,
        see Fenlon, item 490.

493.   Ferrand, Françoise. "La 'juste prière' de Claudio
        Monteverdi." L'Orfeo (item 816), pp. 69-71.

        Provides an analysis of the Orpheus myth and
        cites similarities between Orpheus and Monteverdi.

494.   Fischer, Kurt von. "Eine wenig beachtete Quelle z
        Busenellos L'incoronazione di Poppea." Congress
        internazionale sul tema Claudio Monteverdi (item
        811), pp. 75-80.

        Contends convincingly that the Roman tragedy
        Octavia, generally ascribed to Seneca, provided th
        paradigm for Busenello's libretto L'incoronazione
        di Poppea. Points out numerous parallels between

Octavia and Busenello's libretto. Demonstrates
that Octavia contributed to other forms of theater
during this period such as the German school drama.

495.   ————. "Petit essai sur les opéras de Monteverdi." Anuario musical 37 (1982): 15-24.

Inspired by the Ponelle-Harnoncourt productions
of the operas at Zurich, Fischer reflects on the
importance of Orfeo, Il ritorno d'Ulisse, and
L'incoronazione di Poppea.

496.   ————. "Versuch einer Interpretation von
Monteverdis Opern." Neue Zürcher Zeitschrift
123-24 (May 1977): 2.

Not examined. Summary in RILM Abstracts, 11/2
(May-August 1977): 164, notes that the article is
concerned with the affects in Il ritorno d'Ulisse
and L'incoronazione di Poppea.

497.   Fleuret, Maurice. "L'Orfeo et son temps."
L'Orfeo (item 816), pp. 4-7.

Summarizes the new musical styles of the early
seventeenth century and recognizes Monteverdi's
genius for the new genre of opera.

498.   Forneberg, Erich. "Die Klage der Ariadne.
Zwischen Monteverdi und Orff." Musica 6 (1952):
447-50.

Traces musical settings of the Ariadne legend
from Monteverdi's Arianna (1608) to the twentieth
century. Lauds Carl Orff's edition (1940) of the
Lamento d'Arianna.

499.   Fortune, Nigel. "Correspondence." Music
Review 15 (1954): 88.

Asserts, in a letter to the editor, that the
Florentine Giovanni Gualberto Magli did not sing
the title role in Monteverdi's Orfeo in 1607 and
speculates that the part was sung by Francesco
Rasi.

*   ————. "The Rediscovery of 'Orfeo.'"

Cited below as item 716.

500. Freeman, David. "Telling the Story." Claudio
      Monteverdi: Orfeo (item 588), pp. 156-66.

      Freeman's article describes his rather unorthodo
      approach to staging Orfeo.

501. Gallico, Claudio. "I due pianti di Arianna di
      Claudio Monteverdi." Chigiana: rassegna annuale
      di studia musicologica, vol. 24. Florence:
      Olschki, 1967, pp. 29-42.

      A parallel analysis of Monteverdi's madrigal
      Lasciatemi morire and the monody from which it was
      derived, Lamento d'Arianna. Shows that the sono-
      rous development of the madrigal is continually
      determined by the monody. Speculates that the
      motivation behind the famous Lamento d'Arianna may
      have been the death of Monteverdi's wife just
      before the composition of Arianna.

502. ————. "In modo dorico." Venezia e il melodramm
      nel seicento. Studi di musica veneta 5, edited
      by Maria Teresa Muraro. Florence: Olschki, 197(
      pp. 41-50.

      Recognizes Platonism in Striggio's libretto to
      Monteverdi's Orfeo and notes that the descending
      tetrachord figure found in Monteverdi's musical
      score is reminiscent of Greek musical grammar.

*   George, Graham. "The Structure of Dramatic Music
      1607-1909."

      Cited above as item 83.

503. Ghisi, Federico. "L'orchestra in Monteverdi."
      Festschrift Karl Gustav Fellerer zum sechzigste
      Geburtstag am 7. Juli 1962 überreicht von
      Freunden und Schülern, edited by Heinrich
      Hüschen. Regensburg: G. Bosse, 1962, pp. 187-9.
      ML55 F35 H8

      Documents the use of instruments in the interme
      from 1487 to Monteverdi's Orfeo. Asserts that th
      use of instruments alone and in ensembles was a
      Renaissance practice. Maintains that the Floren-
      tine practice of combining instruments and voices
      together was not really a new practice; it had
      numerous precedents.

504.   Gianuario, Annibale. Orfeo di Claudio Monteverdi.
       Exempla di semeiografia ed armonia nell'edizione
       del 1609. Florence: Edizioni OTOS, 1972. 26, 11
       pp. ML410 M7 G53

       Investigates Monteverdi's musical expression of
       the text in Orfeo and discusses Vito Frazzi's
       recent solutions to basso continuo problems in this
       score. Includes musical examples realized by
       Frazzi. Contains notes, but no bibliography.

505.   Glover, Jane. "The Venetian Operas." The New
       Monteverdi Companion (item 780), pp. 288-315.

       Points out that Monteverdi's operas Il ritorno
       d'Ulisse and L'incoronazione di Poppea differ from
       his first opera, Orfeo, in dramatic format, subject
       matter, musical language, and orchestral forces
       required. Stresses that public performances trans-
       formed opera and that Monteverdi's two Venetian
       operas set standards and precedents for later
       Venetian opera. Includes a description of the
       dramatic action and most significant musical
       portions of Ulisse and Poppea.

506.   Godt, Irving. "A Monteverdi Source Reappears: The
       'Grilanda' of F.M. Fucci." Music and Letters 60
       (1979): 428-39.

       Describes a little-known manuscript of early
       seventeenth-century monody, the Grilanda of F.M.
       Fucci. The collection, which contains over fifty
       songs and arias, is presumably one of the earliest
       sources for Monteverdi's Lamento d'Arianna. Also
       included is a Lamento d'Erminia which, although
       attributed to Monteverdi by Fausto Torrefranca in
       1944, is probably spurious. A complete transcrip-
       tion of the Lamento d'Erminia is provided at the
       end of the article.

507.   Goldschmidt, Hugo. "Claudio Monteverdi's Oper: Il
       ritorno d'Ulisse in patria." Sammelbände der
       Internationalen Musik-Gesellschaft 9 (1907-1908):
       570-92.

       Goldschmidt's second major article on Il ritorno
       d'Ulisse provides an authoritative, thorough
       examination of the opera. Offers the opinion that
       Monteverdi was the outstanding opera composer of
       his time. Also notes that Monteverdi attained an

unprecedented mastery of form and technique with
this opera. See Goldschmidt, item 508.

508. ———. "Monteverdi's Ritorno d'Ulisse." Sammel
      bände der Internationalen Musik-Gesellschaft 4
      (1902-1903): 671-76.

      Asserts the authenticity of the Viennese manu-
      script (Vienna State Library, No. 18763) of Il
      ritorno d'Ulisse.

*   Grout, Donald Jay. A Short History of Opera.

      Cited above as item 90.

509. Haas, Robert. "Zur Neuausgabe von Claudio Monte-
      verdis 'Il Ritorno d'Ulisse in Patria.'" Studi
      zur Musikwissenschaft 9 (1922): 3-42.

      Reports on the first edition, based upon the
      only surviving score of the opera located in the
      Vienna Nationalbibliothek, of Il ritorno d'Ulisse
      prepared by Haas for the Denkmäler der Tonkunst
      Österreich (vol. 29, 1922). Reprints the librett
      of the opera by Giacomo Badoaro in its entirety.

510. Harnoncourt, Nikolaus. "Orfeo tussen Renaissanc
      en Barok." Opera journaal 4 (1973-74): 5. In
      Dutch.

      A very succinct article dealing with Monteverd
      first opera. Considers the work's significance
      the early Baroque period.

511. Hawkins, Sir John. A General History of the
      Science and Practice of Music. London, 1776;
      Novello, 1853; reprint ed. in 2 vols. with an
      introduction by Charles Cudworth. New York:
      Dover, 1963. 963 pp.

      Credits Monteverdi as being the father of the
      theatric style. Describes the composer's use of
      instruments and recitative in Orfeo. Identifies
      Monteverdi as an important composer of madrigals
      and motets. Gives three musical examples from t
      fifth act of Orfeo.

512. Hell, Helmut. "Zu Rhythmus und Notierung des 'V
      ricorda' in Claudio Monteverdis Orfeo." Anale
      musicologica 15 (1975): 87-157.

Offers an extensive, well-researched explanation
based on modern scholarship of the rhythm and
notation problems found in Vi ricorda from the
second act of Orfeo.

513. Heuss, Alfred. "Die Instrumental-Stücke des
      'Orfeo.'" Sammelbände der Internationalen Musik-
      Gesellschaft 4 (1902-1903): 175-224.

      An early, yet thorough examination of the instru-
      mental music of Orfeo. Includes a discussion of
      instrumental music in Italy prior to the advent of
      monody. Also contains a discussion of the Scherzi
      musicali. This article was extracted from the
      author's dissertation completed at the University
      of Leipzig in 1903. See also Heuss, item 97.

514. Hirsch, Hans Ludwig. "Claudio Monteverdis 'Lamento
      d'Arianna': Genesis und Strukturanalyse." Oper
      heute: Ein Almanach der Musikbühne (1978): 9-47.

      Offers a thoughtful analysis of the celebrated
      Lamento d'Arianna. Focuses on the relationship
      between text and music.

515. Kerman, Joseph. "Majesty Restored." Opera News 31
      (November 5, 1966): 8, 10, 12.

      Examines the underlying dramatic ideas of Monte-
      verdi's L'incoronazione di Poppea and discusses
      problems encountered in modern performances of this
      work.

516. ————. Opera as Drama. New York, Alfred A.
      Knopf, 1952; reprint ed., Westport: Greenwood
      Press, 1981. 269 pp. ISBN 0 313 22718 7 ML3854
      K4 1981

      A study of opera from its beginnings through
      Alban Berg's Wozzeck. Describes how drama is
      articulated in opera through music. Chapter 1,
      "Orpheus: the Neoclassic Vision," provides a
      splendid introduction to Monteverdi's Orfeo. A
      portion of the chapter is reprinted in item 517.

517. ————. "Orpheus: The Neoclassic Vision." Claudio
      Monteverdi: Orfeo (item 588), pp. 126-32.

      Reprinted with minor revision from Kerman's book
      Opera as Drama (item 516). Omits the section on
      Gluck's Orfeo ed Euridice found in the original.

*   Kloiber, Rudolf. Handbuch der Oper.
       Cited above as item 101.

518.   Krenek, Ernst. "Zur dramaturgischen Bearbeitung
       von Monteverdis 'Poppea.'" Eine Wiener Musik-
       zeitschrift 31-33 (1937): 22-30.

       Examines Busenello's libretto for Monte-
       verdi's L'incoronazione di Poppea. See Krenek,
       items 805 and 806.

519.   Kretzschmar, Hermann. "Monteverdis 'Incoronazion
       di Poppea.'" Vierteljahrsschrift für Musik-
       wissenschaft 10 (1894): 483-530.

       A major, early monograph offering a perceptive
       view of the importance and historical significanc
       of Monteverdi's last opera. Offers the opinion
       that L'incoronazione di Poppea ranks as the most
       significant opera of the seventeenth century.

520.   Laloy, Louis. "La musique. Un précurseur du dra
       lyrique: Claudio Monteverdi." La revue de Pari
       28 (1921): 653-64.

       Summarizes Monteverdi's biography and provides
       overview of his dramatic works. Touches upon the
       Artusi-Monteverdi controversy and the revival of
       Monteverdi's works in the twentieth century.

521.   Leichtentritt, Hugo. "On the Prologue in Early
       Opera." Proceedings of the Music Teachers'
       National Association 31 (1936): 292-99.

       Compares the prologues of Monteverdi's Orfeo, I
       ritorno d'Ulissse, and L'incoronazione di Poppea.
       Considers these prologues from both musical and
       dramatic points of view.

522.   Leopold, Silke. "Lyra Orphei." Claudio
       Monteverdi: Festschrift Reinhold Hammerstein
       (item 794), pp. 337-45.

       Discusses the problems of performance practice
       related to the instrumentation and instrumental
       pieces in Monteverdi's first opera.

523. Luhring, Alan A. "Monteverdi's <u>Orfeo</u>, Atto Quinto:
      Some Observations Prior to Performance."
      <u>Musicology at the University of Colorado</u>, edited
      by William Kearns. Boulder: University of
      Colorado, 1977, pp. 57-79.

      Presents a helpful analysis of the last act of
      <u>Orfeo</u> based on a study of the libretto and music.

*   McClary, Susan Kaye. "The Transition from Modal to
      Tonal Organization in the Works of Monteverdi."

      Cited above as item 383.

524. McGee, Timothy J. "<u>Orfeo</u> and <u>Euridice</u>, the First
      Two Operas." <u>Orpheus: the Metamorphoses of a</u>
      <u>Myth</u>, edited by John Warden. Toronto: University
      of Toronto Press, 1982, pp. 163-81. ISBN 0 802
      05518 4 BL820.07 O76 1982

      Points out the similarities between Peri's
      <u>Euridice</u> and Monteverdi's <u>Orfeo</u>. Very briefly
      discusses Caccini's <u>Euridice</u>. Concludes that
      Monteverdi's first opera was clearly modeled upon
      Peri's opera.

525. Mâche, François-Bernard. "Méthodes linguistiques
      et musicologie." <u>Musique en Jeu</u> 5 (1971): 79-81.

      Contains an analysis of the overture to the last
      act of <u>L'incoronazione di Poppea</u>.

526. Mahling, Christoph-Hellmut. "Zum Verhältnis von
      'Klangraum' und dramatischer Gestaltung in
      Claudio Monteverdis 'L'Orfeo' (1607) und
      'L'Incoronazione di Poppea' (1642)." <u>Claudio</u>
      <u>Monteverdi: Festschrift Reinhold Hammerstein</u>
      (item 794), pp. 347-58.

      Considers the importance of timbre and tonality
      in the dramatic structure of Monteverdi's first and
      last operas.

527. Michels, Ulrich. "Das 'Lamento d'Arianna' von
      Claudio Monteverdi." <u>Festschrift für Hans</u>
      <u>Heinrich Eggebrecht zum 65. Geburtstag</u>, edited by
      Werner Breig, Reinhold Brinkmann, and Elmar
      Budde. Stuttgart: Franz Steiner, 1984, pp.
      91-109. ISBN 3 515 03662 8 ML5 A63

An excellent examination of the well-known
Lamento d'Arianna. Includes a discussion of its
origins, the libretto, the music, and the differe
settings of the work. Reproduces for comparison
the texts of the Lamento and the Latin contrafact
based upon the Lamento, the Pianto della Madonna.

528.   Monterosso, Raffaello. "Claudio Monteverdi: la
        nouvelle musique." L'Orfeo (item 816), pp. 15-
        19.

        Takes into account the composer's historical an
        geographical background in evaluating the signif-
        icance of Monteverdi's contribution to music.

529.   Monterosso-Vacchelli, Anna Maria. "Elementi
        stilistici nell'Euridice di Jacopo Peri in
        rapporto all'Orfeo di Monteverdi." Congresso
        internazionale sul tema Claudio Monteverdi (ite
        811), pp. 117-27.

        Defends Peri's Euridice against scholars'
        criticism that this work is an act of intellec-
        tualism, devoid of variety. Compares Euridice to
        Monteverdi's Orfeo and concludes that the two wor
        have analogous passages.

*   Moses, Gavriel Josef. "Literary Genre in
        Monteverdi."

        Cited above as item 388.

530.   Müller, Karl F. "Die Technik der Ausdrucks-
        darstellung in Monteverdis monodischen
        Frühwerken." Ph.D. dissertation, University of
        Berlin, 1931.

531.   Müller, Reinhard. "Basso ostinato und die 'imita
        tione del parlare' in Monteverdis Incoronazione
        di Poppea." Archiv für Musikwissenschaft 40
        (1983): 1-23.

        Thoroughly examines the relationship between te
        and music in the opera. Recognizes the exchange
        vocal and instrumental idioms and the importance
        the basso ostinato technique. Concludes that the
        development of the imitatione del parlare
        (parlante) was a prerequisite for the musical and
        dramatic style of Poppea.

532. ————. "Dramatischer Gesang und Instrumentalsatz
bei Claudio Monteverdi." Ph.D. dissertation,
University of Munich, 1978. 243 pp. ML410 M77
M83

Stresses the relationship between words and
music. Contends that the recitative style provides
the foundation of Monteverdi's early operatic
style. Includes footnotes, musical examples, and a
list of works cited. See below, item 533.

533. ————. Der stile recitativo in Claudio Monteverdis Orfeo. Tutzing: Hans Schneider, 1984.
126 pp. ISBN 3 795 20414 3 MT100 M72 M8 1984

Issued as volume 38 in the Münchner Veröffent-
lichungen zur Musikgeschichte, this work is a
revised and expanded version of the first part of
the author's doctoral dissertation (item 532)
presented to the University of Munich in 1978. The
discussion of the music emphasizes Monteverdi's
treatment of the text. Includes explanatory
footnotes, a useful bibliography, and a name and
subject index.

534. Murzilli, Vincenzo. Von Claudio Monteverdi bis
Richard Strauss. Die Opernarie im Laufe der
Jahrhunderte. Halle: Niemeyer Verlag, 1955. 103
pp. ML128 V7 M88

Discusses sixty opera arias composed by forty-
three composers. Numerous musical examples; no
bibliography.

535. Němcová, Alena. "Monteverdiho Lamento d'Arianna a
jeho interpretace." Sborník Janáčkovy akademie
múzickych umĕni 6 (1972): 125-45. In Czech.

Not examined. Summary in RILM Abstracts, 6/2
(May-August 1972): 177, indicates that the article
examines the Lamento d'Arianna in light of contemporary aesthetic principles.

536. Osthoff, Wolfgang. Das dramatische Spätwerk
Claudio Monteverdis. Tutzing: Hans Schneider,
1960. 267 pp. ML410 M77 O8

Originally presented as a doctoral dissertation
to the University of Heidelberg in 1954. Focuses
on a detailed discussion of L'incoronazione di
Poppea and Il ritorno d'Ulisse. Examines some of

the principal elements of structure, including
ostinato technique, walking bass lines, and the u
of purely instrumental pieces. Considers Il combattimento di Tancredi e Clorinda and the Scherzi
musicali of 1632 as forerunners of Monteverdi's
late operatic style. Bibliography, name and
subject index, and extensive footnotes.

537. ———. "Neue Beobachtungen zu Quellen und
     Geschichte von Monteverdis 'Incoronazione di
     Poppea.'" Die Musikforschung 11 (1958): 129-38

     Compares the Venetian and Neapolitan manuscript
     of L'incoronazione di Poppea. Represents an upda
     of an earlier article by Osthoff in Acta musico-
     logica, item 538.

538. ———. "Die venezianische und neapolitanische
     Fassung von Monteverdis 'Incoronazione di
     Poppea.'" Acta musicologica 26 (1954): 88-113.

     An authoritative investigation comparing the
     Venetian manuscript and the Neapolitan manuscript
     (first discovered in 1930) of L'incoronazione di
     Poppea. Focuses on a detailed examination of the
     differences in the two manuscripts. Observes tha
     any effort toward an authentic edition of the ope
     must consider both manuscripts. See also Redlich
     item 559.

539. ———. "Zu den Quellen von Monteverdis 'Ritorno
     di Ulisse in Patria.'" Studien zur Musikwissen
     schaft 23 (1956): 67-78.

     Concerned with the problems of authenticity
     surrounding the Viennese manuscript of the work.
     Compares and contrasts the seven Venetian manu-
     scripts of the libretto. Concludes that the
     connection between the Viennese manuscript and th
     1641 Venetian performance of the opera is valid.
     See Haas, item 509.

540. ———. "Zur Bologneser Aufführung von Monteverd
     'Ritorno di Ulisse' im Jahre 1640." Öster-
     reichische Akademie der Wissenschaften: Anzeige
     der phil.-hist. Klasse 95 (1958): 155-60.

     Establishes 1640 as the correct date of compo-
     sition for Il ritorno d'Ulisse. Blames the Itali
     writer Gaetano Giordani for much of the confusion

and misinformation surrounding the origin of the opera. Reports on Bologna performances of Monteverdi's Ulisse and Francesco Manelli's La Delia.

*   Palisca, Claude V. Baroque Music.

      Cited above as item 126.

541.   Pannain, Guido. "Claudio Monteverdi nell'opera in musica." Musica II (item 813), pp. 35-50.

      Portrays early opera as an ideology of sung words. Examines Monteverdi's Orfeo, Il ritorno d'Ulisse, and L'incoronazione di Poppea and illustrates how Monteverdi's music delineates the characters in these operas. Discusses the authenticity of Il ritorno d'Ulisse, which the author accepts as a work of Monteverdi.

542.   ————. Da Monteverdi a Wagner. Pagine di storia della musica. Milan: Ricordi, 1955. 192 pp. ML160 P17

      A short history of music containing two chapters dealing with Monteverdi. "Atto di nascita dell'arte monteverdiana" emphasizes the importance of Monteverdi's awareness of the close relationship of music and language. Agrees with Redlich that the composer had one style rather than two dissociated ones. In "Le opere di Claudio Monteverdi," Orfeo, Il ritorno d'Ulisse, and Poppea are discussed. Notes the question of the authenticity of Il ritorno, but considers the opera a work of Monteverdi.

543.   ————. "Studi monteverdiani IV." Rassegna musicale 28 (1958): 281-92.

      Compares Monteverdi's Orfeo to Jacopo Peri's Euridice. Discusses recitative in Orfeo and criticizes Anna Amalie Abert's analysis of the opera.

544.   ————. "Studi monteverdiani V." Rassegna musicale 29 (1959): 42-50.

      Continues the author's discussion of Monteverdi's Orfeo from his "Studi monteverdiani IV" (item 543). Stresses the regular symmetry in Orfeo between the

sentiments of the tonality and the words. Draws
from Karl F. Müller's study of Monteverdi's monody
(item 530) and demonstrates that words, melody, an
harmonic structure constitute an organic unity in
Monteverdi's monody.

545. ———. "Studi monteverdiani VI." Rassegna
      musicale 29 (1959): 95-105.

Compares Orfeo's lament in operas of Peri,
Caccini, and Monteverdi based on the Orfeo tragedy
Considers Monteverdi's use of harmony and melody
and comments on Karl F. Müller's analytical study
"Die Technik der Ausdrucksdarstellung in
Monteverdis monodischen Frühwerken" (item 530).

546. ———. "Studi monteverdiani VII." Rassegna
      musicale 29 (1959): 234-46.

Investigates Monteverdi's use of choruses and
instrumental pieces in Orfeo. Considers that the
instrumental pieces in Orfeo serve the same
function as the choruses. Draws on the conclusion
of Anna Amalie Abert (item 438) in the discussion
of the function and structure of choruses and cite
Alfred Heuss (item 513) concerning the instrumenta
pieces in Orfeo.

547. ———. "Studi monteverdiani VIII." Rassegna
      musicale 29 (1959): 301-20.

Discusses Monteverdi's views on imitation in
music, quoting from his letters of December 9,
1616, and October 22, 1633. Defends Monteverdi's
lament from Arianna against the criticism given by
Ambros in his Geschichte der Musik, item 291.

548. Pierce, Terry. "Monteverdi's Use of Brass
      Instruments." Journal of the International
      Trombone Association 9 (1981): 4-8.

Notes Monteverdi's employment of brass instru-
ments with emphasis on his Venetian period.
Asserts that brass instruments predominated in
Venice when Monteverdi was first employed there.
Makes suggestions for the use of brass instruments
in Orfeo, where no indications exist in
Monteverdi's score.

549.   Pirrotta, Nino. "Early Venetian Libretti at Los
       Angeles." Essays in Musicology in Honor of
       Dragan Plamenac on his 70th Birthday, edited by
       Gustave Reese and Robert Snow. Pittsburgh:
       University of Pittsburgh Press, 1969; reprint
       ed., New York: Da Capo, 1977, pp. 233-43. ISBN 0
       306 77408 9 ML3797.1 R44 1977

       Describes the contents of the first four volumes
       of an extensive collection of Venetian opera
       librettos at UCLA. Among those discussed are
       Monteverdi's Il ritorno d'Ulisse and Arianna.
       Discusses the significance of printing librettos
       after the premiere performance.

550.   ————. "Early Venetian Libretti at Los Angeles."
       Music and Culture in Italy from the Middle Ages
       to the Baroque. Studies in the History of Music,
       vol. 1, edited by Lewis Lockwood and Christoph
       Wolff. Cambridge: Harvard University Press,
       1984, pp. 317-24. ISBN 0 674 59108 9 ML290.1
       P57 1984

       Reprinted from Essays in Musicology in Honor of
       Dragan Plamenac (item 549).

551.   ————. "Monteverdi and the Problems of Opera."
       Music and Culture in Italy from the Middle Ages
       to the Baroque. Studies in the History of Music,
       vol. 1, edited by Lewis Lockwood and Christoph
       Wolff. Cambridge: Harvard University Press,
       1984, pp. 235-53. ISBN 0 674 59108 9 ML290.1
       P57 1984

       An English translation by Harris Saunders of
       Pirrotta's article "Monteverdi e i problemi
       dell'opera" (item 552).

552.   ————. "Monteverdi e i problemi dell'opera."
       Studi sul teatro veneto fra rinascimento ed età
       barocca, edited by Maria Teresa Muraro.
       Florence: Olschki, 1971, pp. 321-43.

       Considers influences on Monteverdi's major
       dramatic works. Includes a detailed comparison of
       Monteverdi's Orfeo and Peri's Euridice. Contends
       that Peri's work had a strong impact on Monte-
       verdi's first opera. Cites lesser-known works for
       their influence on other Monteverdi operas. An

English translation of this article appeared as
"Monteverdi and the Problems of Opera" (item 551).

553.   ————. "Teatro, scene e musica nelle opere di
Monteverdi." Congresso internazionale sul tema
Claudio Monteverdi (item 811), pp. 45-67.

This study of first performances of Monteverdi's
operas is concerned with the particular theaters or
halls in which these works were produced and with
their manner of presentation. Describes the San
Giovanni e Paolo, which the author believes was the
place of the premiere of Il ritorno d'Ulisse. Includes a drawing of the layout of the San Giovanni
made in the seventeenth century by Tommaso Bezzi.
This article appeared in an English translation as
"Theater, Sets and Music in Monteverdi's Operas"
(item 554).

554.   ————. "Theater, Sets and Music in Monteverdi's
Operas." Music and Culture in Italy from the
Middle Ages to the Baroque. Studies in the
History of Music, vol. 1, edited by Lewis
Lockwood and Christoph Wolff. Cambridge: Harvard
University Press, 1984, pp. 254-70. ISBN 0 674
59108 9   ML290.1 P57 1984

An English translation by David Morgenstern of
Pirrotta's "Teatro, scene e musica nelle opere di
Monteverdi" (item 553).

555.   Prunières, Henry. "Monteverdi's Venetian Operas."
Musical Quarterly 10 (1924): 178-92.

Acknowledges the influence of Roman opera on the
seventeenth-century Venetian style and, at the same
time, recognizes that Monteverdi's Venetian operas
represent a fusion of his earlier operatic style
and the Roman style. Compares Monteverdi's late
operas with operas by Luigi Rossi and Francesco
Cavalli. Discusses both Il ritorno d'Ulisse and
L'incoronazione di Poppea in some detail.

556.   ————. "L'Orfeo de Monteverdi." Revue musicale
(1923): 20-34.

Presents an examination of Monteverdi's first
opera. Summarizes the historical background
leading to Orfeo, discusses Striggio's libretto,
and examines, with the aid of several musical

examples, arias, recitatives, choruses, and instru-
mental pieces. Reprinted as a chapter in
Prunières's La vie et l'oeuvre de Claudio
Monteverdi, cited as item 329.

557. Quittard, Henri. "L'orchestre de l' 'Orfeo.'"
      Revue d'histoire et de critique musicales 7
      (1907): 380-89, 412-18.

      Written for the 300th anniversary of Orfeo, this
      is one of the earliest essays in any language
      dealing exclusively with Monteverdi's use of the
      orchestra in the opera. Refers to authorities on
      instruments from Monteverdi's own day, such as
      Agostino Agazzari and Michael Praetorius. Deals
      with instrumentation and instrumental form.
      Contends that Orfeo, due to the richness of the
      orchestration, is unique among Monteverdi's operas.

*   Racek, Jan. "Die dramatisierende Funktion der
      Pause in der italienischen Vokal- und
      dramatischen Musik des 17. Jahrhunderts."

      Cited above as item 139.

558. Rapp, Regula. "Claudio Monteverdi: Lamento
      d'Arianna." Neue Zeitschrift für Musik 144
      (November 1983): 23-25.

      Following the definition for "lament" reprinted
      from Walther's Musikalisches Lexikon (1732), Rapp
      provides a brief historical sketch of the genre.
      Includes a good basic introduction to Monteverdi's
      most famous composition.

559. Redlich, Hans F. "Notationsprobleme in Cl.
      Monteverdis 'Incoronazione di Poppea.'" Acta
      musicologica 10 (1938): 129-32.

      Compares the Venetian and Neapolitan manuscripts
      of L'incoronazione di Poppea. Investigates the
      many problems and mistakes in notation (such as the
      indication of clefs) present in the Venetian
      manuscript.

560. ————. "'L'Orfeo' von Claudio Monteverdi." Neue
      Zeitschrift für Musik 118 (July-August 1957):
      411-14.

Cites the importance of the Orpheus myth to
opera. Presents a rather general discussion of
Monteverdi's setting of the myth. Concludes with
comments regarding twentieth-century revivals of
Monteverdi's opera.

561. ————. "Zu Monteverdis letzter Oper." Anbruch 19
      (1937): 108-10.

      Points to the stylistic transformation that
      occurred during the thirty-five year span from
      Orfeo to L'incoronazione di Poppea. Considers
      Monteverdi's last opera the "creative high point"
      of his career.

562. Reiner, Stuart. "Preparations in Parma--1618,
      1627-28." Music Review 25 (1964): 273-301.

      Based upon letters contained in the State Archive
      in Ferrara, this notable article is concerned with
      the music planned for the festivities accompanying
      the wedding of Duke Odoardo II, Farnese of Parma.
      Monteverdi was commissioned to compose dramatic
      music for this important occasion by the Ferrarese
      marchese Enzo Bentivoglio. Reiner concludes that
      Monteverdi and the Ferrarese composer Antonio
      Goretti were both involved in preparations for the
      wedding at Parma.

563. Ringger, Kurt. "Monteverdis Libretti und die
      Anfänge der italienischen Tragödie." Arcadia 13
      (1978): 146-60.

      Considers the momentous role that Monteverdi's
      librettists (Striggio, Badoaro, and Busenello)
      played in the development of early opera.

*   Robinson, Michael F. Opera before Mozart.

      Cited above as item 141.

564. Rogers, Nigel. "'Orfeo' aus der Sicht des Inter-
      preten." Concerto 1 (1983): 43-44.

      Written from the viewpoint of a performer's
      personal involvement with Orfeo.

565. Rolland, Romain. "L'opéra au xvii siècle en
      Italie." Encyclopédie de la musique et
      dictionnaire du conservatoire, edited by Albert
      Lavignac. Paris: Delagrave, 1913-31. Vol. 2.
      1913.

      The third chapter (pp. 695-707) of Rolland's
      extensive essay presents a survey of Monteverdi's
      operas.

566. Rosand, Ellen. "Seneca and the Interpretation of
      L'Incoronazione di Poppea." Journal of the
      American Musicological Society 38 (1985): 34-71.

      Contends that Seneca, not Poppea or Nerone, is
      the principal character of Busenello's libretto.
      Acknowledges Busenello's debt to the Roman play
      Octavia, generally ascribed to Seneca. Thoroughly
      discusses Monteverdi's music for the character of
      Seneca.

567. Rosenthal, Albi. "Monteverdi's 'Andromeda': A Lost
      Libretto Found." Music and Letters 66 (1985):
      1-8.

      Identifies for the first time an extant copy of
      the libretto by Ercole Marigliani to Monteverdi's
      lost opera.

568. Sąsiadek, Eugeniusz. "Partia tytułowa opery
      Orfeusz Claudio Monteverdiego." Zeszyty naukowe.
      Państwowa wyższa szkola muzyczna we Wrocławiu 1
      (1970): 43-68. In Polish.

      Not examined. Summary in RILM Abstracts, 6/2
      (May-August 1972): 129, states that the article
      focuses on the title role in Monteverdi's first
      opera.

569. Savage, Edward B. "Love and Infamy: The Paradox of
      Monteverdi's L'Incoronazione di Poppea." Compar-
      ative Drama 4 (1970): 197-207.

      Argues that Monteverdi, in his characterization
      of Nero and Poppea, maintains with historical
      accuracy the infamous quality of the two lovers.
      Contends that this infamous nature is achieved
      through the use of dramatic irony and the leit-
      motiv, techniques also common to Wagner's Tristan
      und Isolde.

570. Schenkman, Walter. "A Singing Emperor Nero
      Prepares His Part for Poppea." Opera Journal 11
      (1978): 11-24.

      Supported by the writings of the Roman historians
      Tacitus and Suetonius, the author provides a
      tongue-in-cheek comparison of the historical Nero
      with the operatic one.

571. Schrade, Leo. "Monteverdi's Il Ritorno d'Ulisse."
      Musical Quarterly 36 (1950): 422-35.

      After a brief discussion of early seventeenth-
      century opera in Venice, Schrade presents a
      thorough examination and analysis of Il ritorno
      d'Ulisse. Emphasizes Monteverdi's use of such
      musical techniques as stile concertato, stile
      recitativo, and stile concitato. Contends that
      Monteverdi transferred the dramatic madrigal style
      to his operas. This article was extracted from
      Schrade's Monteverdi: Creator of Modern Music, item
      341.

*   Seidel, Wilhelm. "Die Rückkehr des Orpheus zur
      Musik. Die Wirkungen der Musik in Monteverdis
      erster Oper."

      Cited above as item 161.

572. Sirch, Licia. "'Violini piccoli alla francese' e
      'canto alla francese' nell'Orfeo (1607) e negli
      'Scherzi musicali' (1607) di Monteverdi." Nuova
      rivista musicale italiana 15 (1981): 50-65.

      Reviews the literature concerning the designation
      violini piccoli alla francese in the works of
      Monteverdi. Expresses the view that the designa-
      tion canto alla francese refers to a style of
      violin playing which originated in France and was
      described by Muffat in the preface to his
      Florilegium secundum (1698).

*   Smith, Patrick J. The Tenth Muse: A Historical
      Study of the Opera Libretto.

      Cited above as item 163.

*   Solerti, Angelo. Gli albori del melodramma.

      Cited above as item 164.

573.   Sternfeld, Frederick W.   "The Orpheus Myth and the
       Libretto of 'Orfeo.'"   Claudio Monteverdi: Orfeo
       (Item 588), pp. 20-33.

       Interprets the significance of the Orpheus myth
       to early opera. Compares the librettos based upon
       the classical tragedy by Rinuccini and Striggio.

*   Stevens, Denis. Monteverdi: Sacred, Secular, and
       Occasional Music.

       Cited above as item 423.

*   Strainchamps, Edmond.   "The Life and Death of
       Caterina Martinelli: New Light on Monteverdi's
       'Arianna.'"

       Cited above as item 172.

574.   Stuart, Robert Louis.   "Busenello's Libretto to
       Monteverde's 'L'Incoronazione di Poppea': Its
       Place in the History of the Drama and the Opera."
       Musical Times 68 (1927): 891-93.

       Places Busenello's libretto to Poppea in line
       with the dramatic style of Shakespearean drama and
       considers it to be the true ancestor of grand
       opera. Shakespearean traits cited in Busenello's
       libretto are characterization, rapid succession of
       scenes, gradual evolution of plot at the beginning,
       and swiftness of the dénouement. Compares Buse-
       nello's characterization to that in Mozart's Le
       nozze di Figaro.

575.   ————.   "Busenello's 'L'Incoronazione di Poppea.'"
       Musical Opinion 51 (1928): 379-80.

       A brief discussion of characterization in
       Monteverdi's L'incoronazione di Poppea, together
       with a sampling of scholarly thought about the
       opera.

576.   Szweykowska, A.   "Le due poetiche venete e le
       ultime opere di Claudio Monteverdi." Quadrivium
       20 (1977): 149-57.

*   Tarr, Edward H.   "Monteverdi, Bach und die
       Trompetenmusik ihrer Zeit."

       Cited below as item 700.

577. Tegen, Martin. "Monteverdi." _Musikrevy_ 15 (1960):
      84-91. In Swedish.

      Provides a concise overview of Monteverdi's
      madrigals, operas, and church music. The major
      portion of this article is concerned with _Orfeo_.

*   Testi, Flavio. _La musica italiana nel seicento._
      Il melodramma.

      Cited above as item 178.

578. Tiby, Ottavio. _L'incoronazione di Poppea di_
      Claudio Monteverdi e Gian Francesco Busenello.
      Florence: A. Vallecchi, 1937. 27 pp.

579. Tomlinson, Gary A. "Madrigal, Monody, and
      Monteverdi's 'via naturale alla immitatione.'"
      Journal of the American Musicological Society 34
      (1981): 60-108.

      A trenchant article pertaining to Monteverdi's
      setting of text to music. Acknowledges the debt of
      Monteverdi's and Striggio's _Orfeo_ to Peri's and
      Rinuccini's _Euridice_. Recognizes the influence of
      the polyphonic madrigal upon the composer's recita-
      tive style. _Arianna_, composed in collaboration
      with the librettist Rinuccini, is cited as the
      apogee of Monteverdi's union of music and text.
      Portions of the article were adapted from the
      author's Ph.D. dissertation, item 253.

*   ————. "Rinuccini, Peri, Monteverdi, and the
      Humanist Heritage of Opera."

      Cited above as item 253.

*   Towneley, Simon. "Early Italian Opera."

      Cited above as item 179.

580. Vetter, Walther. "Zur Stilproblematik der
      italienischen Oper des 17. und 18. Jahrhunderts."
      Festschrift für Erich Schenk, preface by Othmar
      Wessely. Graz: Hermann Böhlaus, 1962, pp. 561-
      73. ML55 S324

      Includes a discussion of Monteverdi's _Lamento_
      d'Arianna.

*   Waeltner, Ernst Ludwig. "Monteverdi und die
        Entstehung der Oper."

        Cited above as item 181.

581.   Westrup, Jack A. "Monteverdi's 'Lamento
        d'Arianna.'" Music Review 1 (1940): 144-54.

        Includes a discussion of Monteverdi's lost opera
        Arianna (1608), as well as a detailed examination
        of the only surviving portion of the opera, the
        lament. After commenting on various editions of
        the lament and Monteverdi's own arrangements,
        Westrup compares four different manuscript sources
        containing the lament, noting various musical
        discrepancies.

582.   ————. "Monteverde's 'Orfeo.'" Musical Times
        66 (1925): 1096-1100.

        An early article praising Orfeo. After a brief
        discussion and criticism of editions available at
        the time, Orfeo is examined.

583.   ————. "Monteverdi and the Orchestra." Music and
        Letters 21 (1940): 230-45.

        Discusses Monteverdi's use of instruments in
        Orfeo, with special emphasis on the opening
        Toccata. Also focuses on instrumental use in Il
        combattimento di Tancredi e Clorinda. Notes schol-
        arly opinion about Monteverdi's use of instruments
        and compares the composer's instrumental practice
        with that of his contemporaries.

584.   ————. "Monteverde's 'Poppea.'" Musical Times
        68 (1927): 982-87.

        Discusses important features of Monteverdi's
        Poppea in this narrative description. Comments on
        the editorial procedures used by Hugo Goldschmidt
        in his early edition of Poppea.

585.   ————. "The Originality of Monteverde."
        Proceedings of the Musical Association 60
        (1933/34): 1-25.

        After a comparison of Monteverdi with prede-
        cessors such as Peri and Caccini, Westrup focuses
        upon Il ritorno d'Ulisse and L'incoronazione di
        Poppea. Suggests that Monteverdi's late style

developed through a variety of influences, including contemporary opera composers at Rome and
Venice. Concludes that Monteverdi, though not an
innovator, is one of the great composers because of
"the intrinsic musical worth of what he wrote."

586.   ————. "Stages in the History of Opera: Claudio
        Monteverde." Musical Times 70 (1929): 706-708.

An introduction to Monteverdi's first opera.
Outlines precedents for Orfeo, a work which is
often thought to represent more of a departure in
the composer's style than was actually the case.

587.   ————. "Two First Performances: Monteverdi's
        'Orfeo' and Mozart's 'Clemenza di Tito.'" Music
        and Letters 39 (1958): 327-35.

Speculates on the identity of the first performers in the premiers of Monteverdi's Orfeo and
Mozart's La clemenza di Tito. Refutes the idea
that the part of Orfeo was sung by Giovanni
Gaulberto, a name mentioned by Francesco Gonzaga in
a letter to his brother Ferdinando. Discusses
other performers contemporary with Monteverdi.

588.   Whenham, John, ed. Claudio Monteverdi: Orfeo.
        Cambridge: Cambridge University Press, 1986.   216
        pp. ISBN 0 521 24148 0 ML410 M77 C55

A collection of essays by eight eminent scholars.
Published as a volume in the Cambridge Opera Hand-
book series, the book includes new articles as well
as reprinted ones. Contains, in addition to notes,
bibliography, discography, and an index, three useful appendixes entitled: "Correspondence relating
to the early Mantuan performances," "Modern editions and performances," and "A list of Monteverdi's instrumental specifications." The essays
are cited here as items 490, 500, 517, 573, 589,
590, 686, 716, and 753.

589.   ————. "Five Acts: One Action." Claudio Monte-
        verdi: Orfeo (item 588), pp. 42-77.

Contends convincingly that Orfeo was originally
presented without a break between the acts. Concludes with a synopsis detailing stage directions
for the opera.

590. ————. "'Orfeo,' Act V: Alessandro Striggio's
     Original Ending." Claudio Monteverdi: Orfeo
     (item 588), pp. 35-41.

     Publishes Striggio's first ending to Orfeo,
     accompanied by English translation throughout.

591. Winternitz, Emanuel. Musical Autographs from
     Monteverdi to Hindemith. 2 vols. Princeton:
     Princeton University Press, 1955; reprint ed.,
     New York: Dover, 1965. 154 pp. ML96.4 W5

     This study of musical autographs includes a
     facsimile and description of the first three pages
     of the autograph to Monteverdi's L'incoronazione di
     Poppea.

592. Wolff, Christoph. "Zur Frage der Instrumentation
     und des Instrumentalen in Monteverdis Opern."
     Claudio Monteverdi: Festschrift Reinhold Hammer-
     stein (item 794), pp. 489-98.

     Points out the impact and influence of Monte-
     verdi's instrumental writing in his operas upon
     later styles and composers.

593. Wolff, Hellmuth Christian. "L'influsso di
     Monteverdi sull'opera veneziana." Rivista
     italiana di musicologia (item 838), pp. 382-86.

     Discusses the influence of Monteverdi's use of
     secco recitative, text repetition, basso ostinato,
     departure scenes, and dance rhythms on the
     development of Venetian opera. Names Antonio
     Sartorio, Marco Antonio Ziani, Cavalli, and others
     as exhibiting signs of Monteverdi's influence.
     Translated into Italian by Francesco Degrada.

*   ————. "Italian Opera from the Later Monteverdi
     to Scarlatti."

     Cited above as item 190.

*   ————. The Opera I: 17th Century.

     Cited above as item 191.

*   Worsthorne, Simon Towneley. Venetian Opera in the
     Seventeenth Century.

     Cited above as item 192.

3. Sacred Works

*   Anfuso, Nella, and Gianuario, Annibale. Le tre
        Arianne di Claudio Monteverdi.
        Cited above as item 446.

594.   Arnold, Denis. "A Background Note on Monteverdi's
        Hymn Settings." Scritti in onore di Luigi Ronga.
        Milan: Riccardo Ricciardi Editore, 1973, pp.
        33-44. ML55 R77 S43

        Investigates the basis for the musical style of
        the hymn settings in Monteverdi's Selva morale e
        spirituale collection of 1640. Ave Maris Stella,
        from the Vespers of 1610, is cited as an early
        example of Monteverdi's hymn writing, showing some
        rhythmic similarities to the composer's Scherzi
        musicali. Considers Alessandro Grandi and Fran-
        cesco Cavalli among the composers who wrote in a
        style similar to that found in the four hymns in
        the Selva morale.

595.   ————. "Beatus Vir." Music Teacher 58 (February
        1979): 18-19.

        Intended for the general reader, the succinct
        article notes various compositional methods used by
        Monteverdi in Beatus vir from the Selva morale e
        spirituale publication of 1640. Cites four impor-
        tant elements of the setting.

596.   ————. "Formal Design in Monteverdi's Church
        Music." Congresso internazionale sul tema
        Claudio Monteverdi (item 811), pp. 187-216.

        A significant monograph identifying and assessing
        the importance of various structural devices and
        patterns such as the rondo motet, instrumental
        ritornello, strophic variation, walking bass, etc.,
        in the sacred music of Monteverdi and other early
        seventeenth-century composers. Includes several
        musical examples from Monteverdi, Giovanni
        Gabrieli, Claudio Merulo, and Alessandro Grandi.

597.   ————. "Monteverdi and the Technique of
        'concertato.'" The Amor Artis Bulletin 6 (April
        1967): 7-10.

Cites the <u>concertato</u> technique as a powerful
device Monteverdi employed to achieve the contrast
inherent in the text of such poets as Guarini and
Marino. Lauds the use of <u>concertato</u> in the
composer's <u>Vespers</u> of 1610 as being a very
significant application of this principle.

598.   ————. <u>Monteverdi Church Music</u>. BBC Music
        Guides. London: British Broadcasting
        Corporation, 1982. 64 pp. ISBN 0 563 12884 4
        MT115 M7 A689

        A brief overview of Monteverdi's sacred music
        from the motets of 1582 to the <u>Selva morale</u>
        published in 1640. Footnotes, but no bibliography.
        Index of works.

*   ————. "Monteverdi the Instrumentalist."

        Cited above as item 449.

599.   ————. "The Monteverdi Vespers——A Postscript."
        <u>Musical Times</u> 104 (1963): 24-25.

        Questions whether the motets in the <u>Vespers</u> of
        1610 were intended to be performed in a motet-
        psalm-motet order. Cites a 1633 decree of the
        Patriarch of Venice, which indicates that in Venice
        at this time there were insertions of motets into
        the Mass and Offices. Leaves unresolved the
        question as to whether the Monteverdi <u>Vespers</u> were
        sung as a collection of Psalms with motets inter-
        spersed.

600.   ————. "Monteverdi's Church Music: Some Venetian
        Traits." <u>Monthly Musical Record</u> 88 (1958):
        83-91.

        Concludes that Monteverdi utilized the prevalent
        musical techniques of his generation in his church
        music. Compares Monteverdi's <u>Sonata sopra Sancta</u>
        <u>Maria</u> from the <u>Vespers</u> of 1610 with Andrea
        Gabrieli's motet <u>Judica Me</u>. Argues that the <u>Sonata</u>
        must be performed in <u>spezzato</u> style. Points out
        that Monteverdi's church music from Venice employs
        the <u>concertato</u> style more than the <u>spezzato</u> style.

601.   ————. "Notes on Two Movements of the Monteverdi
        'Vespers.'" <u>Monthly Musical Record</u> 84 (1954):
        59-66.

Argues that Monteverdi's church music tends to
follow the standard practices of his day. Compares
two movements from the Vespers of 1610, the Sonata
sopra Sancta Maria and the Duo Seraphim, with
pieces by other composers: the former with a sonata
by Crotti; the latter with settings of the same
text by Banchieri, Crotti, and Croce.

*   Bach, Hans-Elmar. "Die Stellung der Marienvesper
         im Schaffen Claudio Monteverdis--Beitrag zum
         Gedenkjahr anlässlich des 400. Geburtstages des
         Komponisten."

         Cited below as item 660.

602.   Barblan, Guglielmo. Aspetti di umanità e
         religiosità in Claudio Monteverdi. Bolzano:
         Conservatorio di musica 'C. Monteverdi,' 1943.

603.   Biella, Giuseppe. "La Messa, il Vespro e i Sacri
         concenti di Claudio Monteverdi nella stampa
         Amadino dell'anno 1610." Musica sacra (serie
         seconda) 9 (1964): 105-15.

604.   ————. "I 'Vespri dei Santi' di Claudio Monte-
         verdi." Musica sacra (serie seconda) 11 (1966):
         144-53.

         Observes that in the Selva morale e spirituale
         of 1640-41, Monteverdi published a complete musical
         service of the Vespers for most of the Feasts of
         the Saints. Includes the frontispiece and dedi-
         cation for the Selva morale, plus a commentary on
         all the parts of the Selva morale publication.

605.   Blömer, Hermann. "Studien zur Kirchenmusik Claudio
         Monteverdis." Ph.D. dissertation, University of
         Munich, 1935. 173 pp.

606.   Bonta, Stephen. "Liturgical Problems in Monte-
         verdi's Marian Vespers." Journal of the American
         Musicological Society 20 (1967): 87-106.

         Points out problems encountered by Hans Redlich,
         Leo Schrade, Denis Stevens, and others in eval-
         uating the liturgical function of Monteverdi's
         Marian Vespers. Uses Adriano Banchieri's L'Organo
         suonarino as a contemporary source for liturgical
         practice in the early seventeenth century. The
         five non-liturgical motets interpolated between the

psalms are classified as antiphon-substitutes. Concludes that Monteverdi's Marian Vespers is both a liturgical and artistic unity requiring, without deletion, performance in its initial configuration.

607.   Brindle, Reginald Smith.   "Monteverdi's G Minor Mass: An Experiment in Construction."   Musical Quarterly 54 (1968): 352-60.

Contends that new principles of construction are present in some of Monteverdi's church music outwardly employing the stile antico. An extensive analysis of the Messa a 4 voci da cappella of 1650 shows that Monteverdi, utilizing the technique of thematic transformation, derived most of his thematic and harmonic material from one basic theme. Concludes that "far from being merely an exercise in the stile antico, this mass was a tour de force in a new form of constructivism."

608.   Carter, Harry Hardin, Jr.   "A Study of the Concertato Psalm Settings in Monteverdi's Selva Morale e Spirituale."   D.M.A. dissertation, University of Illinois, 1971.   180 pp.   UM Order No. 71-21088

Concentrates upon those works in the Selva morale e spirituale depicting the ideas of the seconda pratica.

609.   Damerini, Adelmo.   "Il senso religioso nelle musiche sacre di Claudio Monteverdi." Collectanea historiae musicae IV, edited by Mario Fabbri.   Florence: Olschki, 1966, pp. 47-60.

Notes the duality of style in Monteverdi's sacred music, which the author attributes to the composer's desire to convey human expression in a variety of musical fashions. Asserts that Baroque mysticism, which dominated the era of the composer, stimulated this need for human expression in the arts. Briefly discusses Monteverdi's three masses and his Pianto della Madonna.

610.   Dangel-Hofmann, Frohmut.   "Eine bisher unbekannte Monteverdi-Quelle." Die Musikforschung 35 (1982): 251-54.

Brings to light for the first time a new source
for the four-voice a cappella Mass from the Selva
morale e spirituale.

611. Davis, Charles R. "Monteverdi's Messa a 4 voci da
      cappella (1651): An Analysis for Performance."
      D.M.A. dissertation, Indiana University, 1970.
      150 pp.

      Examines the Messa a 4 voci da cappella from the
      standpoint of motives, structure, modality, ca-
      dences, and the prima pratica style. Provides a
      practical discussion of rehearsal and performance
      problems.

612. Federhofer, Hellmut. "Die Dissonanzbehandlung in
      Monteverdis kirchenmusikalischen Werken und die
      Figurenlehre von Christoph Bernhard." Congresso
      internazionale sul tema Claudio Monteverdi (item
      811), pp. 435-78.

      Acknowledges the dualism of style present in the
      church music of Monteverdi and the recognition of
      that style by the theorist Christoph Bernhard.
      Bernhard's designation of stylus gravis and stylus
      luxurians, closely resembling the prima pratica and
      seconda pratica of Monteverdi, emphasized the re-
      lationship of words to music and the treatment of
      dissonance. Provides numerous examples.

613. Fenlon, Iain. "The Monteverdi Vespers: Suggested
      Answers to Some Fundamental Questions." Early
      Music 5 (1977): 380-87.

      Reviews the controversy concerning whether the
      Vespers of 1610, apart from the Missa In illo
      tempore, represents an artistic and liturgical
      unity. Fenlon believes that this work was
      performed with the sonata and five solo vocal
      concertos and that the occasion of its first per-
      formance may have been the marriage of Francesco
      Gonzaga to Margherita of Savoy in 1608.

614. Ferrari Barassi, Elena. "Il madrigale spirituale
      nel cinquecento e la raccolta monteverdiana del
      1583." Congresso internazionale sul tema Claudio
      Monteverdi (item 811), pp. 217-52.

      Regards frottole with meditative and spiritual
      texts as the predecessors of the madrigale

spirituale. Credits Petrarch with providing poetic
models for the spiritual madrigals. Traces the
rise of the lauda and madrigale spirituale during
the sixteenth century. Compares Monteverdi's
Madrigali spirituali a quattro voci (1583), of
which only the bass part survives, with his Sacrae
cantiunculae (1582). An appendix includes the text
to Monteverdi's Madrigali spirituali (1583).

615. Hofmann, Friedrich. "Toleranz für Texte? Zum
     theologischen Problem bei Aufführungen der
     Marienvesper von Monteverdi." Der Kirchenmusiker
     28 (1977): 203-204.

     Addresses theological considerations concerning
     the texts of Monteverdi's Vespers of 1610.

616. Holschneider, Andreas. "Zur Aufführungspraxis der
     Marien-Vesper von Monteverdi." Hamburger
     Jahrbuch für Musikwissenschaft 1 (1974): 59-68.

     Asserts that the Vespers of 1610 is Monteverdi's
     boldest church work. Points out the problems
     associated with the five antiphons.

617. Hucke, Helmut. "Die fälschlich so genannte
     'Marien'-Vesper von Claudio Monteverdi." Bericht
     über den internationalen musikwissenschaftlichen
     Kongress Bayreuth 1981, edited by Christoph-
     Hellmut Mahling and Sigrid Wiesmann. Kassel:
     Bärenreiter, 1984, pp. 295-305.

     Reviews the opinions published by a number of
     noted scholars regarding the Vespers of 1610.
     Argues against referring to the collection as the
     "Marian" Vespers.

618. Hust, Gerhard. "Untersuchungen zu Claudio Monte-
     verdis Messkompositionen." Ph.D. dissertation,
     University of Heidelberg, 1970. 231 pp.
     ML410 M77 H8

     Examines in complete detail the Masses of 1610,
     1641, and 1650. Concentrates upon stylistic and
     structural techniques. Provides an extensive
     bibliography.

619.   Hutson, Larry Don.   "A Critical Edition and Per-
       formance Guide to the Magnificat a 7 of Claudio
       Monteverdi."   D.M.A. dissertation, The Universit
       of Oklahoma, 1979.   217 pp.   UM Order No. 791873

       Not examined.   Summary in Dissertation Abstracts
       International, 40 (August 1979): 529-A, indicates
       that this work includes a performing edition of th
       Magnificat a 7 from Monteverdi's Vespers of 1610
       and a conductor's performing guide.

620.   Jeppesen, Knud.   "Monteverdi, Kapellmeister an
       S.ta Barbara?"   Congresso internazionale sul tem
       Claudio Monteverdi (item 811), pp. 313-19.

       Raises numerous questions regarding the litur-
       gical problems associated with the Vespers of 1610
       Compares Monteverdi's work to both the Roman lit-
       urgy and the special liturgy practiced at the cour
       church of Santa Barbara in Mantua.   Concludes that
       the composer did not have any official association
       with the church of Santa Barbara or its liturgy.

*   Kurtzman, Jeffrey G.   "An Early 17th-Century
       Manuscript of Canzonette e Madrigaletti
       Spirituali."

       Cited above as item 380.

621.   ———.   Essays on the Monteverdi Mass and Vespers
       of 1610.   Rice University Studies, vol. 64, No.
       4.   Houston: Rice University, 1978.   182 pp.
       ISBN 0 892 63238 0   ML410 M77

       A collection of essays which represent an ex-
       tension of work beyond the author's doctoral dis-
       sertation (see item 622).   The first chapter
       examines sources for the Mass and Vespers.   Chapte
       two is a general assessment of the artistic merits
       of the Missa In illo tempore.   Chapters three and
       four deal with compositional procedures found in
       these works.   The final chapter is devoted to a
       historical perspective of the sixteenth- and early
       seventeenth-century Italian Vespers repertoire.

622.   ———.   "The Monteverdi Vespers of 1610 and Their
       Relationship with Italian Sacred Music of the
       Early Seventeenth Century."   Ph.D. dissertation,
       University of Illinois, 1972.   1105 pp.   UM Orde
       No. 73-9975

Examines the Vespro della Beata Vergine of 1610
in light of other early seventeenth-century Vespers
collections. Particular attention is given to the
question of liturgical unity and musical unity.
Also included is a large supplement of sacred music
in transcription. Kurtzman's study, consistently
well written and penetrating, represents a significant contribution to Monteverdi research.

623.   ————. "Some Historical Perspectives on the
         Monteverdi Vespers." Analecta musicologica 15
         (1975): 29-86.

Based on the author's significant dissertation
(item 622), this is an important and thorough essay
that compares the Monteverdi Vespers with numerous
Vespers collections published in the late sixteenth
and early seventeenth centuries. Observes the com-
plexity and diversity of Monteverdi's publication
resulting from the wedding of various traditional
and progressive styles and techniques. Considers
the influence, although apparently slight, of
Monteverdi's collection upon later Vespers
settings.

624.   Lowell, John K. "Aspects of Psalmody and Text
         Setting in Monteverdi's Marian Vespers." Musical
         Analysis 2 (1974): 14-26.

Demonstrates Monteverdi's application of psalmody
as a structural device in the Vespers of 1610.
Carefully examines the psalmodic influence in both
the Dixit Dominus and the first Magnificat.

625.   Lupo, Bettina. "Sacre monodie monteverdiane."
         Musica II (item 813), pp. 51-85.

Examines Monteverdi's religious environment.
Discusses the composer's sacred monodies and
divides these works into different categories
according to text. Considers these compositions
to be Baroque rather than Mannerist.

626.   Mack, Gerald Raymond. "A Performance and Analysis
         of the Messa III a Quattro Voci da Capella, by
         Claudio Monteverdi." Ed.D. dissertation,
         Columbia University, 1966. 89 pp. UM Order No.
         66-10,303

Not examined. Abstract in Dissertation Abstracts
International, 27-4 (October 1966): 1074-75-A,
indicates that an examination of Monteverdi's
sacred style is included. Performance practice
issues are also discussed.

627. Masaki, Mitsue. "A Study of the Masses of Claudio
      Monteverdi." Nomura Festschrift. N.p., 1969,
      391-406. In Japanese; summary in German.

      Not examined. Author summary in RILM Abstracts,
      4/1 (January-April 1970): 28, states that the
      Masses of 1610, 1640, and 1650 were composed in th
      stile misto, a combination of the stile antico and
      the stile nuovo.

628. Meier, Bernhard. "Zur Tonart der Concertato-
      Motetten in Monteverdis 'Marienvesper.'" Claudi
      Monteverdi: Festschrift Reinhold Hammerstein
      (item 794), pp. 357-67.

      Carefully examines the four motets found in the
      Vespers of 1610. Offers a detailed analysis of th
      structure of the works.

*   Moore, James H. "Venezia favorita da Maria: Music
      for the Madonna Nicopeia and Santa Maria della
      Salute."

      Cited above as item 120.

*   ————. Vespers at St. Mark's: Music of Alessandr
      Grandi, Giovanni Rovetta and Francesco Cavalli.

      Cited above as item 240.

629. Morche, Gunther. "Monteverdis lateinische Musik
      'da concerto.'" Claudio Monteverdi: Festschrift
      Reinhold Hammerstein (item 794), pp. 369-85.

      Presents an investigation of Monteverdi's
      concerted Latin church music.

630. Noske, Frits. "An Unknown Work by Monteverdi: the
      Vespers of St. John the Baptist." Music and
      Letters 66 (1985): 118-22.

      Based on the travel journal of the Dutchman
      Constantijn Huygens, the author claims the dis-
      covery of an unknown sacred work by Monteverdi.
      Suggests that much of the music for the Vespers of

St. John the Baptist is to be found in the Selva
morale e spirituale of 1640.

631. Osthoff, Wolfgang. "Unità liturgica e artistica
      nei Vespri del 1610." Rivista italiana di
      musicologia (item 838), pp. 314-27.

      Recounts the views of Redlich, Schrade, and
      Stevens concerning the unity of Monteverdi's
      Vespers of 1610. Believes that the Vespers of 1610
      were probably written for the ducal chapel of Santa
      Barbara at Mantua. Identifies a musical unity in
      this work and considers that the liturgy at Santa
      Barbara was possibly unique, allowing for dif-
      ferences in comparison to the Roman liturgy.

632. Parrott, Andrew. "Transposition in Monteverdi's
      Vespers of 1610: An 'Aberration' Defended. Early
      Music 12 (1984): 490-516.

      Advocates the use of transposition where Monte-
      verdi employed high clefs (chiavette). Supports
      this opinion by citing evidence from theoretical
      treatises, musical sources, and the construction of
      selected early Baroque keyboard instruments. See
      the article by Jeffrey Kurtzman, item 692.

*   Prunières, Henry. "Monteverdi à la chapelle de
      Saint-Marc."

      Cited above as item 327.

633. ————. "Monteverdi's Sacred Music." The Sackbut
      3 (1922-23): 259-67.

      Translated from the original French by G.A.
      Pfister, this article provides a general survey of
      Monteverdi's religious music. Divides his sacred
      music into two basic categories: works composed in
      the polyphonic style and works composed in the
      homophonic style.

634. Redlich, Hans F. "Claudio Monteverdis Kirchen-
      musik." Anbruch 17 (1935): 42-44.

      Presents Redlich's first attempt at assessing
      Monteverdi's achievements as a composer of church
      music. Based primarily upon an examination of the
      Missa In illo tempore and the Vespers of 1610.
      Also see Redlich, item 635.

*   ————.   "Early Baroque Church Music."

         Cited above as item 140.

635.   ————.   "Monteverdi's Religious Music."   Music and
         Letters 27 (1946): 208-15.

         Traces the development of Monteverdi's sacred
         music from the Sacrae cantiunculae of 1582 to the
         Messa a 4 voci et Salmi, published posthumously in
         1650.   Notes that the religious works represent a
         mixing of the prima pratica and seconda pratica.
         Praises Malipiero's complete edition of Monte-
         verdi's works yet points out the edition's
         liabilities.

*   Roche, Jerome.   "Liturgical Music in Italy, 1610-
         60."

         Cited above as item 144.

636.   ————.   "Monteverdi: An Interesting Example of
         Second Thoughts."   Music Review 32 (1971):
         193-204.

         Compares two versions of the Confitebor from
         Monteverdi's Messa et Salmi collection of 1650.
         Both settings utilize a chaconne bass with a
         ritornello interpolated between the verses of the
         psalm.   Concludes that the second setting was
         composed after the first and that it is superior
         music.

637.   ————.   "Monteverdi in Church."   Music and
         Musicians 15 (June 1967): 23, 56.

         A cursory survey of Monteverdi's sacred works.
         Contends that Monteverdi's sacred style became more
         expressive between the 1610 and 1640 collections.

638.   Schalz, Nicolas.   "Monteverdi 1610."   Revue
         musicale suisse 123 (1983): 209-18.

         Examines the relationship between Monteverdi's
         two great sacred works of 1610: the Vespers and the
         Missa In illo tempore.   Argues that the signifi-
         cance of the Mass is clarified only in its
         connection to the Vespers.

*   ————. Studien zur Komposition des Gloria.
         Musikalische Formgestaltung von der Gregorianik
         bis zu Monteverdi.

         Cited above as item 154.

639. Sentieri, Alfred Richard. "A Method for the
      Specification of Style Change in Music: A
      Computer-Aided Study of Selected Venetian Sacred
      Compositions from the Time of Gabrieli to the
      Time of Vivaldi." Ph.D. dissertation, Ohio State
      University, 1978. 244 pp. UM Order No. 78-
      19,663

      Not examined. Abstract in Dissertation Abstracts
      International, 39-5 (November 1978): 2612-A, states
      that the study "is a test of a method for speci-
      fying and measuring developments in aspects of
      musical style." Monteverdi is one of six composers
      whose works were examined.

640. Sørensen, Søren. "L'eredità monteverdiana nella
      musica sacra del nord: Monteverdi-Förster-
      Buxtehude." Rivista italiana di musicologia
      (item 838), pp. 341-55.

      A slight revision of Sørensen's article
      "Monteverdi-Förster-Buxtehude," which appeared in
      Dansk aarbog for musikforskning in 1963, item 641.
      Translated into Italian by Guglielmo Barblan.

641. ————. "Monteverdi-Förster-Buxtehude." Dansk
      aarbog for musikforskning 3 (1963): 87-100. In
      German.

      Contends that the church music of Monteverdi
      stands in a direct line of development with the
      cantata style of Buxtehude. The German composer
      Kaspar Förster, who studied in Venice and Rome, is
      cited as providing a connective link between the
      Italian and German styles. A slight revision of
      this article appeared in Rivista italiana di
      musicologia as "L'eredità monteverdiana nella
      musica sacra del nord: Monteverdi-Förster-
      Buxtehude" (item 640).

642. Spinelli, Gianfranco. "Confronto fra le
      registrazioni organistiche dei Vespri di
      Monteverdi e quelle de L'arte organica di
      Antegnati." Congresso internazionale sul tema
      Claudio Monteverdi (item 811), pp. 479-88.

      Compares Monteverdi's organ registration in the
      two settings of the Magnificat from his Vespers o
      1610. Indicates organ registration given by othe
      theorists, composers, and organists of the time.
      The most detailed information found was that of
      Costanzo Antegnati in his L'Arte organica (Bresci
      1608). Describes the organ built by G.B. Facchet
      at Cremona and the one constructed by Graziadio
      Antegnati (Costanzo's father) for Santa Barbara a
      Mantua. Concludes that Monteverdi prescribed onl
      essential registration to achieve an equilibrium
      between the instruments and voices. Monteverdi
      used the organ to sustain and accompany the voice
      and instruments in the two magnificats.

643. Steele, John. "The Concertato Synthesis: Monte-
      verdi's 'Beatus Primo.'" Claudio Monteverdi:
      Festschrift Reinhold Hammerstein (item 794), pp
      427-34.

      Attempts to explain the popularity of Monte-
      verdi's first setting of Psalm 111 through an
      investigation of the structural elements of the
      work. Views the construction of Beatus vir on fi
      interlocking levels: basso ostinato, imitation an
      repetition, refrain, ritornello, and da capo. Co
      cludes that it is the combination of these elemen
      in forming a whole that makes the composition
      distinctive.

644. Stevens, Denis. "Claudio Monteverdi: Selva moral
      e spirituale." Congresso internazionale sul te
      Claudio Monteverdi (item 811), pp. 423-34.

      Discusses numerous aspects associated with the
      large, diverse collection of works published in t
      Selva morale e spirituale. Notes the abundance o
      errors in the original printed edition. Identifi
      the musical material in two of the psalms as bein
      derived from madrigals by Monteverdi. Points out
      that one of the monodies in the Selva is based on
      the Lamento d'Arianna. Also discusses performanc
      practice.

*   ———. Monteverdi: Sacred, Secular, and
         Occasional Music.

         Cited above as item 423.

645.   ———. "Monteverdi's Double-choir Magnificat."
         Musical Times 110 (1969): 587-89.

         Clarifies the editorial problems in Novello's
         reconstructed edition of Monteverdi's eight-voice
         Magnificat (1610) edited by Denis Stevens and John
         Steele. Compares Monteverdi's polychoral style to
         that of Andrea and Giovanni Gabrieli.

646.   ———. "Monteverdi's Other Vespers." Musical
         Times 120 (1979): 732-37.

         Theorizes that a large portion of Monteverdi's
         church music composed between 1610 and 1641 was
         later published in the two major collections of
         1641 and 1650: the Selva morale e spirituale and
         the Messa...Salmi...Letanie. Suggests that
         practical sets of Vespers can be extracted from
         these two publications. Stevens's edition of
         Monteverdi's Christmas Vespers (Novello, 1979) uses
         this procedure.

647.   ———. "Monteverdi's Venetian Church Music."
         Musical Times 108 (1967): 414-17.

         A succinct overview of Monteverdi's church music,
         stressing lesser-known compositions. Recognizes
         for the first time that Petrarch was the author of
         the first two spiritual madrigals in the Selva
         morale e spirituale.

648.   ———. "Monteverdi's Vespers Verified." Musical
         Times 102 (1961): 422.

         Examines the Nigra sum, Pulchra es, Duo
         Seraphim, Audi coelum, and Sancta Maria in the
         Vespers of 1610. Argues that these pieces are not
         to be performed as antiphons to the adjacent psalm
         verses in this collection but should be presented
         as separate cantatas for solo voice. This article
         later appeared in an Italian translation as "Altri
         Vespri di Monteverdi" in Nuova rivista musicale
         italiana 14 (1980): 167-77.

649.   ———. "Where Are the Vespers of Yesteryear?"
         Musical Quarterly 47 (1961): 315-30.

Attempts to clarify the confusion associated with the significance and purpose of the various items published collectively as Monteverdi's Vespers of 1610. Argues that the disparate conclusions reached by Redlich and Schrade are both incorrect. Concludes that stylistic or liturgica] unity was not Monteverdi's plan for this publication.

650. Tagliavini, Luigi Ferdinando. "Registrazioni organistiche nei Magnificat dei 'Vespri' monteverdiani." Rivista italiana di musicologia (item 838), pp. 365-71.

Observes that Monteverdi's organ registration in the two Magnificats from the Vespers of 1610 represents a sonorous ideal. Compares Monteverdi organ registration with registration given in contemporary treatises. Notes the composer's exclusive use of the registration d'organo, the sole exception being his employment of the voce umana.

651. Tagmann, Pierre M. "The Palace Church of Santa Barbara in Mantua, and Monteverdi's Relationshi to Its Liturgy." Festival Essays for Pauline Alderman, edited by Burton L. Karson. Provo: Brigham Young University Press, 1976, pp. 53-60 ML55 A4 1976 ISBN 0 8425 01010

Presents background information concerning the planning and construction, under the guidance of Giovan Battista Bertani, of the Basilica Palatina di Santa Barbara. Contains a brief history of th special liturgy proposed by Duke Guglielmo and approved by Pope Gregory XIII in 1583. Poses several questions concerning Monteverdi's association with the church and its liturgy. Argues, contrary to the conclusion of Leo Schrade, that Monteverdi had little connection with the palace church. See the studies by Knud Jeppesen (item 620) and Tagmann (item 174).

*   Tegen, Martin. "Monteverdi."

Cited above as item 577.

652. Witzenmann, Wolfgang. "Stile antico e stile nuovo
     nella musica sacra di Claudio Monteverdi."
     Rivista italiana di musicologia (item 838), pp.
     372-81.

     Considers that the stile antico for Monteverdi
     was the a cappella style of the sixteenth century
     and that the new style of church music in the
     seventeenth century was the stile concertato.
     Cites the use of the liturgical cantus firmus in
     the Vespers of 1610 as a sign of an earlier style
     and the use of ostinato and ritornello as a move to
     a more personal style.

               4. Prima and Seconda Pratica

653. Abert, Anna Amalie. "Die Opernästhetik Claudio
     Monteverdis." Congresso internazionale sul tema
     Claudio Monteverdi (item 811), pp. 35-55.

     Based primarily upon Monteverdi's letters, Abert
     emphasizes the composer's ideas concerning the
     relationship of music to text as formulated in his
     seconda pratica.

654. Anfuso, Nella, and Gianuario, Annibale. Prepara-
     zione alla interpretazione della 'poiësis' monte-
     verdiana. Florence: Otos e Centro Studi Rinasci-
     mento Musicale, 1971. 393 pp.

     Views Monteverdi's seconda pratica in light of
     Plato's Republic and Aristotle's Poetics. Looks at
     humanistic Renaissance movements, both Italian and
     French, in relation to Monteverdi's works. Reviews
     the criticism of a number of twentieth-century
     Monteverdi scholars, including Prunières, Schrade,
     de' Paoli, and Cimbro.

655. Arnold, Denis. "Monteverdi and the Art of War."
     Musical Times 108 (1967): 412-14.

     Emphasizes the effect of Monteverdi's partici-
     pation in Prince Vincenzo Gonzaga's Hungarian
     military campaign of 1595 upon his musical style.
     Contends that this experience obviously had an
     impact upon the development of the stile concitato.

656.   ————. "'Seconda pratica': A Background to
        Monteverdi's Madrigals." Music and Letters 38
        (1957): 341-52.

        Approaches the seconda pratica by questioning w.
        Monteverdi's music seemed so original to the con-
        temporary theorist Artusi. After a glance at
        Artusi's theoretical works, the author discusses
        Monteverdi's melody and harmony in light of other
        seconda pratica composers.

657.   Artusi, Giovanni Maria. L'Artusi overo delle
        imperfettioni della moderna musica. Venice:
        Giacomo Vincenti, 1600; facsimile ed., Biblio-
        theca musica bononiensis, Sezione II. n. 36.
        Bologna: Forni, 1968. 71 pp. ML171 A83

        A controversial, theoretical treatise divided
        into two arguments. The first criticizes Ercole
        Bottrigari's Il Desiderio (1594) and the second
        critically analyzes two madrigals by Monteverdi,
        without naming the composer, which were unpublishe
        at the time Artusi's work was written. The secon
        part of this work appears in English translation
        Strunk, item 288.

658.   ————. Discorso secondo musicale di Antonio
        Braccino da Todi per la dichiaratione della
        lettera posta né Scherzi musicali del sig.
        Claudio Monteverdi. Venice: Giacomo Vincenti,
        1608; facsimile ed., Milan: n.p., 1924; reprint
        ed., Milan: Bollettino Bibliografico Musicale,
        1934. 15 pp. ML171 A83 D5

        Thought to be by Giovanni Maria Artusi, this
        discourse answers Giulio Cesare Monteverdi's
        Dichiaratione in Monteverdi's 1607 volume of
        Scherzi musicali. Criticizes Monteverdi's use of
        time signatures and claims that rhythm should be
        the master of both text and harmony.

659.   ————. Seconda parte dell'Artusi overo delle
        imperfettioni della moderna musica. Venice:
        Giacomo Vincenti, 1603; facsimile ed., Biblio-
        theca musica bononiensis, Sezione II. n. 36.
        Bologna: Forni, 1968. 56 pp. ML171 A83

Responds to letters from L'Ottuso Accademico,
whose identity is unknown, defending Monteverdi's
madrigals against earlier criticisms made by Artusi
in L'Artusi, overo delle imperfettioni della
moderna musica (1600). The second part of this
work criticizes statements made by Ercole
Bottrigari. See also Artusi, items 657 and 658.

660. Bach, Hans-Elmar. "Die Stellung der Marienvesper
im Schaffen Claudio Monteverdis--Beitrag zum
Gedenkjahr anlässlich des 400. Geburtstages des
Komponisten." Musica sacra 87 (1967): 284-90.

Not examined. Summary in RILM Abstracts, 2/2
(May-August 1968): 14, indicates that the article
notes the emphasis of the seconda pratica in
Monteverdi's Vespers.

661. Dahlhaus, Carl. "Seconda pratica und musikalische
Figurenlehre." Claudio Monteverdi: Festschrift
Reinhold Hammerstein (item 794), pp. 141-50.

Deals with Monteverdi's use of dissonance and its
relationship to the seconda pratica.

662. Fano, Fabio. "Il Monteverdi sacro, la 'prima
prattica' e la scuola veneziana." Rivista
italiana di musicologia (item 838), pp. 264-69.

Refutes the common assumption that in Monteverdi's seconda pratica the music is the servant of
the text. Draws attention to early and late works
which were written in the prima pratica style and
cites portions of Orfeo which the author contends
were influenced by this style. Notes a similarity
of style between some works of Monteverdi and
Giovanni Gabrieli.

663. Fortune, Nigel. "Monteverdi and the seconda
prattica: From Madrigal to Duet." The New
Monteverdi Companion (item 780), pp. 198-215.

Beginning with examples from the fourth madrigal
book, Fortune sketches Monteverdi's development of
duet texture (two voices and continuo). This
article first appeared in The Monteverdi Companion
(item 779).

664. ———. "Monteverdi and the seconda prattica:
      Monody." The New Monteverdi Companion (item
      780), pp. 183-97.

      Surveys Monteverdi's production of solo songs.
      Notes the paucity of monodies in comparison with
      the composer's overall output. Reflects upon the
      influence of the Lamento d'Arianna. This article
      first appeared in The Monteverdi Companion (item
      779).

665. Gianuario, Annibale. "Proemio all' 'Oratione' di
      Monteverdi." Rivista italiana di musicologia
      (1969): 32-47.

      Clarifies the idea that Monteverdi's musical ex-
      pression of oratione (concepts expressed phoneti-
      cally) was based on his understanding of Plato, a
      Monteverdi revealed in a letter of October 22,
      1633. Cites Vicentino, Zarlino, Galilei, and Per
      to illustrate divergent, contemporary views on th
      study of oratione.

666. Isgro, Robert Mario. "The First and Second Prac-
      tices of Monteverdi: Their Relation to Contem-
      porary Theory." D.M.A. dissertation, Universit
      of Southern California, 1968. 460 pp. UM Orde
      No. 68-17029

      Deals with the Artusi-Monteverdi controversy
      regarding the prima pratica and the seconda
      pratica. The author's stated purpose "is to
      examine in detail the nature of Monteverdi's two
      practices with a view toward establishing their
      connections with the theory of his day."

667. Konen, Valentina. "Claudio Monteverdi."
      Sovetskaia muzyka 31 (May 1967): 89-96. In
      Russian.

      Not examined. Summary in RILM Abstracts, 1/2
      (May-August 1967): 16, indicates that the article
      discusses the variegated nature of Monteverdi's
      music, emphasizing the relationship of music to
      text and the expression of human passions.

668. Malipiero, G. Francesco. "Claudio Monteverdi da
      Cremona." Rassegna musicale (item 819), pp.
      53-58.

Emphasizes that there are two different musical styles evident in Monteverdi's works. Cites Padre Martini's statement concerning Monteverdi's use of dissonance in his madrigals. Includes a transcription of the Sanctus from Monteverdi's Messa a 4 voci da cappella found in the Selva morale collection.

669.   Massera, Giuseppe. "Dalle 'imperfezioni' alle 'perfezioni' della moderna musica." Congresso internazionale sul tema Claudio Monteverdi (item 811), pp. 397-408.

Describes the contents and arguments in Seconda parte dell'Artusi, overo delle imperfettioni della moderna musica (1603) and Discorso secondo musicale di Antonio Braccino da Todi (1608). Argues that L'Ottuso, the writer of anonymous letters in the former treatise, was probably not Monteverdi and that, based on its emphasis, the latter treatise may not have been written by Artusi.

670.   Palisca, Claude V. "The Artusi-Monteverdi Controversy." The Monteverdi Companion (item 779), pp. 133-66.

Clarifies statements made in L'Artusi, overo delle imperfettioni della moderna musica (1600) and Seconda parte dell'Artusi, overo delle imperfettioni della moderna musica (1603) concerning the use of dissonance. Speculates on the identity of L'Ottuso Accademico, the person cited in the latter treatise, and concludes that he was most likely a composer active at Ferrara or Mantua. Includes a translation of the statement made by Monteverdi in the foreward to his fifth book of madrigals (1605). Cites numerous seventeenth-century theorists who either continued to define the two practices (prima pratica and seconda pratica) or continued the controversy started by Artusi and Monteverdi.

671.   ————. "The Artusi-Monteverdi Controversy." The New Monteverdi Companion (item 780), pp. 127-58.

A slight revision of the author's article (item 670) in The Monteverdi Companion. Refers to Stuart Reiner's review of Palisca's earlier article in which Reiner suggests that L'Ottuso may have been Giulio Cesare Monteverdi. Palisca doubts this possibility.

672.   ———. "Vincenzo Galilei's Counterpoint Treatise
        A Code for the Seconda pratica." Journal of the
        American Musicological Society 9 (1956): 81-96.

        Summarizes Vincenzo Galilei's views on the
        treatment of dissonance found in his 1588-1591
        counterpoint treatises, Il primo libro della
        prattica del contrapunto intorno all'uso delle
        consonanze and Discorso intorno all'uso delle
        dissonanze. Also discusses his essay Discorso
        intorno all'uso dell'enharmonio et di chi fusse
        autore del cromatico, to which Galilei later added
        a supplement. Palisca sees Galilei's counterpoint
        treatise as fulfilling the void left by Monte-
        verdi's intended treatise on the seconda pratica,
        which he promised in the preface to his fifth book
        of madrigals. Observes that this empirical theory
        of composition is possibly the earliest treatise o
        harmony.

*   Pereyra, M.L. Explication de la lettre qui est
        imprimée dans le cinquième livre de madrigaux de
        Claudio Monteverde.

        Cited above as item 277.

673.   Reich, Willi. "Claudio Monteverdi--sein bahn-
        brechendes musikalisches Lebenswerk." Universi-
        tas 22 (1967): 955-59.

        Not examined. Summary in RILM Abstracts, 4/1
        (January-April 1970): 28, states that the article
        deals with Monteverdi's theory of word over harmor
        in the seconda pratica.

674.   Roche, Jerome. "Monteverdi and the prima prat-
        tica." The New Monteverdi Companion (item 780),
        pp. 159-82.

        Sheds light on the development of the prima
        pratica in Monteverdi's sacred style through an
        examination of the musical milieu of the time.
        Compares his church music with similar works by
        Soriano, Anerio, Bernardi, and Palestrina. This
        article first appeared in The Monteverdi Companion
        (item 779).

675.   Tessier, André. "Les deux styles de Monteverde."
        Revue musicale 3 (1922): 223-54.

Characterizes the dramatic change in musical
style that occurred at the beginning of the seventeenth century. Considers the role of the prima
pratica and seconda pratica in the music of Monteverdi. Includes sections on the madrigals, monodies, and L'incoronazione di Poppea.

676. ————. "Monteverdi e la filosofia dell'arte."
Rassegna musicale (item 819), pp. 59-68.

States that although Monteverdi did not complete
his philosophical treatise Melodia overo seconda
pratica musica, he did leave the essence of that
work in letters and prefaces written by him and his
brother, Giulio Cesare Monteverdi. Considers the
importance of the third book of Plato's Republic on
the philosophy of Monteverdi. Stresses the significance of imitation for the purpose of express-
ing truth in Monteverdi's art.

677. Yamaguchi, Hiroko. "Seconda pràtica--Monteverdi no
madrigal ni miru atarashii ongaku no sôzô." M.A.
thesis, Tokyo Geijutsu Daigaku, 1977. 2 vols.
344 pp. In Japanese.

Not examined. Summary in RILM Abstracts, 11/1
(January-April 1977): 32, indicates that the author
views, in light of the Monteverdi-Artusi polemic,
the composer's seconda pratica style as a reaction
against traditional forms and practices.

5. Studies in Performance and
Performance Practice

678. Apel, Willi. "Anent a Ritornello in Monteverdi's
Orfeo." Musica disciplina 5 (1951): 213-22.

Investigates rhythmic problems found in the
ritornello connected to Orfeo's Vi ricorda in the
second act of Monteverdi's Orfeo. Compares eight
transcriptions of this piece with the original,
offering a solution which clarifies the fact that
in the sixteenth century "3" was not equivalent to
our modern triplet and that proportio triplia can
indicate trisected values in groups of two or four
as well as in groups of three or six.

679. Arnold, Denis. "Monteverdi's Singers." _Musical_
      Times 111 (1970): 982-85.

      A short essay, based upon Monteverdi's letters
      and other contemporary records, describing Monte-
      verdi's opinions on singing. In addition, names
      singers associated with Monteverdi.

680. ————. "Performing Practice." _The New Monteverd_
      Companion (item 780), pp. 319-33.

      Advocates that modern performances of Monte-
      verdi's music must be prepared with an awareness o
      the drastic style changes that occurred between th
      composer's early and late periods. Divides Monte-
      verdi's output into two categories: the Renaissanc
      composer and the Baroque _maestro di cappella_. Con
      cludes that the twentieth-century musician must
      "trust the composer."

*   Boyden, David D. "Monteverdi's _violini piccoli_
      alla francese and _viole da brazzo_."

      Cited above as item 459.

*   Cammarota, Lionello. "L'orchestrazione dell'
      'Orfeo' di Monteverdi."

      Cited above as item 465.

681. Carse, Adam. "Monteverde and the Orchestra." _The_
      Sackbut 2 (1921): 12-17.

      One of the earliest articles dealing with
      Monteverdi's innovations and contributions to the
      development of the Baroque orchestra.

*   Collaer, Paul. "Notes concernant l'instrumentatic
      de _L'Orfeo_ de Claudio Monteverdi."

      Cited above as item 471.

682. ————. "L'orchestra di Claudio Monteverdi."
      Musica II (item 813), pp. 86-104.

      Contends that in _Orfeo_, the _Madrigali guerrieri_
      et amorosi, and in parts of the _Vespro della Beat_
      Vergine (1610), Monteverdi makes his orchestral
      requirements clear. Warns that much of the com-
      poser's expression is lost by reconstructing thes
      works. Introduces the instruments found in Monte-
      verdi's works, comparing them to their modern

equivalent, if possible. Discusses in some detail
specific passages from Monteverdi's works, illus-
trating how the architecture of these works is
determined by Monteverdi's choice of instruments.

*   Corboz, Michel. "Michel Corboz: A propos de
         L'Orfeo."

       Cited above as item 472.

683.   Curtis, Alan. "Claudio Monteverdi in zijn ware
         gedaante." Opera journaal 4 (1973-74): 1-4. In
         Dutch.

       Deals with performance practice considerations in
       the music of Monteverdi.

*   Epstein, Peter. "Zur Rhythmisierung eines
         Ritornells von Monteverdi."

       Cited above as item 486.

684.   Fortune, Nigel. "Duet and Trio in Monteverdi."
         Musical Times 108 (1967): 417-21.

       After observing the paucity of solo songs in
       Monteverdi's output, the author stresses the
       composer's use of sonority as a structural device.
       Affirms that Monteverdi's duets and trios were
       instrumental in establishing the sectional chamber
       cantata in Italy.

685.   Frobenius, Wolf. "Zur Notation eines Ritornells in
         Monteverdis L'Orfeo." Archiv für Musikwissen-
         schaft 28 (1971): 201-204.

       Addresses the problem of proportion and
       sesquialtera found in arias and ritornellos from
       Orfeo.

686.   Glover, Jane. "Solving the Musical Problems."
         Claudio Monteverdi: Orfeo (item 588), pp. 138-55.

       Offers sensible solutions to several performance
       practice questions associated with Orfeo. Should
       be consulted by any prospective conductor of the
       opera.

687. Gottwald, Clytus. "Sendbrief vom Dolmetschen: Übe
      die Interpretation alter Musik." _Musica_ 34
      (1980): 349-52.

      Debates the performance practice question of
      recreating the original "sound idea" in early
      music.

688. Harnoncourt, Nikolaus. "Het klank-karakter van
      Monteverdi's Maria-Vespers." _Opera journaal_ 4
      (1973-74): 6-8. In Dutch.

      Stresses the instruments and instrumental
      practices of Monteverdi's day.

689. ————. "Werk und Aufführung bei Monteverdi."
      Österreichische Musikzeitschrift 33 (1978):
      193-99.

      Addresses numerous problems associated with the
      performance of early music. Cites the reproductio
      of Baroque opera as being particularly problem-
      atical.

*   Hell, Helmut. "Zu Rhythmus und Notierung des 'Vi
      ricorda' in Claudio Monteverdis _Orfeo_."

      Cited above as item 512.

690. Jürgens, Jürgen. "Urtext und Aufführungspraxis be
      Monteverdis _Orfeo_ und _Marien-Vesper_." _Congresso
      internazionale sul tema Claudio Monteverdi_ (item
      811), pp. 269-304.

      Reports on aspects of performance practice
      associated with _Orfeo_ and the _Vespro della Beata
      Vergine_. Compares recordings and performances of
      both works.

691. Krell, Friedrich. "Aufführungspraktische
      Prinzipien bei der Interpretation der Madrigale
      von Marenzio, Gesualdo und Monteverdi." _Wissen-
      schaftliche Beitr. der U. Halle, Rheihe G_ 8
      (1968): 41-63.

      Not examined. Summary in _RILM Abstracts_, 2/2
      (May-August 1968): 119, indicates that the music
      examined from the _cinquecento_ provides the basis
      for a performance practice.

692. Kurtzman, Jeffrey G. "Observations: An Aberration
      Amplified." Early Music 13 (1985): 73-76.

      Supports Andrew Parrott's article (item 632),
      which calls for the use of transposition when high
      clefs are employed by Monteverdi.

*   Leopold, Silke. "Lyra Orphei."

      Cited above as item 522.

693. Mori, Rachele Maragliano. "Claudio Monteverdi
      'Maestro di Canto.'" Rassegna musicale 21
      (1951): 33-38.

      Discusses vocal production as described by
      Monteverdi. Stresses the importance of a natural
      voice with tonal resonance. Emphasizes the use of
      the diaphragm in performing the trillo.

*   Parrott, Andrew. "Transposition in Monteverdi's
      Vespers of 1610: An 'Aberration' Defended."

      Cited above as item 632.

*   Praetorius, Michael. Syntagma musicum.

      Cited above as item 137.

694. Razzi, Fausto. "Polyphony of the seconda prattica:
      Performance Practice in Italian Vocal Music of
      the Mannerist Era." Early Music 8 (1980):
      298-311.

      Stresses the importance of a rhythmic flexibility
      and intelligent declamation of poetic text in the
      performance of seconda pratica secular vocal music.
      Cites examples from Monteverdi's fifth and seventh
      madrigal books and gives detailed information on
      how the text should be declaimed.

695. Redlich, Hans F. "Sull'edizione moderna delle
      opere di Claudio Monteverdi." Rassegna musicale
      8 (1935): 23-41.

      Written after fourteen volumes of Malipiero's
      edition of Monteverdi's works had appeared, Redlich
      calls for more practical performance editions based
      on the performance practices of Monteverdi's time.
      Offers solutions to numerous performance practice
      problems in the Vespers of 1610. Cites

Monteverdi's correspondence and the Syntagma
musicum III of Michael Praetorius as holding the
key to performance practice problems concerning
instrumentation found in the composer's works.

696.   Righini, Pietro. "Contributo per le ricerche sul
       linguaggio musicale originario dell'epoca
       monteverdiana." Congresso internazionale sul
       tema Claudio Monteverdi (item 811), pp. 539-41.

       Criticizes the use of modern temperament in
       performances of Monteverdi's works. Maintains that
       the only way to realize the musical sound of Monte-
       verdi's era is to use the temperament of the time.
       Notes a 1967 performance of Il combattimento di
       Tancredi e Clorinda in Turin which used a
       historically correct temperament.

697.   Sąsiadek, Eugeniusz. "O technice wokalnej i
       realizacji ozdobników w utworach Monteverdiego."
       Ruch muzyczny 21 (July 1977): 6-7. In Polish.

       Not examined. Summary in RILM Abstracts, 11/2
       (May-August 1977): 224, states that the essay
       considers questions of vocal technique in the
       Vespers of 1610 and Orfeo.

698.   Stevens, Denis. "Ornamentation in Monteverdi's
       Shorter Dramatic Works." Bericht über den
       siebenten internationalen musikwissenschaftlichen
       Kongress Köln 1958. Kassel: Bärenreiter, 1959,
       pp. 284-87. ML36 I628 1958

       Surveys four books on ornamentation published in
       Italy in the decade before Peri's Dafne. Demon-
       strates how these texts influenced singers in the
       early seventeenth century and briefly discusses
       ornamentation in the works of Monteverdi.

699.   ————. "Wagner Versus Monteverdi." American
       Choral Review 12 (1970): 95-98.

       Discusses recent performances of the two Magnif-
       icats from Monteverdi's Selva morale e spirituale
       (1640). Gives emphasis to the problematic missing
       alto and bass parts in choir II of the double choir
       Magnificat primo.

STUDIES OF MONTEVERDI'S MUSIC   213

700. Tarr, Edward H. "Monteverdi, Bach und die Trompe-
      tenmusik ihrer Zeit." Bericht über den inter-
      nationalen musikwissenschaftlichen Kongress Bonn
      1970. Kassel: Bärenreiter, 1972, pp. 592-96.

      Not examined. Summary in RILM Abstracts, 7/3
      (September-December 1973): 257, indicates that the
      article is concerned with the use of the trumpet in
      the Baroque era. Notes Monteverdi's utilization of
      the trumpet in Orfeo.

701. Uberti, Mauro, and Schindler, Oskar. "Contribution
      à la recherche d'un art vocal monteverdien: la
      couleur." L'Orfeo (item 816), pp. 78-82.

      An analytical essay focusing on vocal coloration.
      See also Uberti and Schindler, item 702.

702. —————. "Contributo alla ricerca di una vocalità
      monteverdiana: il 'colore.'" Congresso inter-
      nazionale sul tema Claudio Monteverdi (item 811),
      pp. 519-37.

      Examines Monteverdi's use of the voice, partic-
      ularly in secular works, based on comments made by
      the composer and others. Advocates that in these
      compositions a delicate, resonant voice should be
      used that is capable of producing the varied tone
      colors necessary to render the affetti of the
      musical style. The authors have studied the
      "flowing" voice with the use of an oscilloscope and
      have provided evidence of the varying tone colors
      required to perform works such as Monteverdi's Il
      combattimento. See also Uberti and Schindler, item
      701.

703. Westrup, Jack A. "The Continuo in Monteverdi."
      Congresso internazionale sul tema Claudio
      Monteverdi (item 811), pp. 497-502.

      Examines the role of the continuo in the music
      of Monteverdi. Argues against those who contend
      that improvisation played a large part in Baroque
      performance. Cautions editors and performers
      against placing too much emphasis upon theorists of
      the time for rules of interpretation.

*   —————. "Two First Performances: Monteverdi's
      'Orfeo' and Mozart's 'Clemenza di Tito.'"

      Cited above as item 587.

704. Worsthorne, Simon T. "Venetian Theatres:
      1637-1700." Music and Letters 29 (1948): 263-75.

      Surveys the layout of Venetian theaters in the
      seventeenth century and emphasizes performance
      practice in those theaters. Includes information
      on the San Cassiano, SS. Giovanni e Paolo, San
      Moisè, Teatro Novissimo, SS. Apostoli, Sant'
      Apollinare, San Salvatore, Ai Saloni, Sant' Angelo,
      San Giovanni Crisostomo, and Canaregio. Draws
      information from Cristoforo Ivanovich's Minerva al
      tavolino (item 99) and Pompeo Molmenti's Storia di
      Venezia nella vita privata (item 11).

705. Zimmerman, Franklin B. "Performance Practices and
      Rehearsal Techniques." College Music Symposium 9
      (1969): 101-11.

      Advocates greater flexibility and freedom in the
      performance of early music. Interpretation
      problems are discussed using examples from the
      madrigals of Monteverdi and the music of other
      composers.

V

MONTEVERDI TODAY

1. Revival of Monteverdi's Works

706. Bachmann, Claus-Henning. "Monteverdi-Renaissance."
     Musica 13 (1959): 788.

     Reviews a performance of L'incoronazione di
     Poppea, edited by Walter Goehr and conducted by
     Ernest Bour, at Hamburg's Staatsoper. Asserts that
     a satisfactory performance of the opera is not
     viable without some revisions.

707. Brown, Howard M. "Proms." Musical Times 114
     (1973): 1029-30.

     Favorably reviews a performance of Monteverdi's
     Vespro della Beata Vergine (1610) presented at
     Westminster Cathedral under the direction of John
     Eliot Gardiner. The performance used modern
     instruments.

708. Buchau, S. Von. "San Francisco." Opera News 45
     (May 1981): 37.

     Reviews a performance of Monteverdi's Il ballo
     delle ingrate based on the Denis Stevens edition
     and conducted at the harpsichord by Willie Anthony
     Walters. The performance is criticized for being
     "monotonously relentless."

709. Castéra, René de. "L'Orfeo de Monteverdi." Guide
     musical 1 (1904): 286-88.

Reviews the 1904 revival of <u>Orfeo</u> in Paris. For
other reviews of the performance, see items 752 and
766.

710. Collaer, Paul. "Les soirées de Bruxelles." <u>Le
      monde musical</u> 47 (April 1936): 108.

      Reviews performances at the Palais des Beaux-Arts
      of Cavalieri's <u>La rappresentazione di anima e di
      corpo</u> and Monteverdi's <u>Il ballo delle ingrate</u>.
      Contains a brief plot synopsis for the Monteverdi
      work. Notes the importance of Monteverdi as an
      opera composer and concludes by discussing the
      significance of his orchestration for the ballet.

711. Dobbins, Frank. "Monteverdi." <u>Musical Times</u> 121
      (January 1980): 43-44.

      Comments on performances by Musica nel Chiostro
      of <u>Il combattimento di Tancredi e Clorinda</u>, staged
      according to Monteverdi's preface, and <u>Il ballo
      delle ingrate</u>.

712. Dubreuil, Dominique. "Traduire les conflits de la
      nuit intérieure." <u>Musique en Jeu</u> 29 (1977):
      12-14.

      Considers the historical position of <u>L'incoro-
      nazione di Poppea</u> in relation to Venetian art.
      Includes a review of a performance of the work at
      the Opéra de Lyon.

713. Eberle, Gottfried. "Von der wahren Art historische
      Musik zu spielen." <u>Neue Zeitschrift für Musik</u> 49
      (January-February 1981): 49.

      Enthusiastically reviews a Berlin performance of
      Monteverdi's <u>Vespers</u> of 1610.

714. Epstein, Eugene V. "Zurich." <u>Opera News</u> 44
      (October 1979): 50.

      Reviews a staged performance of excerpts from
      Monteverdi's eighth book of madrigals, conducted by
      Nikolaus Harnoncourt and produced by Jean-Pierre
      Ponnelle. The basis for this very successful pres-
      entation of Monteverdi madrigals, according to
      Epstein, is Harnoncourt's belief that Monteverdi
      thought of the madrigals in scenic terms while
      composing them.

MONTEVERDI TODAY

MONTEVERDI TODAY   217

715. Fabian, I. "München ehrt Orff." Opernwelt 21
      (1980): 19-21.

      Reports on performances at the Bavarian Staats-
      oper of Carl Orff's third edition (Dresden, 1940)
      of Monteverdi's Orfeo and of Orff's own popular
      opera Die Kluge. These productions were presented
      in honor of Orff's eighty-fifth birthday. For
      other reviews of these performances, see items 732
      and 750.

716. Fortune, Nigel. "The Rediscovery of 'Orfeo.'"
      Claudio Monteverdi: Orfeo (item 588), pp. 78-118.

      A highly informative and thoroughly researched
      study. Traces the twentieth-century revival of
      Orfeo in editions and performances.

717. Freund, Erich. "Claudio Monteverdi's 'Orfeo':
      Deutsche Uraufführung in Breslau." Die Musik,
      Jg. 12, vol. 48 (1912-13): 26-27.

      Presents a review of the 1913 Breslau resur-
      rection of Orfeo. For other reviews of the
      performance, see items 739 and 751.

718. Gerhartz, Leo Karl. "Regietheater im Opern-
      haus-Sakrileg oder Auftrag?" Österreichische
      Musikzeitschrift 36 (1981): 537-38.

      Favorably comments on 1979 productions in Zurich
      by Harnoncourt and Ponnelle of three dramatic works
      by Monteverdi. Praises the historical accuracy of
      these performances.

719. Goertz, Harald. "Zürcher Premieren: Mozart-Oper
      und Monteverdi-Film." Österreichische Musik-
      zeitschrift 35 (1980): 237-39.

      Applauds the Zurich Theater production of
      L'incoronazione di Poppea, filmed and released by
      Unitel-Films.

720. Guérillot, F. "L'Orfeo de Monteverde." Société
      internationale de musique revue musicale
      mensuelle 7 (1911): 77-78.

      A terse review of the important May 2, 1911
      performance of Orfeo at the Théâtre Réjane in
      Paris. Recognized as the first modern stage

production of the opera. The performance employed
the d'Indy edition of the opera.

721. Hofmann, Peter. "Kassel: Theorie und Praxis."
      Opernwelt 2 (February 1968): 40.

      For the most part, an approving review of the
      first production in Kassel of L'incoronazione di
      Poppea. The performance employed Walter Goehr's
      edition of the opera.

722. Howes, Frank. "Notes on Monteverde's Orfeo."
      Musical Times 65 (1924): 509-11.

      Reflects upon the first English performance of
      Orfeo, produced by M. Louis Bourgeois and using
      Vincent d'Indy's edition, given at the Cromwell
      Gardens in London in 1924. The opera was presented
      in concert form with piano accompaniment. Con-
      siders the orchestration desirable for a modern
      performance of Orfeo. Succinctly compares editions
      of the opera then available.

*   Hunkemöller, Jürgen. "Strawinsky rezipiert
      Monteverdi."

      Cited below as item 802.

723. Hust, Gerhard. "Claudio Monteverdi in Darstel-
      lungen und Wertungen der ersten Hälfte des 19.
      Jahrhunderts." Claudio Monteverdi: Festschrift
      Reinhold Hammerstein (item 794), pp. 249-69.

      An account of the revival of interest in Monte-
      verdi's music during the first half of the nine-
      teenth century.

724. Jacobson, Bernard. "Murder at Aix." Music and
      Musicians 13 (October 1964): 34-35.

      Reviews a performance of L'incoronazione di
      Poppea at Aix-en-Provence on August 23, 1964.
      Highly critical of the use of an edition prepared
      by Gian Francesco Malipiero because of the exten-
      sive cuts evident in this performance.

725. Kammerer, Rafael. "The Coronation of Poppea."
      Musical America 81 (February 1961): 38-39.

Enthusiastically reviews a performance of the opera presented in concert form under the direction of Nicola Rescigno. The American Opera Society production was a new revision of the opera in English translation.

726. Kerner, Leighton. "Venetian Evocations." Village Voice 26 (June 1981): 82.

Reports on the first biennial Boston Early Music Festival and Exhibition. Particularly praises a production of L'incoronazione di Poppea, performed in English and edited by Martin Pearlman, co-produced by the Boston Lyric Opera and Banchetto Musicale.

727. Krause, Ernst. "Monteverdi at the Komische." Opera 31 (1980): 1227-28.

Reviews with mixed opinions a performance of L'incoronazione di Poppea at the East Berlin Komische Oper. The production was by Göran Järvefelt and used the Raymond Leppard realization of this opera.

728. Leipsic, Jeffrey A. "Munich: Monteverdi Cycle." Music and Musicians 28 (April 1980): 54-55.

A mixed review of the Zurich Opera's productions in Munich of Orfeo, Il ritorno d'Ulisse, and L'incoronazione di Poppea, all staged by Jean-Pierre Ponnelle and conducted by Nikolaus Harnoncourt.

729. Leslie, Murray. "Innsbruck: Curtis's Poppea." Opera 31 (1980): 1091.

Reviews favorably a performance of Monteverdi's L'incoronazione di Poppea at the Festival of Early Music at Innsbruck, directed by Alan Curtis in collaboration with Filippo Sanjust.

730. Lewinski, Wolf-Eberhard von. "Die Entdeckung einer Monteverdi-Bühne: 'Orfeo' in Wiesbaden." Opern-welt 18 (1977): 37.

Wiesbaden's 1977 performance of Orfeo, conducted by Hans-Werner Pintgen and utilizing the setting of August Wenzinger, is favorably reviewed. Praises the conductor's knowledge of ornamentation.

731.   ———. "Grosse Oper-Nah Gesehen: Zu aktuellen
        Bestrebungen des Fernsehens, Opern zu Senden."
        Opernwelt 20 (1979): 10-11.

        Includes reviews of several different opera
        performances. Concludes with a discussion of the
        Zurich Opera House filmed production of Orfeo.

732.   Lohmüller, Helmut. "München: Carl Orff-
        Geburtstag." Die Bühne 260 (1980): 24-25.

        Unenthusiastically reviews performances of
        Monteverdi's Orfeo and Orff's Die Kluge, both
        produced in honor of Orff's eighty-fifth birthday.
        Applauds, however, Hermann Prey's interpretation of
        the title role. For other reviews of these perfor-
        mances, see Reed, item 750, and Fabian, item 715.

733.   McCann, John. "Brussels: Disjointed Season."
        Opera 30 (1979): 984-87.

        Lavishes praise on an Alan Curtis 1978 pro-
        duction, based on the Venetian manuscript, of
        L'incoronazione di Poppea at La Monnaie in
        Brussels.

734.   Malipiero, G. Francesco. "Claudio Monteverdi."
        Musica II (item 813), pp. 1-3.

        A brief essay written as a tribute to Monteverdi
        on the 300th anniversary of his death. The essay
        serves as a preface to five articles about Monte-
        verdi contained in Musica II (item 813).

735.   ———. Così parlò Claudio Monteverdi. La coda di
        paglia N.4. Milan: Vanni Scheiwiller, 1967.
        ML410 M77 M165

        Malipiero offers personal reflections on
        Monteverdi at the time of the composer's 400th
        birthday. Contains facsimiles from Monteverdi's
        works and a bibliography of Malipiero's writings.

736.   ———. "Eine reine Quelle: Claudio Monteverdi."
        Anbruch 10 (1928): 357-58.

        Praises Monteverdi as the most original, in-
        fluential, and important composer of his time.
        Translated by Paul Stefan.

737. Mompellio, Federico. "Discorso conclusivo."
      Congresso internazionale sul tema Claudio
      Monteverdi (item 811), pp. 613-20.

      Briefly summarizes the results of the Monteverdi
      conference held in Cremona, Mantua, and Venice from
      May 3-7, 1968. Asserts that we are still lacking
      sufficient information on Monteverdi and his time
      to write the definitive volume on the composer.

738. Montagu, George. "The Monteverdi Revival."
      Musical Opinion 96 (1973): 234-35.

      Attributes the revival of Monteverdi's music in
      England to John Christie, who engaged Raymond
      Leppard to provide a new edition of L'incoronazione
      di Poppea for the Glyndebourne Festival of 1962.
      Mentions several other performances as well as
      selected recordings.

739. Neufeldt, Ernst. "Monteverdi's 'Orfeo' in
      Breslau." Signale für die musikalische Welt 29
      (1913): 1090-93.

      Describes the 1913 Breslau performance of Hans
      Erdmann-Guckel's edition of the opera in German
      translation. For other reviews of the performance,
      see items 717 and 751.

740. Osthoff, Wolfgang. "Claudio Monteverdi in unserer
      Zeit." Musica 21 (1967): 203-16.

      Written for the 400th anniversary of Monteverdi's
      birth, Osthoff's article convincingly demonstrates
      relationships and similarities between the music of
      Monteverdi and selected twentieth-century composi-
      tions. Provides numerous musical examples.

741. Parry, C. Hubert H. "The Significance of
      Monteverde." Proceedings of the Royal Musical
      Association 42 (1915-16): 51-67.

      An early essay attempting to evaluate the
      importance of Monteverdi in the development of
      modern music.

742. Porter, Andrew. Music of Three More Seasons: 1977-
      80. New York: Alfred A. Knopf, 1981. 613 pp.
      ISBN 0 394 51813 6 ML60 P894

A collection of essays which were first presented in <u>The New Yorker</u>. Contains numerous references to performances of Monteverdi's works.

743.   ————. <u>Music of Three Seasons: 1974-1977</u>. New York: Farrar Straus Giroux, 1978. 668 pp. ISBN 0 374 21646 0   ML60 P895 M88

Another collection of essays written by the music critic of <u>The New Yorker</u>. Contains reviews of performances of various Monteverdi works.

744.   ————. <u>A Musical Season</u>. New York: The Viking Press, 1974. 313 pp. ISBN 670 49650 2   ML60 P8.95 M9

Contains informative essays originally published by the author in <u>The New Yorker</u>. Reviews 1973 performances of Monteverdi's <u>L'incoronazione di Poppea</u> produced by the New York City Opera (pp. 190-99) and the Opera Society of Washington (pp. 243-46).

745.   Prunières, Henry. "Le couronnement de Poppée." <u>Revue musicale</u> 19 (1938): 135-36.

Reviews a performance of <u>Poppea</u> at the Théatre National de l'Opéra Comique. Generally praises the quality of the singing, especially the performance of Reneé Gilly in the title role. Comments, for the most part in an appreciative tone, on the Malipiero edition.

746.   Puffett, Derrick. "Orfeo." <u>Music and Musicians</u> 23 (April 1975): 38-39.

Comments on a performance of <u>Orfeo</u> given by the Oxford University Opera Club in February of 1975, conducted by Jane Glover. Puffett endorses Glover's treatment of unspecified instrumental parts but criticizes her use of an English translation in a performance of a work so dependent on the declamation of the recitatives.

747.   Rasponi, Lanfranco. "Spoleto." <u>Opera News</u> 44 (December 1979): 38.

Reviews a Spoleto performance at the Caio Melisso theater of <u>L'incoronazione di Poppea</u>, produced by Filippo Sanjust and using the Alan

Curtis edition. The editor conducted the orchestra
of authentic Baroque instruments.

748. Rebling, Eberhard. "Monteverdi-gesungen und
      getanzt." Musik und Gesellschaft 19 (1969):
      245-46.

      Reports on a performance of Il ballo delle
      ingrate, edited by Denis Stevens, at the Deutschen
      Staatsoper.

749. Redlich, Hans F. "Monteverdi-Renaissance."
      Atlantis 8 (1936): 768.

750. Reed, Herbert E. "Munich." Opera News 44 (1980):
      40-41.

      Criticizes a Munich production of Orfeo produced
      by Pierre Jean Valentin and utilizing the Carl Orff
      edition. For other reviews of this performance,
      see items 715 and 732.

751. Riesenfeld, Paul. "L'Orfeo." Allgemeine Musik-
      Zeitung 11 (1913): 997-98.

      Reviews a historically significant 1913 perfor-
      mance of Orfeo presented at the Breslau Stadt-
      theater. Discusses difficulties encountered by H.
      Erdmann-Guckel in preparing the opera for the
      stage. For other reviews of the performance, see
      items 717 and 739.

*   Rogers, Nigel. "'Orfeo' aus der Sicht des Inter-
      preten."

      Cited above as item 564.

752. Rolland, Romain. "Chronique musicale." La revue
      d'art dramatique et musical 19 (1904): 49-54.

      Reviews the historic 1904 performances of Orfeo
      at the Schola Cantorum in Paris, presented in
      concert version under the direction of Vincent
      d'Indy and using his own edition. For other
      reviews of the performance, see items 709 and 766.
      For an English translation of this review, see item
      753.

753. ————. "A Review of Vincent d'Indy's Performance
      (Paris, 1904)." Claudio Monteverdi: Orfeo (item
      588), pp. 119-25.

Rolland's perceptive review of the two Parisian performances in 1904 is reprinted here in English translation by Wendy Perkins. The original article is cited as item 752.

*   Rosenthal, Albi. "Monteverdi's 'Andromeda': A Lost Libretto Found."

Cited above as item 567.

754.   Rosenthal, Harold. "The Coronation of Poppea: Guildhall School of Music and Drama, London." Opera 31 (1980): 613-14.

Lauds a Guildhall student performance utilizing the Alan Curtis edition in the English translation of Arthur Jacobs. The costumes and sets, portraying Monteverdi's day rather than ancient Rome, were a unique feature of the production.

755.   ———. "Orfeo: English National Opera at the London Coliseum." Opera 32 (October 1981): 1079-81.

Praises both David Freeman's staging and John Eliot Gardiner's performing edition in this production of Orfeo.

756.   Sadie, Stanley. "Il ballo delle ingrate; Venus and Adonis; Kent Opera at Sadler's Wells Theatre." Opera 32 (1981): 743-44.

Lauds these performances for the careful attention given to Baroque performance practice and yet criticizes the lack of authenticity demonstrated in the dancing.

757.   ———. "The Return of Ulysses. St. Mary's Church, Oxford." Opera 32 (1982): 761-62.

Reviews a performance of Il ritorno di Ulisse by the Oxford University Opera Club conducted by Denis Arnold. Criticizes the performance because of numerous cuts and for being slow-paced.

758.   Salvetti, Guido. "Alcuni criteri nella rielaborazione ed orchestrazione dell' 'Incoronazione.'" Rivista italiana di musicologia (item 838), pp. 332-40.

Considers the problem of performing Monteverdi's
L'incoronazione di Poppea by focusing on per-
formances directed by Gaetano Cesari in 1907,
Giacomo Benvenuti in 1937, and Giorgio F. Ghedini
in 1953 and 1965. Finds both the Benvenuti and
Cesari productions more faithful to the extant
Marciana manuscript. This study concentrates
mostly on instrumentation. Published editions were
available for the productions of Benvenuti and
Ghedini. Concludes with a discussion by Salvetti,
Cavicchi, and Monterosso on instrumentation and the
realization of basso continuo.

759.   Sartori, Claudio. "News: Italy." Opera 5 (1954):
        505-506.

        Reviews a performance of Il ballo delle ingrate
        at La Scala, Milan. Gives some historical
        background on this work.

760.   Schelp, Arend. "Een uniek Monteverdi-project:
        Nederlandse Operastichting." Mens en melodie 29
        (1974): 73-78. In Dutch.

        Discusses performances in the Netherlands of the
        Vespers of 1610, Orfeo, Il combattimento di
        Tancredi e Clorinda, and Il ballo delle ingrate.
        Concludes with observations by Marius Flothius
        regarding performance practice.

761.   Schott, Howard. "Boston Early Music." Musical
        Times 122 (1981): 620.

        Reports favorably on a performance by the
        Banchetto Musical and the Boston Lyric Opera of
        Monteverdi's L'incoronazione di Poppea, directed by
        Martin Pearlman and based on his performing version
        of the work.

762.   Schumann, Karl. "Barockes Weihnachtsmärchen."
        Musica 23 (1969): 36.

        Reviews the Munich premiere of Orfeo, conducted
        by Matthias Kuntzsch, in the Cuvilliés theater.

763.   Stoeckl, R. "Orffs Welttheater." Opernwelt 21
        (1980): 42.

        Reports on performances of Monteverdi's Orfeo
        and Orff's Carmina burana at Augsburg's

Stadttheater, both staged in honor of Carl Orff's
eighty-fifth birthday.

764. Sutcliffe, James H. "West/East Berlin." Opera
      News (October 1980): 29-31.

      Briefly discusses an East Berlin Komische Oper
      production in German of L'incoronazione di Poppea.

765. Taylor, Peter. "Opera and Ballet in London."
      Musical Opinion 104 (1980): 20-21.

      Reports on an English National Opera production
      of L'incoronazione di Poppea conducted by Kenneth
      Montgomery. Applauds Raymond Leppard's edition of
      the score.

766. Tiersot, Julien. "L'Orfeo de Monteverde." Le
      ménestrel 70 (1904): 75-76.

      Reports on the significant 1904 Parisian
      performance of Orfeo produced by Vincent d'Indy.
      For other reviews of the performance, see items 709
      and 752.

767. Trevor, Claude. "Claudio Monteverdi (1567-1643)."
      Monthly Musical Record 11 (1910): 149-51.

      Reports on early twentieth-century Italian
      performances of Orfeo, presented in concert version
      with the edition prepared by Giacomo Orefice in
      1909. Includes a synopsis of the plot, as well as
      an assessment of Monteverdi's historical
      importance.

768. Trilling, Ossia. "Wenn Mäzene helfen: Beethoven,
      Monteverdi und Haydn in Glyndebourne." Opernwelt
      20 (1979): 25-26.

      Comments favorably on a revival of Il ritorno
      d'Ulisse featuring Frederica von Stade and Richard
      Stillwell in the leading roles.

769. Walker, Thomas. "Monteverdi Vespers." Musical
      Times 115 (1974): 406.

      Reviews a performance of the Vespers of 1610,
      conducted by Roger Norrington. Supports the
      practice followed in this performance of including
      the concertos between the psalms.

770. Wolff, Hellmut Christian. "Incoronazione di
      Poppea." Music Review 14 (1953): 299-300.

      Reviews a 1953 performance of Poppea produced by
      Ludwig Berger. The production is noted to be the
      first performance of this work in German. The
      review is translated by Hans Keller.

771. Wolff, Stéphane. "Le billet de Stéphane Wolff."
      Le courrier musical de France 62 (1978): 75.

      Provides a brief history of Parisian performances
      of L'incoronazione di Poppea. Reviews a perfor-
      mance of the opera, utilizing the Raymond Leppard
      edition, with Gwyneth Jones singing the role of
      Poppea and Jon Vickers as Nero.

772. Zijlstra, Miep. "Bij de Monteverdi-herdenking in
      het Holland Festival." Mens en melodie 22
      (1967): 132-36. In Dutch.

      Reports on performances in Amsterdam for the
      1967 Holland Festival celebrating the 400th
      birthday of Monteverdi. Also discusses Orfeo and
      the Vespers of 1610. Notes performance practice
      problems associated with modern revivals of early
      Baroque music.

773. ————. "Het Monteverdi-project van het Koninklijk
      Conservatorium." Mens en melodie 27 (1972):
      162-65. In Dutch.

      Deals with the Monteverdi celebration, organized
      under the leadership of Kees van Baaren and Jan van
      Vlijmen, at the Royal Conservatory in The Hague.
      The festival featured the Concentus Musicus under
      the direction of Nikolaus Harnoncourt.

774. ————. "L'incoronazione di Poppea, een belan-
      grijke Monteverdi-restauratie." Mens en melodie
      26 (1971): 341-43. In Dutch.

      Concerned with a Netherlands Opera House revival
      of L'incoronazione di Poppea. Provides background
      information pertaining to the two manuscript
      versions of the opera. Praises the work of Gustav
      Leonhardt and Alan Curtis in resurrecting the
      opera.

2. Research, Editions, and Recordings

775.   Abert, Anna Amalie. "Die Barockoper: Ein Bericht
       über die Forschung seit 1945." Acta musicologica
       41 (1969): 121-64.

       A comprehensive survey updating the state of
       research on Baroque opera after 1945. Provides an
       extensive bibliography for each individual topic.
       Concludes with a list of editions published since
       1945.

776.   Arnold, Denis. "Early Opera on Record."
       Gramophone 59 (December 1981): 871-72.

       Comments on recordings of Monteverdi's operas
       and other dramatic works by the composer such as Il
       ballo delle ingrate and Il combattimento di
       Tancredi e Clorinda.

777.   ———. "More Monteverdi Vespers." Musical Times
       108 (1967): 637-38.

       Cites the inherent problems associated with
       editing Monteverdi's Vespro della Beata Vergine of
       1610 and points out the strengths and weaknesses of
       Gottfried Wolters's edition of the Vespers.

778.   ———. Review of Claudio Monteverdi: Christmas
       Vespers, edited by Denis Stevens. Early Music 8
       (1980): 395-96.

       Reviews favorably Denis Stevens's compilation of
       five psalms and a hymn taken from Monteverdi's
       Selva morale and Messa a quattro voci et Salmi.

779.   Arnold, Denis, and Fortune, Nigel, ed. The
       Monteverdi Companion. London: Faber and Faber,
       1968; reprint ed., New York: Norton, 1972, pp.
       257-76. ISBN 0 393 00636 0   ML410 M77 A82 1972

       A collection of ten articles intended to shed
       light on Monteverdi's music and his environment.
       See items 206, 207, 256, 421, 455, 482, 663, 664,
       670, and 674 for individual articles. Contains an
       extensive bibliography of editions, books, and
       articles. An updated version of this work appeared
       in 1985 as The New Monteverdi Companion (item 780).

780.   ————. The New Monteverdi Companion. London:
        Faber and Faber, 1985. 353 pp. ISBN 0 571 13148
        4 ML410 M77 N5 1985

        An update of the earlier publication The
        Monteverdi Companion (item 779), with some articles
        reprinted from that volume. The eleven articles in
        The New Monteverdi Companion address Monteverdi's
        correspondence, his musical environment, the theory
        behind Monteverdi's art, the composer's music, and
        performance practice. See items 206, 207, 287,
        435, 491, 505, 663, 664, 671, 674, and 680 for
        individual articles. Contains a list of editions
        and an extensive bibliography.

781.   Barblan, Guglielmo. "Malipiero e Monteverdi."
        L'approdo musicale 3 (1960): 122-33.

        Describes the ambitious task of Malipiero in
        undertaking the complete edition of the works of
        Monteverdi. Briefly comments on his transcriptions
        and the publication of the works. Barblan notes
        that Malipiero believed he was guided by the spirit
        of Monteverdi when confronting transcription
        problems. Comments on the effect of this project
        on Malipiero's own compositions and his interest in
        early music.

782.   ————. "Nota bibliografica monteverdiana."
        Rivista italiana di musicologia (item 838), pp.
        387-89.

        Comments, in his review of the Universal edition
        of Tutte le opere di Claudio Monteverdi (Malipiero
        reprint), that only a small portion of this work is
        revised from the original printing. Volume VII
        carries the indication "revised," but no editor is
        indicated. Volumes XV and XVI indicate Denis
        Arnold as the editor. Also reviews volume XVII
        (Supplemento) of the Malipiero edition, which
        contains works found in anthologies.

783.   ————. Problemi monteverdiani. Rome: Accademia
        di S. Cecilia, 1954. 12 pp.

784.   Bedford, Steuart. "The Problems of 'Poppea.'"
        Opera 20 (1969): 94-100.

        Deplores the lack of authenticity found in most
        editions of L'incoronazione di Poppea. The author

discusses the problems encountered in the
preparation of his own edition of the opera.

785.   Blume, Friedrich.   "Saluto al convegno conquiste e
        prospettive monteverdiane." Rivista italiana di
        musicologia (item 838), pp. 203-206.

        Presents Blume's opening remarks at the Convegno
        internazionale di studi monteverdiani which took
        place in Siena, April 28-30, 1967. Gives an
        account of the state of Monteverdi research with a
        plea for more attention to be given to performance
        practice and for the need for a new Monteverdi
        complete edition. Translated into Italian by
        Guglielmo Barblan.

786.   Cesari, Gaetano.   "L' 'Orfeo' di Cl. Monteverdi
        all' 'Associazione di amici della musica' di
        Milano." Rivista musicale italiana 17 (1910):
        132-78.

        Critically reviews the Giacomo Orefice edition
        of Orfeo published by the 'Associazione di Amici
        della Musica' of Milan. Cesari compares the Eitner
        and d'Indy editions of Orfeo with the Orefice one.
        Criticizes the historical information in the
        preface of the Orefice edition. Includes
        considerable information on the use of instruments
        in dramatic works during the early seventeenth
        century and documents the use of ornamentation at
        this time.

787.   Dallapiccola, Luigi.   "Per una rappresentazione de
        'Il ritorno di Ulisse in patria' di Claudio
        Monteverdi." Musica II (item 813), pp. 121-36.

        Traces the discovery of the copy of Il ritorno
        di Ulisse at the National Library in Vienna and
        documents the subsequent debate over whether the
        work is by Monteverdi. Describes a transcription
        of the work by Dallapiccola and the rationale
        behind his edition.

788.   de' Paoli, Domenico.   "A Few Remarks on 'Orfeo' by
        Claudio Monteverdi." The Chesterian 20 (1939):
        61-67.

        Argues against editorial emendations in preparing
        an edition of Orfeo. Suggests a spiritual affinity

between Monteverdi's opera and Debussy's <u>Pelléas et Mélisande</u>.

789. Dobrodinský, Ján Mária. "Claudia Monteverdiho <u>Vespro della beata Vergine</u>. Poznámky k interpretácii." <u>SlovenskáHud</u> 12 (February 1968): 60-64. In Slovak.

Not examined. Summary in <u>RILM Abstracts</u>, 2/2 (May-August 1968): 145, notes that the article compares Redlich's edition (1934) and Goehr's edition (1956) of the <u>Vespro della Beata Vergine</u>.

790. Donington, Robert. Review of Claudio Monteverdi: <u>Orfeo (1607), favola pastorale in due parti</u>, edited by Bruno Maderna; and <u>L'Orfeo, favola in musica</u>, edited by Denis Stevens. <u>Music Library Association Notes</u> 25 (1968): 112-14.

Reviews Bruno Maderna's edition (Zerboni, 1967) of <u>Orfeo</u> and Denis Stevens's edition of the same work (Novello, 1967). Criticizes Maderna's edition for its arbitrary transpositions and praises the one by Stevens for being scholarly yet practical.

791. Epstein, Peter. "Monteverdi in unserer Zeit." <u>Die Musik</u> 22 (1929-30): 86-88.

Evaluates available editions of Monteverdi's music, with particular emphasis on <u>Orfeo</u>. Praises and discusses Malipiero's progress toward a complete edition of Monteverdi's works.

792. Fenlon, Iain. Review of <u>Monteverdi</u>, by Paolo Fabbri. <u>Musical Times</u> 127 (1986): 92.

Praises Fabbri (item 303) for presenting evidence of the cultural climate in Cremona, Mantua, and Venice. The reviewer considers this study to be "the most detailed account of Monteverdi's activities yet produced."

793. Finke, G. W. "Monteverdis Werke in Gesamtausgabe." <u>Neue Musikzeitung</u> 23 (1974): 15.

794. Finscher, Ludwig, ed. <u>Claudio Monteverdi: Festschrift Reinhold Hammerstein zum 70. Geburtstag</u>. Laaber: Laaber-Verlag, 1986. 508 pp. ISBN 3 890 07105 8 ML410 M77 C53 1986

Published in honor of the seventieth birthday of Reinhold Hammerstein, this volume contains a collection of twenty-three essays dealing with various aspects of Monteverdi's music. Also includes a list of Monteverdi's compositions. For individual articles, see items 93, 161, 222, 227, 232, 355, 374, 428, 432, 447, 461, 484, 489, 522, 526, 592, 628, 629, 643, 661, 723, 802, and 842.

795. Fox, Charles Warren. Review of Monteverdi: Create of Modern Music, by Leo Schrade (item 341). Musical Quarterly 37 (1951): 272-78.

An informative and complimentary review. Suggests that Schrade was more interested in the earlier stages of Monteverdi's output than in his mature style.

796. Gallico, Claudio. "Per la nuova edizione nazional di tutte le opere di Claudio Monteverdi." Congresso internazionale sul tema Claudio Monteverd (item 811), pp. 505-17.

Summarizes views by Blume, Redlich, and Barblan concerning the lack of a new edition of Monteverdi's works. Announces a proposed new complete edition of the works of Monteverdi. Give a list of editorial procedures to be used in this edition and outlines the contents of the proposed volumes.

797. Gianuario, Annibale. "Correspondence." Music and Letters 52 (1971): 466-67.

Written as a rebuttal to Westrup's review (item 855) of a book by Gianuario and Anfuso. Five majc points of issue are cited by Gianuario. Music and Letters includes a response from the reviewer.

798. Glover, Jane. "The Metamorphoses of 'Orfeo.'" Musical Times 116 (1975): 135-39.

Critically reviews editions of Monteverdi's Orfe from Eitner's 1881 edition to the editions of Deni Stevens, Bruno Maderna, and Raymond Leppard, all c which appeared in 1967. Criticizes most of the earlier versions for their extensive cuts and lack of faithfulness to Monteverdi's and Striggio's text.

799. ————. Review of Claudio Monteverdi: Orfeo,
      recorded by the Monteverdi Choir and the
      Hamburg/Instrumental Ensemble, conducted by
      Jürgen Jürgens. Musical Times 116 (1975): 149-
      50.

      Reviews a recording of Orfeo (Archive 2723 018)
      conducted by Jürgen Jürgens which used the
      conductor's edition of the score. Criticizes the
      performance for the excessive number of string
      instruments used and for the addition of string
      instruments to the brass sinfonias in Acts 3 and 4.

800. Graubart, Michael. "Letters to the Editor:
      Monteverdi's Instrumentation." Musical Times 116
      (1975): 339.

      Offered as a reply to Jane Glover's review (item
      799) of Jürgens's recording of Orfeo. Contends
      that strings should play the five-part sinfonia
      prior to "Possente spirto" in the third act.

801. Hübsch-Pfleger, Lini. "Monteverdi als Theater-
      musiker." Musikhandel 18 (1967): 105-107.

      Written in honor of Monteverdi's 400th birthday,
      this article provides a cursory examination of
      Monteverdi as an opera composer. Considers new
      editions of his operas.

802. Hunkemöller, Jürgen. "Strawinsky rezipiert
      Monteverdi." Claudio Monteverdi: Festschrift
      Reinhold Hammerstein (item 794), pp. 237-47.

      Begins with a brief discussion of twentieth-
      century composers who have edited works by
      Monteverdi. Considers Monteverdi's influence upon
      the music of Stravinsky.

803. Hutchings, Arthur. "Monteverdi's Vespers."
      Musical Times 102 (1961): 572.

      Praises Denis Stevens's edition of Monteverdi's
      Vespers of 1610 as published by Novello.

804. Kerman, Joseph. Review of Claudio Monteverdi, by
      Hans F. Redlich (item 332). Musical Quarterly 39
      (1953): 120-26.

      Kerman's highly informative review criticizes
      Redlich for presenting Monteverdi as the composer

chiefly responsible for several musical innovation
of the early Baroque.

805. Krenek, Ernst. "Meine Textbearbeitung von Monteverdis 'Poppea.'" Anbruch 18 (1936): 106-108.

One of three articles by the author on his
performing edition of L'incoronazione di Poppea.
See also Krenek, items 518 and 806.

806. ————. "Zur musikalischen Bearbeitung von
Monteverdis 'Poppea.'" Schweizerische
Musikzeitung 76 (1936): 545-55.

Contains a thorough discussion of the author's
often-criticized practical performing edition of
L'incoronazione di Poppea. See also Krenek, items
518 and 806.

807. Kurtzman, Jeffrey G. Review of Claudio Monteverdi
Madrigali à 5 voci, libro primo, edited by
Raffaello Monterosso; and Claudio Monteverdi: Il
primo libro di madrigali à cinque voci, edited b
Bernard Bailly de Surcy. Journal of the America
Musicological Society 27 (1974): 343-48.

Compares the editorial procedures used in
Raffaello Monterosso's edition of Monteverdi's
first book of madrigals, published by Athenaeum
Cremonense (1972), with Bernard Bailly de Surcy's
edition of the same collection, published by Les
Editions Renaissantes (1972). Considers the
Monterosso edition an "objective and scholarly"
edition and de Surcy's work to be a performing
version. Criticizes the notational practices,
musica ficta, and performance practice recom-
mendations in the de Surcy edition.

808. ————. Review of The New Monteverdi Companion
(item 780), edited by Denis Arnold and Nigel
Fortune. Musical Quarterly 72 (1986): 418-21.

Criticizes the volume's lack of new research and
argues that it contains a limited viewpoint due to
the fact that the essays were written by only
British scholars.

809. Lincoln, Stoddard. "Monteverdi Madrigals." Stere
Review 46 (August 1981): 98.

Criticizes the Philips recording of Monteverdi's eighth book of madrigals, under the direction of Raymond Leppard, for its virtuosic, nineteenth-century style.

810.   Lippmann, Friedrich, and Witzenmann, Wolfgang. "Convegno di studi monteverdiani." Die Musikforschung 21 (1968): 64-65.

Reports on the Monteverdi Congress held under the auspices of the Società Italiana di Musicologia at Siena, Italy, in April of 1967.

811.   Monterosso, Raffaello, ed. Congresso internazionale sul tema Claudio Monteverdi e il suo tempo. Verona: Stamperia Valdoneza, 1969.   638 pp.   ML410 M77 C6

Contains papers read at the 1968 International Congress celebrating the Monteverdi quatercentenary, which took place in Venice, May 3-4; Mantua, May 5; and Cremona, May 6-7.   The theme of the conference was "Claudio Monteverdi and His Time."   Includes a greeting to the Congress by Giovanni Favaretto Fisca, a celebration address by Piero Caleffi, and a concluding statement by Federico Mompellio.   Reprints music programs presented at the conference.   For individual articles, see items 22, 114, 118, 189, 212, 220, 225, 237, 358, 376, 400, 401, 407, 443, 471, 479, 494, 529, 553, 596, 612, 614, 620, 642, 644, 653, 669, 690, 696, 702, 703, 737, 796, 841, and 861.

812.   Moore, James H.   Review of The Letters of Claudio Monteverdi (item 273), edited by Denis Stevens. Journal of the American Musicological Society 35 (1982): 554-65.

A very informative review which generally praises this volume of Monteverdi's letters in English translation.   Maintains that the commentaries provided for each letter represent a significant contribution to the composer's biography.

813.   Musica II.   Florence: Officina Grafica Fratelli Stianti, 1943.   281 pp.

A collection of articles devoted principally to Monteverdi in commemoration of the 300th anniversary of the composer's death.   The

introductory essay is by G.F. Malipiero (item 734)
Other articles are listed as items 4, 362, 541,
625, 682, and 787. Thirty-two plates in this
volume contribute to Monteverdi iconography.

814. Newcomb, Anthony. Review of Claudio Monteverdi:]
      primo libro de' madrigali a cinque voci, edited
      by Bernard Bailly de Surcy. Musical Quarterly (
      (1974): 118-26.

      Reviews an edition of Monteverdi's first book of
      madrigals, published by Les Editions Renaissantes
      (1972). Discusses the salient characteristics of
      Monteverdi's madrigal style and compares two of th
      madrigals with settings of the same text by Orazic
      Vecchi and Luca Marenzio. Questions some of the
      editorial procedures of the editor. See also item
      807.

815. Norrington, Roger. "A New Edition of Poppea."
      Music and Musicians 22 (July 1974): 22-23.

      Reports on Roger Norrington's realization of
      L'incoronazione di Poppea based on a collation of
      available manuscripts by Alan Curtis. Cites the
      restricted use of the orchestra and performance at
      the original pitch as unique aspects of this
      production.

816. L'Orfeo. Avant-scène opéra 5 (September-October
      1976): 1-89.

      Contains a collection of ten essays devoted to
      Monteverdi's initial opera. The volume also
      includes Striggio's libretto with a French trans-
      lation provided by Denyse Wettstein and a
      commentary written by Henry Barraud. Offers a
      discography, a list of performances to 1976, a
      selective bibliography, and English summaries of
      the articles by François Pouget. The essays are
      cited here as items 451, 452, 453, 472, 474, 478,
      493, 497, 528, and 701.

817. Osthoff, Wolfgang. "Monteverdi-Funde." Archiv fü
      Musikwissenschaft 14 (1957): 253-80.

      An extensive report of twelve compositions
      attributed to Monteverdi not included in
      Malipiero's complete edition. Osthoff edited and
      published these works for Ricordi under the title

Monteverdi: 12 Composizioni vocali profane e sacre
(Milan, 1958).

818. ————. "Per la notazione originale nelle pubbli-
      cazioni di musiche antiche e specialmente nella
      nuova edizione Monteverdi." Acta musicologica 34
      (1962): 101-27.

      Argues that editions of Monteverdi's works which
      alter the original note values or the original
      clefs only serve to distort the music. Claims that
      the reduction in note values used by many editors
      of early music is more appropriate for instrumental
      than vocal music. Cites numerous examples from
      Monteverdi's works to make his point.

819. Rassegna musicale 2 (October 1929): 453-511.

      This issue of Rassegna musicale is devoted to
      Claudio Monteverdi. See items 13, 406, 668, and
      676.

820. Redlich, Hans F. "Aufgaben und Ziele der
      Monteverdi-Forschung." Die Musikforschung 4
      (1951): 318-32.

      A lengthy essay criticizing Leo Schrade's book
      Monteverdi: Creator of Modern Music (item 341),
      focusing primarily upon Schrade's use of the
      Malipiero edition. Schrade later defended his book
      against Redlich's attack in a letter to the editor
      of Music Review (item 843).

821. ————. "Claudio Monteverdi (1567-1643), Some
      Editorial Problems of 1967." The Consort 24
      (1967): 224-32.

      Discusses editions of Monteverdi's works with
      emphasis on the Malipiero complete edition.
      Criticizes Malipiero's editorial judgement and the
      mistakes he made in his transcriptions. Cites
      several examples of these errors in the edition and
      offers his own solutions. Notes sources other than
      the original printed works which should be
      consulted for a more accurate edition of
      Monteverdi's music.

822. ————. "Claudio Monteverdi: Some Problems of
      Textual Interpretation." Musical Quarterly
      41 (1955): 66-75.

A critical review by Leo Schrade (see item 845)
of Redlich's edition of Monteverdi's Vespro della
Beata Vergine 1610 (Universal, 2nd revised editic
1952) seems to have prompted this defense of
Redlich's editorial practices. The discussion
centers on realization of the figured bass, use c
instruments, and ornamentation. Redlich also mak
observations on the continuo problems in Monteverdi's fifth book of madrigals.

823. ————. "Claudio Monteverdi's 'L'incoronazione d
Poppea.'" Schweizerische Musikzeitung 77 (1937
617-27.

Concerns the author's edition of L'incoronazion
di Poppea, published in 1937. Divided into five
parts: history and bibliography, libretto, music,
musical criticism of the text, and problems of th
musical edition.

824. ————. "Correspondence: Editions of Monteverdi'
Vespers of 1610." The Gramophone 31 (1954): 50

Defends, in the form of a letter to the editor,
his edition of the Monteverdi Vespers against
criticisms made by Leo Schrade. Claims that
Schrade's edition of the same work borrowed
features from the Redlich edition.

825. ————. "Correspondence: Monteverdi." Music
Review 15 (1954): 87-88.

Defends his 1959 practical edition of
Monteverdi's Vespers of 1610 in light of Leo
Schrade's comments in a letter to Music Review
(item 843).

826. ————. "Dreissig Jahre Monteverdi-Renaissance."
Österreichische Musikzeitschrift 8 (1953): 85-9

Primarily an account of Redlich's Monteverdi
activities from 1922 until 1952. Concludes with
list of the author's Monteverdi publications.

827. ————. "The Editing of Monteverdi."
Renaissance News 7 (1954): 18-20, 50-52.

Points out problems associated with the editing
of Monteverdi's music. Cites several examples of
editorial problems in specific pieces.

828.   ————. "Monteverdi and Schütz in New Editions."
        Music Review 19 (1958): 72-76.

        Contains a thorough review and comparison of
        modern editions of works by Monteverdi and Schütz,
        all published in the 1950s. Criticizes three
        different editions of the Vespers of 1610,
        published respectively by Ghedini, Wolters, and
        Goehr. Includes a generally complimentary
        discussion of two editions of Orfeo, one edited by
        Wenzinger and the other by Hindemith.

829.   ————. "Monteverdi-Gesamtausgabe." Anbruch 10
        (1928): 207-11.

        Offers an assessment of Malipiero's complete
        edition (in progress at that time) of Monteverdi's
        works. Praises the editor for achieving a
        synthesis between the scientific approach and the
        pragmatic approach.

830.   ————. "Neue Monteverdiana." Anbruch 13 (1931):
        127-28.

        Redlich's report on the publication of volumes
        VII through XIII of Malipiero's Collected Edition.

831.   ————. "Notes to a New Edition of Monteverdi's
        Mass of 1651." Monthly Musical Record 83 (May
        1953): 95-99.

        Includes a concise list of editorial changes
        that Redlich recommends which differ from the
        Malipiero edition of Monteverdi's Messa a 4 voci da
        cappella of 1651. These changes are made on the
        basis of observations from the 1651 printing of
        this work and are incorporated in the Eulenburg
        (1952) edition of this work edited by Redlich.

832.   ————. "Problemi monteverdiani." Rivista
        italiana di musicologia (item 838), pp. 328-31.

        Mentions several attempts at earlier Monteverdi
        complete editions, yet comments that, as of the end
        of 1967, the 1926-42 Malipiero edition, with its
        Universal Edition reprint, stands as the only
        realized collected edition. Rather than wait for a
        totally new edition, Redlich advocates a total
        revision of the Malipiero one. Translated into
        Italian by Guglielmo Barblan.

833. ————. "The Re-Discovery of Monteverdi, on the
     Occasion of a New Edition of L'Incoronazione di
     Poppea." Music Review 23 (1962): 103-108.

     Recaps the rediscovery of Monteverdi from Carl
     von Winterfeld's early assessment to the more
     recent practical editions of Monteverdi's works.
     Includes a brief history of Monteverdi's
     L'incoronazione di Poppea, along with some of the
     editorial problems prevalent in this work.

834. ————. "Zur Bearbeitung von Monteverdis 'Orfeo.
     Schweizerische Musikzeitung 76 (1936): 37-42;
     74-80.

     Presents the author's editorial conclusions
     relating to his performing edition of Orfeo
     produced at Zurich in 1936. Attempts to place the
     opera in its proper historical position and briefl
     discusses other editions of the work. Criticizes
     Malipiero's printing of Orfeo for its numerous
     editorial mistakes.

835. Redlich, Hans F., and Stevens, Denis. "Monte-
     verdi's Vespers." Musical Times 102 (1961): 56-
     65.

     Contains a letter to the editor by Redlich
     criticizing Stevens's article "Monteverdi's Vespe
     Verified" (item 648). Also includes a letter of
     rebuttal by Stevens to Redlich's criticisms.

836. Reiner, Stuart. Review of Claudio Monteverdi e i
     suo tempo (item 811), edited by Raffaello
     Monterosso. Music Library Association Notes 26
     (1970): 747-48.

     This book, published as the result of the Italia
     congress held in honor of the 400th anniversary o
     Monteverdi's birth, is held in high regard by the
     reviewer. Notes the contents of the volume which
     among other items, contains 35 scholarly essays.
     Criticizes the volume for the absence of an index.

837. ————. Review of The Monteverdi Companion (item
     779), edited by Denis Arnold and Nigel Fortune.
     Journal of the American Musicological Society 2
     (1970): 343-49.

     Comments on each essay in the book. Criticizes
     the volume for its uneven quality.

838. Rivista italiana di musicologia 2/2 (1967), pp.
       201-389.

      This volume of Rivista italiana di musicologia
      contains papers presented in Siena, April 28-30,
      1967 at the Convegno internazionale di studi
      monteverdiani sponsored by the Società Italiana di
      Musicologia. For individual articles, see items
      211, 213, 218, 228, 368, 371, 426, 440, 458, 480,
      593, 631, 640, 650, 652, 662, 758, 782, 785, and
      832.

839. Roche, Jerome. "New Vespers". Musical Times
       121 (1980): 387.

      Takes issue with some of the editorial practices
      used by Denis Stevens in his Christmas Vespers
      publication.

840. Ronga, Luigi. "Su Monteverdi e sull'opera italiana
       del seicento." Rivista musicale italiana 57
       (1955): 140-50.

      Reviews in detail Anna Amalie Abert's Claudio
      Monteverdi und das musikalische Drama (item 438)
      and comments on Simon Towneley Worsthorne's
      Venetian Opera in the Seventeenth Century (item
      192). Praises Abert's study of seventeenth-century
      opera for its inclusion of literary, pictorial, and
      theatrical materials, as well as its musical
      analysis. Ronga is critical of Abert's speculation
      on the origin of the Venetian opera aria and her
      conclusion that only Monteverdi was successful in
      blending the theatrical/festival characteristic of
      Roman opera with the public celebration of Venetian
      opera. Worsthorne's study is considered valuable
      for its information on scenic conditions and organ-
      ization of the performances, but it falls short of
      being a thorough study of Venetian opera.

*   Salvetti, Guido. "Alcuni criteri nella rielabo-
       razione ed orchestrazione dell' 'Incoronazione.'"

      Cited above as item 758.

841. Schenk, Erich. "Festansprache." Congresso inter-
       nazionale sul tema Claudio Monteverdi (item 811),
       pp. 627-33.

      The concluding paper presented to the Inter-
      national Monteverdi Congress held in 1968.

242 MONTEVERDI TOD

Stresses the connection between Monteverdi and
Austria.

842. Schneider, Herbert. "Carl Orffs Neugestaltung vc
Monteverdis 'Orfeo' und ihre Vorgeschichte."
Claudio Monteverdi: Festschrift Reinhold
Hammerstein (item 794), pp. 387-407.

Thoroughly discusses and compares the editions
Orfeo prepared by Carl Orff. Reports on the history of Orfeo editions beginning in 1881. Compar
the editions of the opera by Robert Eitner and
Vincent d'Indy.

843. Schrade, Leo. "Correspondence: Monteverdi." Mus
Review 14 (1953): 336-40.

Schrade's letter to the editor is in response
to an article (item 820) by Hans Redlich which
contains criticisms of Schrade's book on Monteverdi.

844. ————. Review of Claudio Monteverdi: Beatus Vir
Laudate Dominum, and Ut queant laxis, recorded
the vocal ensemble and chamber orchestra of the
Scuola Veneziana, conducted by Angelo Ephrikian
Claudio Monteverdi: Combattimento di Tancredi e
Clorinda, Ballo della Ninfe d'Istro, Mentrê Vag
Angioletta, same performers as above; and Claud
Monteverdi: Domine Ad Adjuvandum, Nigra sum, Av
Maris Stella, and Magnificat, same performers a
above. Musical Quarterly 39 (1953): 328-39.

Reviews three recordings of Monteverdi's works
(Period SPLP 536, Period SPL 551, and Period SPL
558) conducted by Angelo Ephrikian. Includes a
description of the works recorded and comments on
the performances. Finds many aspects of the performances favorable but considers some tempos too
slow.

845. ————. Review of Claudio Monteverdi: Vespro del
Beata Vergine (1610), recorded by the Swabian
Chorale Singers and the Stuttgart Bach Orchestr
conducted by Hans Grischkat. Musical Quarterly
40 (1954): 138-45.

Cites as "adequate" the recording of Monteverdi
Vespro della Beata Vergine (Vox PL 7902) conducte
by Hans Grischkat, which uses the Hans Redlich

edition. Criticizes Redlich's version for its de-
pendence on Malipiero's edition and for its instrumentation, expression markings, and realization of
the thorough-bass.

846. Seay, Albert. Review of Adrian Willaert: Memento
      Domine David, edited by Joan Long; and Claudio
      Monteverdi: Gloria concertata a 7 voci, edited by
      John Steele. Music Library Association Notes 26
      (1970): 837-40.

      Reviews favorably Joan Long's edition of Memento
      Domine and John Steele's edition of Monteverdi's
      Gloria concertata, both published in the Penn State
      Music Series. Considers Steele's score of the
      Gloria excellent but criticizes the preparation of
      the orchestral parts.

847. ————. Review of Claudio Monteverdi: Orfeo,
      edited by Edward H. Tarr. Music Library Asso-
      ciation Notes 32 (1975): 125-26.

      The reviewer praises Edward Tarr's edition of
      Monteverdi's Orfeo for its scholarship and for its
      usefulness as the basis of an authentic perform-
      ance.

848. Siegmund-Schultze, Walther. "Beiträge zu einem
      neuen Monteverdi-Bild." Wissenschaftliche Beitr.
      der U. Halle, Reihe G 8 (1968): 11-40.

      Not examined. Author summary in RILM Abstracts,
      2/3 (September-December 1968): 266, reveals that
      the monograph consists of two essays originally
      presented at the 1967 Halle Symposium on Monte-
      verdi. Monteverdi's compositions are viewed from
      the standpoint of their historical position.

849. Steele, John. "Tre Missae: Claudio Monteverdi."
      Early Music (1975): 170.

      Questions the authenticity of three masses at-
      tributed to Monteverdi by Don Cisilino in a Uni-
      versal Edition publication.

850. Stevens, Denis. "Communications." Journal of the
      American Musicological Society 24 (1971): 320-23.

      Strongly criticizes the translations of selected
      Monteverdi letters which appear in The Monteverdi
      Companion (item 779).

851.   ———. "New Vespers." <u>Musical Times</u> 121
        (1980): 490.

        A response, in the form of a letter to the
        editor, to Jerome Roche's review of Stevens's
        edition of Monteverdi's <u>Christmas Vespers</u>.

852.   ———. "A Preface to Monteverdi's Orfeo." <u>Amer</u>
        <u>ican Choral Review</u> 9 (1967): 3-11.

        This article is a reprint of the preface to
        Stevens's edition of <u>Orfeo</u> for the subscribers of
        the <u>American Choral Review</u>. The preface is divid
        into the following sections: historical backgroun
        editorial problems, orchestra, woodwind, brass,
        strings, continuo, basic realization, and notatio
        Especially helpful are the editor's pragmatic sol
        tions to various problems of performance practice

853.   Weber, J.F. "A Remarkably Fine New Orfeo."
        <u>Fanfare</u> 5 (1982): 201-203.

        Reviews favorably Siegfried Heinrich's recordin
        of Monteverdi's <u>Orfeo</u> on the Jubilate label (JU
        85810-12) and gives an overview of the recordings
        of this work. Includes an annotated discography
        Monteverdi's operas.

854.   Westrup, Jack A. "Monteverdi's 'Il ritorno
        d'Ulisse in patria.'" <u>Monthly Musical Record</u>
        58 (1928): 106-107.

        Reviews a BBC broadcast performance of Monte-
        verdi's <u>Ulisse</u> and criticizes the d'Indy edition
        used in the performance for its additional string
        parts in recitatives, for its inappropriate reali
        zation of the basso continuo, and for the numerou
        cuts in the edition. Concludes with a brief com-
        parison of the musical style of Monteverdi's
        operas.

855.   ———. "Review of <u>Claudio Monteverdi: Lamento</u>
        <u>d'Arianna. Studio e interpretazione</u> (item 445),
        N. Anfuso and A. Gianuario." <u>Music and Letters</u> 5
        (1971): 200-201.

        A scathing review of almost every facet of the
        book. Especially critical of the fact that only
        one manuscript source was used, the Florence
        manuscript. Also see Gianuario (item 797).

856. ————. "Review of Claudio Monteverdi: L'Orfeo,
       edited by Denis Stevens. Music and Letters 48
       (1967): 400-402.

       A generally favorable review of Stevens's
       edition of Orfeo published by Novello in 1967.
       Includes a list of corrections for the Malipiero
       edition of Orfeo from the collected works, Vol. XI.

857. ————. Review of Tutte le opere di Claudio
       Monteverdi, vols. XII, XII, VIV, pt. i, and XIV,
       pt. ii, edited by G. Francesco Malipiero. Music
       and Letters 48 (1967): 171-78.

       Compares Malipiero's edition of L'incoronazione
       di Poppea (Tutte le Opere, vol. XIII) with the
       editions of W. Goehr and R. Leppard. Suggests
       solutions to problems of continuo realization in
       Poppea.

858. Witzenmann, Wolfgang. "Die italienische Kirchen-
       musik des Barocks--ein Bericht über die Literatur
       aus den Jahren 1945 bis 1974." Acta musicologica
       48 (1976): 77-103.

       A substantial article focusing on research and
       literature about early Baroque Italian church music
       produced from 1945 to 1974. Concludes with an
       excellent bibliography.

       3. Bibliographies, Catalogs, and Discographies

859. An Alphabetical Index to Claudio Monteverdi tutte
       le opere novamente date in luce da G. Francesco
       Malipiero, Asolo 1926-1947, MLA Index Series:
       Number one, edited by the Bibliography Committee
       of the New York Chapter MLA. New York: Music
       Library Association, 1964? 17 pp. ML134 M66 A2

       An alphabetical index of Monteverdi's works con-
       tained in the Malipiero collected edition. Cites
       volume, page, year of composition, number of parts,
       and basso continuo, if extant. Lists contents for
       the sixteen volumes of the Malipiero edition.

860.   Barblan, Guglielmo, ed. <u>Catalogo della Bibliotec</u>
       <u>del Conservatorio di Musica 'G. Verdi' di Milan</u>
       <u>Fondi speciali 1: Musiche della Cappella di S.</u>
       <u>Barbara in Mantova.</u> Biblioteca di Bibliografia
       Italiana, 68. Florence: Olschki, 1972.   530 pp.
       ML136 M6 V49

       An important catalog of music from the church
       of Santa Barbara in Mantua. Asserts, in the pref-
       ace, that the absence of Monteverdi's name from
       this collection suggests that the composer's activ
       ities may have been limited to the theater and
       court at Mantua. Contains a thematic index of
       incipits, an index of printers and editors, and ar
       index of text incipits. See also Jeppesen (item
       620).

861.   Cè, Nivia. "Saggio di discografia monteverdiana."
       <u>Congresso internazionale sul tema Claudio Monte-</u>
       <u>verdi</u> (item 811), pp. 543-56.

       An annotated discography of Monteverdi's sacred
       music and dramatic works, excluding madrigals.
       Annotations contain information on editions used
       and evaluations of performances.

*   Galvani, Livio Niso. <u>I teatri musicali di Venezi</u>
       <u>nel secolo XVII (1637-1700): memorie storiche e</u>
       <u>bibliografiche.</u>

       Cited above as item 80.

*   Ivanovich, Cristoforo. <u>Minerva al tavolino.</u>

       Cited above as item 99.

862.   Lowenberg, Alfred. <u>Annals of Opera, 1597-1940.</u>
       3rd ed. Totowa, New Jersey: Rowman and Little-
       field, 1978. ISBN 0 874 71851 1 ML102.06 L6
       1978

       A standard reference work on opera performances.
       Arranged chronologically, each entry identifies tl
       composer, the original title, the date and locatic
       of the first performance, the librettist, and sub-
       sequent performances. Includes entries for <u>Orfeo</u>
       <u>Arianna</u>, <u>Adone</u>, <u>Il ritorno d'Ulisse</u>, and <u>L'incoro-</u>
       <u>nazione di Poppea</u>. Contains a name, location, an
       topic index as well as indexes for operas, compos-
       ers, and librettists.

863. Marco, Guy. Opera: A Research and Information
      Guide. Garland Reference Library of the
      Humanities, vol. 468. New York: Garland, 1984.
      373 pp. ISBN 0 824 08999 5 ML128.04 M28 1984

      An annotated bibliography of writings on opera.
      Cites general music reference works, opera refer-
      ence works, opera yearbooks, opera periodicals, and
      studies of individual opera composers. Lists
      Monteverdi studies on page 114. Contains a check-
      list of opera composers and their major works, an
      author-title index, and a subject index.

864. Monterosso, Raffaello, ed. Mostra bibliografica
      dei musicisti cremonesi: catalogo storico-critico
      degli autori e catalogo bibliografico. Cremona:
      Biblioteca Governativa e Liberia Civica, 1951.
      149 pp.

      Dedicated to the memory of the Cremonese musi-
      cologist Gaetano Cesari, this volume contains a
      catalog of the 1949 exhibition pertaining to
      composers active in Cremona from the Renaissance
      through the nineteenth century. Presents brief,
      critical profiles, written by Monterosso, of
      musicians active in Cremona (the Monteverdi entry
      can be found on pages 36-40). The second part of
      this work is a catalog of works by Cremonese
      musicians located in nineteen libraries in Italy,
      France, and Austria. Includes an anthology of
      music by Cremonese composers. Offers an index to
      the music anthology, an index for the bibliographic
      catalog, and an index of illustrations.

*   L'Orfeo. Avant-scène opéra.

      Cited above as item 816.

865. Parsons, Charles H. The Mellen Opera Reference
      Index, Opera Composers and Their Works. 4 vols.
      Lewiston, New York: The Edwin Mellen Press, 1986.
      1966 pp. ISBN 0 889 46400 6 ML102.06 P25

      This index cites composers and their works
      with place and date of first performance and
      locations of manuscript sources. Monteverdi's
      works are listed in volume three, pp. 1226-27.

866. Pincherle, Marc. "Monteverdi." Journal musical
     français musica-disques 161-62 (1967): 20-23.

867. Répertoire international des sources musicales,
     A/I/6. Einzeldruck vor 1800, edited by Karlheinz
     Schlazer. Vol. 6. Kassel: Bärenreiter, 1976.
     670 pp.

     Lists musical works printed before 1800. Monte-
     verdi's printed works are cited with bibliographic
     citations and locations of printed sources.

868. Répertoire international des sources musicales.
     Recueils imprimés XVIe-XVIIe siècles, I Liste
     chronologique, published under the direction of
     François Lesure. Kassel: Bärenreiter, 1960.   639
     pp. ML113 I6 vol. BI

     A chronological list of music collections pub-
     lished in the sixteenth and seventeenth centuries.
     The entries identify composers and the number of
     works contributed to the collections but not the
     specific works included. Cites the locations of
     the anthologies by means of library sigla. Con-
     tains an index of titles and authors of collections
     and an index of publishers and printers. Collec-
     tions which contain Monteverdi works are cited in
     this bibliography.

869. Salzman, Eric. "Opera: How It Began." Stereo
     Review 36 (1976): 56-60.

     A concise survey of the development of opera
     from its beginnings with the Florentine Camerata
     to Venetian opera of the late seventeenth century.
     Includes information on available recordings of
     early operas.

870. Sartori, Claudio. Bibliografia della musica
     strumentale italiana, stampata in Italia fino al
     1700. Florence: Olschki, 1952.   652 pp.   ML120
     I8 S3

     A bibliography of instrumental music printed
     before 1700 which also includes vocal works with
     instruments. Monteverdi's Vespers of 1610 and his
     fifth through eighth books of madrigals are cited.
     Bibliographic entries include prefaces, table of
     contents, and locations of printed sources.

*   Solerti, Angelo. "Le rappresentazioni musicali di
        Venezia dal 1571 al 1605 per la prima volta
        descritte."

        Cited above as item 167.

871.   Sommerfield, David. "A Monteverdi Discography."
        Current Musicology 8-9 (1969): 215-32.

        Lists Monteverdi recordings available at the time
        of publication. Gives detailed information on
        recordings not found in the Schwann record catalog.

872.   Sonneck, O.G. "Italienische Opernlibretti des 17.
        Jahrhunderts in der Library of Congress." Sam-
        melbände der Internationalen Musik-Gesellschaft
        13 (1911-12): 392-99.

        Primarily a catalog of seventeenth-century opera
        librettos contained in the Library of Congress.
        Identifies the composer, title, place of publica-
        tion, and the likely or certain dates of publica-
        tion. Includes three librettos set by Monteverdi.

873.   ————. Library of Congress Catalogue of Opera
        Librettos printed before 1800. 2 vols.
        Washington: Government Printing Office, 1914;
        reprint ed., New York: Johnson Reprint Corp.,
        1968. 1172, 1674 pp. ML136 U55 C45 1968

        Catalogs, with brief commentaries, opera libret-
        tos in the Library of Congress printed before 1800.
        Volume 2 contains an author list, composer list,
        and an aria index. Cites librettos set by
        Monteverdi.

874.   Stattkus, Manfred H. Claudio Monteverdi Verzeich-
        nis der erhaltenen Werke. Bergkamen: Stattkus,
        1985. 183 pp. ML134 M66 S72 1985

        A catalog of Monteverdi's works. Contains a
        works index divided into three parts: collections,
        individual works, and works of questionable authen-
        ticity. Presents a list of both printed and manu-
        script sources. Also contains an alphabetical list
        of titles, subtitles, and incipits. Provides lists
        of instrumental settings, contrafacta, arrange-
        ments, editors, publishers, modern editions, and a
        chronology of printing. Includes a bibliography
        and illustrations.

875. Vogel, Emil. Bibliothek der gedruckten weltlichen
      Vocalmusik Italiens aus den Jahren 1500-1700. 2
      vols. Hildesheim: Olms, 1962. 530, 832 pp.
      ML120 I8 V8

      Contains bibliographic information for Italian
      secular vocal music printed from 1500 to 1700. The
      first part, arranged alphabetically by composer,
      lists the contents of collections devoted mainly to
      one composer. The second part, arranged chrono-
      logically by date of publication, lists the con-
      tents of anthologies. This work, first published
      in Berlin in 1892, was greatly expanded by Alfred
      Einstein. The first part of this work has been
      superseded by item 876.

876. Vogel, Emil; Einstein, Alfred; Lesure, François;
      and Sartori, Claudio. Bibliografia della musica
      italiana vocale profana pubblicata dal 1500 al
      1700. 3 vols. Pomezia: Staderini-Minkoff
      Editori, 1977. 946, 1888, 615 pp. ML120 I8 B18

      A comprehensive catalog of secular vocal music
      published between 1500 and 1700. Volumes one and
      two contain collections devoted to one composer.
      Volume three contains an index to works in the
      previous two volumes, including poets of works, if
      known. Cites bibliographic information on Monte-
      verdi's madrigals, Scherzi musicali, and Orfeo.
      This volume supersedes the first part of Vogel's
      Bibliothek der gedruckten weltlichen Vocalmusik
      Italiens (item 875).

877. Westerlund, Gunner, and Hughes, Eric. Music of
      Claudio Monteverdi: A Discography. London:
      British Institute of Recorded Sound, 1972. 72
      pp. ISBN 0 900 20805 8 ML156.5 M65 W5

      Provides information for 324 records issued
      prior to October 31, 1971. Divides the musical
      items into three categories: I. Madrigals, Can-
      zonette, and Scherzi musicali; II. Stage Works; and
      III. Church Music. Concludes with a numerical list
      of records arranged alphabetically by label and
      number.

878. Wiel, Taddeo. I codici musicali contariniani del
      secolo XVII nella R. Biblioteca di San Marco in
      Venezia. Venice: Ongania, 1888; reprint ed.,
      Bologna: Forni, 1969. 121 pp. ML136 V44 S3

A description of over 100 manuscript scores
located in the Contarini collection of the Biblioteca di San Marco, now at the Biblioteca Nazionale
Marciana. Monteverdi's L'incoronazione di Poppea
is among the manuscripts in this collection.
Contains an index.

AUTHOR INDEX[*]

[*]In the following indexes, numbers refer to item numbers in the bibliography.

INDEX OF COMPOSITIONS BY MONTEVERDI

GENERAL INDEX OF PROPER NAMES